Compromised Compliance

Recent Titles in Contributions in Political Science
Series Editor: Bernard K. Johnpoll

The Right Opposition: The Lovestoneites and the International Communist Opposition of the 1930s
Robert J. Alexander

Quantification in the History of Political Thought: Toward a Qualitative Approach
Robert Schware

The Kent State Incident: Impact of Judicial Process on Public Attitudes
Thomas R. Hensley with James J. Best, James L. Kotschwar, Marlyn G. Heller, and Judith W. Reid

Representation and Presidential Primaries: The Democratic Party in the Post-Reform Era
James I. Lengle

Heroin and Politicians: The Failure of Public Policy to Control Addiction in America
David J. Bellis

The Impossible Dream: The Rise and Demise of the American Left
Bernard K. Johnpoll

Eurocommunism: The Ideological and Political-Theoretical Foundations
George Schwab, editor

American-Soviet Relations: From 1947 to the Nixon-Kissinger Grand Design
Dan Caldwell

The First Amendment Under Siege: The Politics of Broadcast Regulation
Richard E. Labunski

Political Culture, Foreign Policy, and Conflict: The Palestine Area Conflict System
Basheer Meibar

The Politics of Wilderness Preservation
Craig Willard Allin

Nationalism: Essays in Honor of Louis L. Snyder
Michael Palumbo and William O. Shanahan, editors

Compromised Compliance

IMPLEMENTATION OF THE 1965 VOTING RIGHTS ACT

Howard Ball, Dale Krane, and Thomas P. Lauth

Contributions in Political Science, Number 66

GREENWOOD PRESS
Westport, Connecticut . London, England

Library of Congress Cataloging in Publication Data

Ball, Howard, 1937-
Compromised compliance.

  (Contributions in political science, ISSN 0147-1066;
no. 66)
  Bibliography: p.
  Includes index.
  1. Afro-Americans—Politics and suffrage.
2. Voters, Registration of—United States. I. Krane,
Dale. II. Lauth, Thomas P. III. Title. IV. Title:
Voting Rights Act. V. Series: Contributions in
political science; no. 66.
KF4893.B35   342.73′072′0269   81-6342
                  347.302720269   AACR2
ISBN 0-313-22037-9 (lib. bdg.)

Library of Congress Catalog Card Number: 81-6342
ISBN: 0-313-22037-9
ISSN: 0147-1066

First published in 1982

Greenwood Press
A division of Congressional Information Service, Inc.
88 Post Road West
Westport, Connecticut 06881

Printed in the United States of America

10 9 8 7 6 5 4 3 2 1

For Carol,
Maria,
and Jean

Contents

Figures

Tables

Acknowledgments

Our research on the implementation of the 1965 Voting Rights Act has gone on since the spring of 1977. Many people have helped us over the intervening years. We would like to thank all those who have, by their advice, counsel, and criticism, assisted us as we made our way through the implementation process of a very important piece of civil rights legislation in a highly complex intergovernmental-federal-political system.

Research support for certain facets of this project was provided by the Office of Research and Graduate Studies, Mississippi State University, under the leadership of Vice President Marion T. Loftin. Without Dr. Loftin's timely aid, in the form of research assistance and printing and mailing costs, much of the information garnered by us about the views of local officials in Mississippi and Georgia would have been unavailable. In addition, Georgia State University and Mississippi State University provided travel and secretarial support for the gathering of basic research in 1977-1978 and for the typing of earlier drafts of this manuscript for presentation at professional meetings in 1978-1980.

From the very beginning of our research in this area, we have had the cooperation of dedicated officials in the Voting Section, Civil Rights Division, U.S. Department of Justice, in Washington, D.C. We would like to thank Gerald Jones, Chief, Voting Rights Section; Kay Butler, staff attorney; Mike Corley, staff attorney; Janet Blizzard, paralegal supervisor; Liz Dunagin, research analyst; James Turner, Deputy Assistant Attorney General, Civil Rights

xiv   *Acknowledgments*

Division; Drew Days, III, Assistant Attorney General, Civil Rights Division; and, most especially, a truly committed public servant, David Hunter, staff attorney, Civil Rights Division.

In addition to these federal administrators in the Department of Justice, other federal officials provided us with insights and data. These helpful people are Deborah P. Snow, Project Director, Office of Program and Policy Review, U.S. Commission on Civil Rights; John Ols, Assistant Director, General Government Division, U.S. General Accounting Office; and Howard Glickstein, Director, President's Task Force on Civil Rights Reorganization (OMB).

Just as we benefited from the assistance of the federal administrators responsible for implementing the 1965 Voting Rights Act, we gained invaluable information and insights from many local citizen-participants in the arena of voting rights policy. We are most grateful to Vivian Jones, Executive Director, Voter Education Project, Atlanta, Georgia; Armand Derfner, Lawyer's Committee for Civil Rights Under Law, Charleston, South Carolina; Henry Kirksey, Mississippi House of Representatives; John Guyton, City Attorney, Kosciusko, Mississippi; and John Ferguson, County Attorney, Fulton County, Georgia.

We have presented various chapters of this book before our peers in the disciplines of political science and public administration. Our views about voting rights policy have been honed by the frank comments and helpful suggestions we received from our colleagues. Included in this group are Glenn Abney and Phillip Cooper, Georgia State University; Richard Engstrom, University of New Orleans; Stephen Wasby, SUNY/Albany; James Harvey and Leslie McLemore, Jackson State University; and John Gruhl, University of Nebraska at Omaha.

Typing and editorial assistance by Dixie Jennings has been excellent; working with three authors located in two states has, we are sure, proven to be an interesting experience for her. She survived without breaking down. We have appreciated her stamina and good cheer throughout this endeavor and we thank her for her fine support.

Finally, we want to take this opportunity to acknowledge the support and love our wives have given us throughout this protracted, yet always stimulating, research activity. Carol, Maria, and Jean, all professionals in their own fields of work, were quick with their support and understanding and tolerance when we were on the road collecting data, discussing our studies, and presenting reports to colleagues in the profession. For this support, and for so much else, we thank them so much.

Since 1977, when we first began to raise questions about voting rights policy and about its impact on human values in the covered jurisdictions, we have greatly expanded our understanding of the complexity of policymaking and policy implementation in a federal system. We have examined the merits and deficiencies of a radical voting rights policy that was created in response to violence and death in Selma, Alabama. Voting and the ultimate consequence of political participation was the promise and the purpose of the 1965 Voting Rights Act. Fulfilling the promise, in our federal system, has proven to be a difficult venture. That is what we have tried to discuss in this book.

Many friends and colleagues have helped us in making our assessments. We, however, have made the judgments and the evaluations regarding the value and worth of the voting rights implementation process. We alone, not those we have mentioned above, are responsible for these judgments. We thank all those who have led us to this point. However, if there are faults in the book, they are ours and ours alone.

Compromised Compliance

Prologue: The Night They Moved the Voting Machines in Jackson, Mississippi, or Compromised Compliance with the 1965 Voting Rights Act

The time, October, 1978; the place, Jackson, Mississippi; the event, the race for the U.S. Senate seat vacated when U.S. Senator James O. Eastland retired after serving for decades in Congress. It was a three-man race. Maurice Dantin, a longtime conservative lawyer was running on the Democratic ticket. Thad Cochran, a youngish, dynamic lawyer, and U.S. Congressman (R), was the Republican officeseeker. Charles Evers, longtime state leader of the National Association for the Advancement of Colored People (NAACP) and mayor of Fayette, Mississippi, was the black independent candidate. It had been a tough campaign, typical in many ways of elections in Mississippi; however, the Evers candidacy greatly concerned state Democrats who were troubled by the fact that the black vote (traditionally Democratic) would go to Evers, thereby taking away voting strength from Dantin, who was in some trouble in October, 1978. The outcome was in some doubt because of the incertitude of voter behavior in the three-man race. The *Jackson Clarion-Ledger* the morning of the election stated that "the election of Cochran, a Republican, or Evers, a black, would give the state its first U.S. Senator in either category since Blanch K. Bruce—a black Republican—served during the Reconstruction era."[1]

On October 16, 1978, just a few weeks before the election, the Hinds County Election Commission, consisting of five commissioners (all white Republican Party members) and chaired by Charlotte Davis, submitted a request to receive "preclearance" for a change in voting procedures in Hinds County to the U.S. Department of Justice's Voting Rights Section.[2] The Election Commission asked permission to move 30 polling places in populous Hinds County, Mississippi, to the location of the state capital, Jackson. Eleven of these polling places were in predominantly black electoral precincts. The justification for the move offered by the Commission was that it was desirous that the polling places be located on public property such as schools and armories rather than at private dwelling locations such as the all-black New Hope Baptist Church in Jackson, Mississippi (which had been used as a polling place for over two decades). As of Monday evening, November 6, 1978 (the evening before the election), the Justice Department had not formally approved the voting change.

That day, however, the Hinds County Election Commission moved the voting machines from their old polling places to the new locations. The first candidate to notice this last minute change was a Democrat running for the Fourth Congressional District seat in the House of Representatives, John Hampton Stennis (son of U.S. Senator, John C. Stennis). Alan Moore, Stennis' campaign director, said "It's an obvious attempt to confuse the voters. It's irresponsible not to have publicized [the change in polling places]."[3] Moore then contacted Charles Evers and told the senatorial candidate what was happening.

Evers immediately conferred with Frank Parker, a well-known civil rights attorney from Jackson, Mississippi. Parker hurriedly spoke with U.S. District Court Judge Dan Russell and then formally asked the federal judge to restore the 30 polling places to their original locations. Parker claimed that Evers might very well lose the election because of the great confusion created by the "midnight" change of polling places, the lack of adequate notice about the change to the 8,500 or so voters living in these precincts, and the lack of final preclearance by the Department of Justice.

Candidate Evers complained: "I can win this thing tomorrow and they know it. That's why the Hinds County Election Commission is playing these tricks."

The discussion with the federal judge consisted of two half-hour conference calls. During the first discussion, held early

Monday evening, the Jackson civil rights attorney requested that the machines be returned to the old polling places. The Hinds County Commissioners, the other participants in the conference call, argued that there was a good reason for changing the polling places, that there was not enough time to transport the machines to the old locations and that, anyway, the U.S. Department of Justice had informally told them to proceed with the change. Said Chairman Davis: "The Department of Justice told us to proceed as though the changes had been approved because we were so close to the election."

After the first of the two conference calls ended with the news that Justice officials had informally approved the change that no one in the region knew about except the five Commissioners, Parker immediately called up the U.S. Department of Justice and spoke with Drew Days, III, a black attorney who was appointed Assistant Attorney General/Civil Rights Division by Democratic President Jimmy Carter, in 1977.[4] Parker complained that the Hinds County Election Commission violated the 1965 Voting Rights Act by not getting formal Section 5 approval. Furthermore, there was no prior knowledge of the possible voting change passed onto interested parties by either the Department of Justice or by the Hinds County Election Commission. Parker told Days that there was inadequate parking at the new polling places and that, because of the lack of publicity surrounding the move, the voters might get lost trying to find the new polling places.

Days, however, rejected the plea from Parker that the Department of Justice step in and order the machines moved back to the old polling places. Days suggested that the Jackson Police Department direct the voters to the new polling places. Parker, enraged at this seemingly gratuitous comment by the chief of the Civil Rights Division, then told Days: "Evidently you don't know the price we paid for the right to vote [in Mississippi]." Parker then broke off the conversation with Days, commenting bitterly afterwards that the Department of Justice "was trying to convince the [all white] Hinds County Election Commission to do right by the blacks in Mississippi."

Gil Jonas, an Evers backer, was in the office when Parker spoke with Drew Days. He said that "Days was helpless to act because he is under the Attorney General Griffin Bell and President Carter." Said Jonas sarcastically, "Carter has bent over backwards to endorse Democrat Maurice Dantin in the Mississippi Senate race. I'm sure Days got his marching orders!"

After the fruitless effort to get the Civil Rights Division to intercede on behalf of the black voters by objecting to the voting change, Parker then had his second, and final, conference call with Federal Judge Russell. Parker suggested that there might be a lawsuit, introduced by Evers, challenging the constitutionality of the election if the voting machines were not moved back to the old locations. However, the argument was to no avail. After the half-hour conversation, Russell ruled that: (1) it would prove too difficult for Hinds County to arrange for the return of the voting machines to their original polling places before the scheduled opening of the polls at 7 a.m. the following morning, and (2) Hinds County must double the number of people at the old polling places to direct voters to the new locations and that the County must provide emergency parking facilities at some of the new places. Russell, however, did not address himself to the legality of the move. The federal judge's ruling came shortly before midnight—barely seven hours before the opening of the polls on election day, November 7, 1978.

On election day, there were few election workers at the old polling places; a few policemen on extra duty directed the voters to some of the new polling places. Dr. Emmett Burns, NAACP Field Secretary and Pastor of the New Hope Baptist Church in Jackson, Mississippi (one of the old polling places that had been closed due to the voting change), said: "When you pull a switch like [this] at the last minute, it confuses our people. We're talking about 10,000 to 12,000 votes."

Charles Evers lost the election in 1978. Thad Cochran, the first Republican since the days of Reconstruction to win an election for a seat in the U.S. Senate, took his place in Congress in January, 1979. Evers did not challenge the results of the senatorial election. "I am not going to press the issue," he said. The voting machine caper ended as quickly as it had begun.

This incident, one of countless hundreds that have taken place in Mississippi and across the South since the passage of the 1965

Voting Rights Act, serves as an introduction to this assessment of its implementation by the U.S. Department of Justice (DOJ). The 1965 Voting Rights Act was thought by many to be the definitive, even radical (by American political standards), answer to the persistent dilemma of racially motivated voting discrimination in the South.

Some of the provisions of the Act dealt with outright vote denial through the use of literacy tests and other devices. Suspension of such devices was mandated by the Act in the covered states; marshals were to be called into these local areas to ensure that blacks would be registered to vote without undue delay and harrassment by local white registrars. Section 5 of the Act was written to deal with the prospect of dilution of black voting strength after the black communities had been registered and were allowed to vote. Dilution of the voting power of newly enfranchised voters could take place by voting changes such as moving the polling places (the Jackson, Mississippi, caper), redistricting, annexations, at-large elections, reregistrations, etc., that would have the effect of neutralizing the vote of the black citizens. To counter these kinds of activities that would have the effect of nullifying the registration gains made by the blacks using the Voting Rights Act, Section 5 called for prior approval, "preclearance," by federal officers (either federal judges or DOJ attorneys) in Washington, D.C., of all voting changes the covered jurisdictions sought to introduce after November, 1964.

Section 5 was a federal effort to prevent new discriminatory voting practices from being implemented in the South that would dilute the voting strength of blacks. The success of this effort, however, depended upon the ability and the motivation of the men and women who were responsible for its implementation: the U.S. Attorneys and paraprofessionals in the Voting Rights Section, Civil Rights Division, DOJ.

As the "voting machine caper" suggests, there have been major problems in the implementation of the Voting Rights Act by the DOJ. Gaining compliance with Section 5 has not been an easy task nor a straightforward process. In many ways, as will be shown in this book, voting rights legislation is unique among federal policies; that is, several differences distinguish voting rights enforcement from the achievement of compliance in more typical policy areas. For example, conventional wisdom underlying most federal policy suggests that a "financial carrot" can either lure or induce compliance from unwilling subnational partners.[5] However, voting rights policy is fiscally dry. Of course, the Department of Justice could resort to disincentives such as the criminal penalties provided for in the Act, but these penalties have never been used. Compounding this resource deprivation, the existence of a 60-day time limit within which the Attorney General must make the preclearance decision means, unlike other bureaucrats, the Submission Unit in the Department of Justice that handles the preclearances cannot delay judgment. To make matters worse (or better, depending on whose ox is being gored), the Voting Section in Justice does not possess its own field personnel stationed throughout the region of covered jurisdictions.

This book will focus on the question of implementation of a radical voting rights policy with these kinds of factors as the springboard for analysis. In addition to these dynamics, we seek to examine this important public policy by concentrating on administrative management of a potentially explosive subject, and focusing on the intergovernmental environment—including federal judicial responses to legal controversies surrounding the management of this policy—and its impact on federal bureaucrats in their effort to implement a policy that many persons thought would lead to an intolerable situation where the covered states would be treated like "conquered provinces."

This book seeks to lay out the nature and character of these implementation problems and, in so doing, to describe the interactions between the major actors (DOJ attorneys, political leaders at various levels of government, civil rights groups, federal judges, election commissioners, county and city attorneys, voter groups—black and white) in the Section 5 implementation process. The issues revealed and the questions raised in the "voting machine" caper in Jackson, Mississippi, indicate why the authors of this book believe that Section 5 enforcement is an important subject for scholarly investigation.

NOTES

1. Dates and quotes in this introduction are from the Jackson, Mississippi *Clarion-Ledger*, November 7, 1978, Johanna Neuman, "Evers Challenge Could Reverse Last Minute Relocation of Polls," p. 1, and November 8, 1978, Patrick Larkin, "Evers Decides Not to Contest Voting Results," p. 1.

2. The 1965 Voting Rights Act in part (Section 5) requires that all those jurisdictions covered by the Act submit all changes in voting procedures to either the U.S. District Court in the District of Columbia or to the U.S. Department of Justice's Voting Rights Section, also in the District of Columbia, for preclearance by the federal agency. No voting change can be implemented without the submission and without the issuance of either a declaratory judgment or receipt of a "no objection" letter from the Justice Department.

3. Hinds County Chancery Clerk Pete McGee claimed part of the blame for the lack of publicity. He submitted copy concerning the changes to the local newspapers to run from November 1-November 5, 1978. McGee thought the notice would be printed as a public service; the newspapers did not run the announcement because there was no payment of fees for advertising copy. It was not until the day the polls were changed, November 6, 1978, that McGee found out that there was no announcement in the Jackson, Mississippi, papers.

4. Days was the judicial administrator in the Justice Department who reviewed recommendations of the Voting Section attorneys. All preclearances, extensions of time, or objections have to be approved by Days, the Assistant Attorney General, Civil Rights Division.

5. Helen Ingram, "Policy Implementation Through Bargaining: The Case of Federal Grants-In-Aid," *Public Policy* 25, 4 (Fall 1977); 499-526.

PART ONE

A GENERAL FRAMEWORK

1 Voting Rights Enforcement as Policy Implementation

INTRODUCTION

The Voting Rights Act of 1965 was both an affirmation of the principles embodied in the Civil Rights Acts of 1957, 1960, and 1964 and a statement of objectives regarding the elimination and prohibition of abhorrent practices of racial discrimination in voting in the United States. With the passage of the Act, it became the policy of the U.S. government to eliminate the use of those devices that had traditionally been employed to prevent black citizens from registering and voting in the states of the deep South, and to prohibit those states from introducing new processes or devices that would dilute or abridge the voting rights of black citizens.

Public policy is, in one sense, a statement of goals and objectives articulated at a particular moment in time in a legislative enactment, executive order, or judicial decision. However, in another sense, it is the corpus of practices, procedures, and determinations that unfolds during administrative implementation of those laws, orders, and decisions. Implementation decisions by administrators, particularly in a conflict-laden area such as voting rights, are decisions that determine whose interests and values will be accorded protection of the law. The Voting Rights Act[1] was amended and extended in 1970 and 1975, and in 1982 the Congress will determine whether or not the Act is to be further extended or amended. As that decision date approaches, it is a propitious time to examine and assess the manner in which the Act has been implemented during the 16 years of its existence.

This book is about the performance of voting rights policy. It is an investigation of the factors and forces that have contributed to the attainment of the policy objectives set forth in the Voting Rights Act of 1965. Before proceeding, it will be useful to indicate what we do not purport to do here. First, the inquiry is not primarily about the process through which the Voting Rights Act became a law, although inevitably we will refer from time to time to the determinants of voting rights policy. Second, it is not an attempt to measure the ultimate impact of voting rights policy on the quality of life of black or minority language citizens, although voting rights policy surely assumes that equality of voting opportunities will have such an impact. Carl Van Horn and Donald Van Meter have noted that "successful program performance may be a necessary— but not sufficient—condition for the attainment of positive ultimate outcomes."[2] Recognizing that exogenous factors will also influence the life opportunities of black and minority language citizens, the degree to which the implementation of the Voting Rights Act achieved the policy objective of nondiscrimination in voting practices in covered jurisdictions is, nevertheless, an interesting and important concern. Thus, the purpose of this book is to assess the manner in which, and the degree to which, policy implementation by the Department of Justice has brought about changes in the voting practices of jurisdictions covered by the 1965 Act. Whether or not the successful implementation of voting rights policy results in concomitant changes in the life opportunities of black and minority language citizens is a question that is beyond the scope of this volume. In the language of social scientists, this is a study of policy implementation, rather than a study of policy impact.

THE VOTING RIGHTS ACT

The Voting Rights Act of 1965, as amended, was enacted to ensure that the right of citizens to vote would not be denied or impaired because of racial or language discrimination.* The Act contains several general provisions, which apply throughout the country, as well as special provisions, which apply only in selected states and local jurisdictions. For example, the Voting Rights Act set maximum residence requirements (30 days before the election) for voting in any state in presidential elections; established criminal penalties for certain acts related to vote denial; and authorized federal courts to impose some or all of the special provisions of the Act in jurisdictions not automatically covered in cases where major violations of federally protected voting rights are found.

In addition to the general provisions that apply throughout the United States, the Act has special provisions that apply in states and local jurisdictions that meet certain conditions delineated in the law. Jurisdictions are covered by the special provisions of the Act if they meet one or more of the following tests: (1) the jurisdiction maintained on November 1, 1964, a test or device (such as a literacy test) as a condition for registering or voting, and less than 50 percent of its total voting-age population was registered or actually voted in the 1964 presidential election; (2) the jurisdiction maintained on November 1, 1968, a test or device as a condition for registering or voting, and less than 50 percent of its total voting-age population was registered or actually voted in the 1968 presidential election; (3) more than 5 percent of the citizens of voting age in the jurisdiction were members of a single language minority group on November 1, 1972, and the jurisdiction provided registration and election materials only in English on November 1, 1972, and less than 50 percent of the citizens of voting age had been registered or had voted in the 1972 presidential election; and (4) more than 5 percent of the citizens of voting age in the jurisdiction are members of a single language minority group, and the illiteracy rate of such persons as a group is higher than the national illiteracy rate.[3] Jurisdictions covered by the first and second "triggers" are subject to the special provisions of the original 1965 Act. Jurisdictions covered by the third trigger are subject to both the special provisions of the original Act and the

* See Appendix A. The 1965 Voting Rights Act and Amendments.

minority language provisions added by the 1975 amendments, and those covered by the fourth trigger are subject only to the minority language provisions.[4] The states originally covered by the Act were: Alabama, Georgia, Louisiana, Mississippi, South Carolina, Virginia, and portions of North Carolina. The state of Texas was added as a result of the 1975 extension of the Act (the third trigger), as were counties from 14 states. The special provisions of the Voting Rights Act are temporary inasmuch as all four triggers have "bail out" features. A jurisdiction may bail out by proving in a suit in the U.S. District Court for the District of Columbia that its voting practices or procedures were not used in a discriminatory manner for a prior period (17 years in the case of the first two triggers and 10 years under the third). All jurisdictions covered by the special provisions of the original Act will be able to bail out in 1982 if they have refrained from using a discriminatory test or device since 1965, while those covered under the 1975 amendments will be able to bail out after 1985.[5]

According to Sections 4 and 6 of the Act, examiners from the Department of Justice and observers from the U.S. Civil Service Commission (now the Office of Personnel Management) were to be sent into the covered jurisdictions for the purpose of guaranteeing that black citizens would be duly registered and permitted to vote. A number of tests and devices for discrimination in voting were suspended as part of the Section 4 enforcement process. In an effort to prevent recurrences of black vote dilution, Section 5 of the Act requires covered jurisdictions to obtain "preclearance" before any changes in "voting qualification or prerequisite to voting, or standard, practice, or procedure with respect to voting" different from that in effect on November 1, 1964, can be enforced. Submissions are examined to determine if they have either the purpose or effect of denying or abridging the right to vote on account of race or color. The inclusion of such a section was primarily designed to prevent the substitution of new discriminatory practices for old ones that had been eliminated by previous legislative or judicial actions. Covered jurisdictions may seek preclearance of voting changes from either the U.S. District Court for the District of Columbia or from the U.S. Attorney General. However, because filing with the Department of Justice enables the states and local jurisdictions to obtain a more rapid determination of the acceptability of proposed changes, virtually all of the changes have been sent to the Attorney General rather than to the U.S. District Court.

Unlike Section 4, which requires a decision by the Attorney General before federal examiners or observers are sent to a covered jurisdiction, Section 5 is automatic in that all vote changes in covered jurisdictions must be submitted for Section 5 review. Section 5 places the burden on covered jurisdictions to submit all vote changes for prior approval, and it places the burden of proof on covered jurisdictions to demonstrate that those changes are not discriminatory. The Attorney General must act on a submission within 60 days. Failure to do so would result in preclearance even though the submitted change might be discriminatory. The inclusion of Section 5 in the Voting Rights Act was based on two basic assumptions: first, local jurisdictions bent on preventing blacks from voting can be, and in the past have been, rather ingenious in devising new tests and devices to replace old ones that have been declared illegal; and second, the limited resources of the Department of Justice make it nearly impossible to investigate independently, on the Department's own initiative, changes with respect to voting enacted by states and local jurisdictions covered by the Act. For these reasons, the somewhat unusual remedy was adopted of requiring covered jurisdictions to come to Washington, D.C. for a federal imprimatur on their proposed voting changes.

The Section 5 preclearance requirement makes use of what Andrew Dunsire has called the "bottle-neck" principle. According to Dunsire, "if the target population can be brought to pass through a central point rather than having to be sought out by the controllers, the work is greatly eased."[6] Ideally, the bottle neck is most effective where it is unavoidable (for example, customs inspection at arriving international flights) and where avoiding it is made an offense in itself. This form of constraint is especially appropriate when the target population (such as covered jurisdictions) is an unwilling partner in the implementation of government policy. Whereas Section 4 voids all attempts to prevent black citizens from registering and voting, Section 5 is designed to prevent covered jurisdictions from instituting new tests or devices that would dilute or abridge voting rights.

Although enactment of the Voting Rights Act was a necessary condition for protecting the voting rights of black and minority language citizens in the South, it is in the administrative implementation of the Act (particularly Section 5) that the voting rights policy goals set forth by the Congress and the President are transformed into civil rights protections for minority group citizens. The principal focus of this book, therefore, will be on the implementation of Section 5 of the Act.

THE IMPLEMENTATION PERSPECTIVE

In recent years, studies of public policy have tended with increasing frequency to focus on the implementation process. Implementation has been defined as "the stage of policymaking between the establishment of a policy—such as the passage of a legislative act, the issuing of an executive order, the handing down of a judicial decision, or the promulgation of a regulatory rule—and the consequences of the policy for the people whom it affects."[7] It has also been identified as "those actions...that effect the achievement of objectives set forth in prior policy decisions";[8] "the process of carrying out authoritative public policy decisions";[9] and "the relevant actions and inactions of public officials who have responsibility to achieve objectives contained in previously enacted policies.[10] Although some writers are of the view that there is not a distinction to be made between the concept "implementation" and what has traditionally been known as public administration,[11] implementation in its contemporary meaning refers to an interaction process among individuals and organizations aimed at putting a program into effect. It is the complex "process of assembling numerous and diverse program elements"[12] in order to "penetrate through bureaucratic/political layers in trying to reach a final set of actors—those who manage the treatment or service, those who deliver it and those who receive it."[13] In short, implementation is the ability to link policy choice to policy performance.[14]

Typically, there have been two major ways of thinking about the relationship between policy and administration. The classical model of administration posited that administrative actions were

essentially technical, nonpolitical activities dictated by the decisions of elected and appointed policy makers.[15] In this model,
policy implementation was viewed as routine bureaucratic activity. Although rooted in quite different soil, the rational comprehensive decision-making model also tends to hold that once policy
objectives are selected from among a range of alternatives, the task
of administration is to bring about previously agreed upon objectives efficiently and effectively. However, another major way of
thinking about policymaking is to argue that prior to implementation, "policy" is little more than an expression of hopes and
expectations—that policy actually emerges only as it is implemented.

Eugene Bardach has characterized policy implementation as a
"process of assembling numerous and diverse program elements"
in order to turn out some product or service.[16] However, because
these elements are often in different hands, most of which are
independent of each other, bargaining is necessary to induce
individuals and groups to contribute those elements to the policy
enterprise. In the area of voting rights enforcement, policy implementation depends less upon "assembling program elements"
than it does upon obtaining compliance with rules and regulations. However, just as the necessary elements of a social service
program are in the hands of different individuals and groups, the
capacity to comply (or not to comply) with the requirements of
the Voting Rights Act is in the hands of officials in covered
jurisdictions who are relatively independent of those federal
government officials who are seeking to obtain compliance. If
voting rights enforcement is viewed as a bargaining process
between Department of Justice officials and officials from covered
jurisdictions, then voting rights "policy" is that which emerges
during implementation as well as that which is embodied in the
original Act. A major question to be addressed throughout the
following chapters will be the extent to which the voting rights
policy that has emerged from the practices and procedures of
implementation is consistent with the voting rights policy mandated by political decision makers in the adoption of the Voting
Rights Act. The analytical task will be to identify the factors and
forces that have affected the manner in which the statutory objectives of the Act have been achieved.

It is this explicit consideration of pluralist politics as it operates during administrative implementation that distinguishes the "implementation" approach from the more traditional subject matter of public administration.[17] It is the purpose of implementation analysis "to identify factors which affect the achievement of statutory objectives."[18]

Interest in implementation as a framework for analyzing the policy process has been accompanied by more programmatic concerns over the apparent failure of many of the Great Society social service programs.[19] However, the rationale for this study of the implementation of the Voting Rights Act, particularly Section 5 of the Act, is not that it is a failed program. Although some critics argue that Section 5 implementation has fallen short of expectations, the implementation of this dimension of voting rights policy has in many ways been successful. Paul Sabatier and Daniel Mazmanian have suggested that one of the factors that affects the achievement of statutory objectives is the "tractability" of the problem being addressed by the statute.[20] Tractability in this context means that some problems are simply more difficult to deal with than others. One aspect of the tractability of a problem is the percentage of the population within a jurisdiction whose behavior needs to be changed. Sabatier and Mazmanian point out that the successful implementation of the Voting Rights Act of 1965 can partially be explained by the fact that it sought to eliminate a specific set of abuses engaged in by readily identifiable actors—voting officials in the states of the deep South. As compared with other areas of civil rights policy such as housing and education where the relevant population whose behavior needs to be changed is both larger and much less readily identifiable, the tractability problem has been less severe in voting rights policy implementation. A closely related aspect of tractability is the amount of changed behavior required of the target population in order to achieve policy objectives. A Department of Justice official with direct responsibility for voting rights enforcement has noted:

Section 5 is probably easier than a lot of areas. We're not asking them to do anything special—spend money that they wouldn't have otherwise, or have new programs. We're just asking them to do their normal business, but not discriminate.[21]

Nevertheless, for voting officials in many covered jurisdictions, compliance with both the letter and the spirit of the Voting Rights Act requires substantial behavior modification. Although the task of voting rights enforcement has been facilitated because the problem is somewhat easier to solve than problems in other policy areas, including other areas of civil rights policy, it is not free from the tractability problem.

IMPLEMENTATION: CONTROL AND DISCRETION

In a constitutional democracy, Paul Appleby reminded us, citizens are the sovereigns.[22] Authority to govern, having initially been conferred with the ratification of the basic instrument of governance, is periodically reconferred through popular participation in the process of leadership selection. Through the electoral process, the sovereigns authorize their representatives to act on behalf of their individual and collective interests.[23] Although elections are at best clumsy vehicles for determining the will of the people, democratic theory holds that policies enacted by the elected representatives of the people are authoritative expressions of public purposes and objectives. The Voting Rights Act is, of course, one such expression.

Legislatures, however, are not particularly well suited for the implementation of public policies, and responsibility for that task has come to reside with administrative officials who are, as Frederick Mosher puts it, "thrice removed" from direct popular control.[24] Career administrators are three times removed in that they report to political executives, who in turn are appointed by an elected chief executive. Despite their distance from direct popular control, career administrators in executive branch agencies are expected to pursue the public policy objectives formulated by political decision makers, and political decision makers are ultimately accountable for the performance of administrators. In short, administration is subordinate to the political direction and supervision exercised by the representatives of the people.[25]

There are, however, limitations on the ability of political decision makers to exercise control over administrators. The ability of elected and appointed decision makers to penetrate the bureaucracy tends to be limited by administrative expertise and professionalism. From the perspective of political decision makers, expertise is a double-edged sword. On the one hand, it means that political decisions "will be guided by competent technical advice and carried out by skilled personnel";[26] on the other hand, expertise increases the potential for administrative preferences and values to prevail over the preferences and values of political decision makers.

Administrative expertise partially results from the presence of highly trained professionals (lawyers at the Department of Justice, for example) who possess the skills needed by agencies for the accomplishment of their program objectives. Francis Rourke has noted that expertise also results from the practical knowledge that comes with experience. As administrators concentrate their attention on specific problems and continually perform the same functions, they tend to develop experience-based expertise. One consequence of this development, he notes, is the near monopoly on information that comes with it[27]—an important source of agency power.

Another centrifugal force that limits political decision makers in exercising control over administrative agency programs is the opportunity for administrators to exercise discretion in the implementation of those programs. Discretion is exercised in interpreting legislative intent and applying it to particular situations. Frequently, the ability of the legislature to arrive at consensus on important policy questions is facilitated by agreements to delegate to administrators the responsibility for making judgments about specific (and potentially divisive) policy applications. Initially, agencies refine policies formulated by the legislature and produce a framework for implementing them by "the drafting and adoption of rules and regulations that define further the intent of the policy and guide administrators in its eventual application to specific cases and programs."[28]

From the perspective of political decision makers, administrative discretion, like professional expertise, may be both functional and dysfunctional. It is functional in that agency personnel have the flexibility to accommodate unanticipated situations and individualize policy applications to meet the needs of particular jurisdictions. On the other hand, discretion may be dysfunctional whenever administrative actions alter the intent of policies established by political authorities.

Sometimes those political authorities whose interests did not prevail in the policy formulation stage have an opportunity to protect their interests during policy implementation. The implementers of voting rights policy have operated in an environment in which their discretionary actions have been constrained by political authorities in an interesting way. Historically, those members of Congress who have been less than enthusiastic supporters of civil rights legislation often occupied key positions on such powerful committees as Judiciary and Appropriations. There they have been in a position to affect program and appropriations decisions important to the Department of Justice. That reality has not escaped the attention of Department of Justice officials in their dealings with covered jurisdictions from the states and districts of key members of Congress. Thus, the issue of political control over administration takes a somewhat unusual twist in voting rights implementation. The typical concern has been to ensure that administrators exercise their discretion in a manner that is compatible with legislative intent. However, if those individuals with primary responsibility for conducting legislative oversight are not strong supporters of the intent of the law, political control over administration can lead to less, rather than greater, rigor in administrative implementation.

ROLE OF THE JUDICIARY IN THE INTERPRETATION AND REFINEMENT OF VOTING RIGHTS POLICY

From time to time, legislative enactments or administrative practices and procedures developed for the implementation of legislative enactments are called into question by citizens, government agencies, or governments at other levels within the federal system. Occasionally, the federal judiciary is called upon to validate a piece of national legislation challenged by states as unconstitutional, or to rule on the legitimacy of implementation practices and procedures established by administrative agencies. Although federal courts sometimes function to create public policy *de novo* through constitutional interpretation, they frequently function in the role of norm enforcers by validating, refining, and interpreting policies previously established by the legislative branch or executive branch agencies. This norm enforcement function of federal courts will be particularly evident in our subsequent consideration of voting rights enforcement.[29] In 1966, the Supreme Court validated the 1965 Voting Rights Act, and in 1969, it encouraged the Department of Justice to formulate administrative regulations for the enforcement of Section 5 of the Voting Rights Act.[30] In the decade following, 1971-1980, the Court validated portions of the regulations, as well as administrative decisions rendered by the Department of Justice officials based on those regulations.[31]

Consideration of the role of the judiciary in voting rights policy implementation poses a potentially troublesome conceptual difficulty, which needs to be dealt with at the outset. The public law literature and the literature of policy implementation have attached different meanings to common words. As Lawrence Baum has pointed out, the public law literature has tended to view "compliance" with court decisions as a matter of obedience or disobedience with rules of law laid down by the Court. Stephen Wasby, for example, in an early statement on the subject, defined compliance as the degree to which "a specific decision is obeyed."[32] Although compliance surely refers to the degree to which a decision is obeyed, it is problematical to think of compliance as simply a matter of obedience or disobedience in relationships between superordinates and subordinates. In policy implementation situations, those being called upon to comply with court decisions are frequently policy makers in their own right at some lower level in the judicial or administrative hierarchy or at another level of government in the federal system who have available to them a range of responses to decisions by courts.[33] Court decisions can, however, be accommodated in the policy implementation perspective. Lawrence Baum writes:

From the implementation perspective, judges and administrators are seen as policy makers whose responsibilities may include the implementation of particular court decisions. The task of implementation is not a legal obligation but an action requested by a policy making agency that stands higher in a legal structure. The central question for analysis then is not whether officials "obey" a decision but simply how they respond to it.[34]

Thus, it will be useful to treat bureaucratic compliance with court decisions as consisting of a range of acceptable responses that fall within some zone of acceptability[35] to the court. Similarly, it will be useful to treat compliance with the requirements of Section 5 as being represented by a range of possible responses by covered jurisdictions which fall within some zone of acceptability established by the policy implementers at the Department of Justice, rather than as a bipolar response set consisting of either compliance or noncompliance. For example, a voting change might be precleared with no objection so long as it achieved a threshold level of nondiscrimination, even if some potential for discrimination remained. According to this way of thinking about compliance, only those responses from covered jurisdictions that fall outside the zone of acceptability are regarded as noncompliance. From this perspective, policy implementation can be portrayed as an interaction process between those who interpret and apply the policy and those who must comply with it, and compliance can be considered more a matter of bargaining and compromise than obedience.

INTERGOVERNMENTAL DIMENSIONS OF VOTING RIGHTS ENFORCEMENT

Federalism confounds the task of voting rights enforcement because policy implementation must transpire within the structure of the federal system and compliance must be achieved within the context of intergovernmental relations. Following the passage of the Voting Rights Act, especially the preclearance provision of Section 5, federal-state relations in the area of voting rights could have gone off in one of several directions: federal domination of the covered jurisdictions, massive state resistance, or—as the title of this book suggests—a form of intergovernmental accommodation that resulted in compromised compliance.

In the American federal system, functional responsibilities and decision-making authority are divided between two major levels of government, the states and the national government. In principle, the national government is a government of enumerated powers (and as the result of judicial interpretation also implied powers), while the states are governments of reserved powers. Each level derives its powers from the citizens within its sphere of jurisdiction and is, therefore, presumed to enjoy supremacy in exercising those powers assigned to it provided, however, that the national government when acting within its assigned sphere, has supremacy over any conflicting assertions of state power. Each level is also presumed to have the prerogative of acting directly upon all persons within its territorial limits. As a result, citizens possess dual citizenship, as citizens of the United States and of the states in which they reside. Local governments are participants in the federal relationship in that, as agents of state government, they from time to time have direct relationships with the national government.

Richard Leach provides us with a useful summary of the various interpretations of American federalism under two major categories: competitive theories and cooperative theories.[36] The earliest of the competitive theories to be advanced held that since the U.S. Constitution was derived from the people as a whole, the government that the whole people established should be the center of political power in the nation. A second view has the Constitution resulting from state action and sees the chief concern of the states and their citizens to be vigilance against enlargement of national power. A third competitive view held that the Constitution created dual sovereignties with separate and equal power centers. Each of these approaches to federalism emphasized the competitive character of the relationship and worried about the enlargement of the powers of one at the expense of the other.

According to competitive theories of federalism, the areal division of powers between levels of government serves to prevent the concentration of power and thus reduces the likelihood of governmental infringement of individual rights. However, the history of the voting rights struggle in the United States suggests a different interpretation of the areal division of power thesis. In general, the pattern of discrimination in voting has been one of majorities (political if not numerical) locally situated perpetrating a denial of the franchise on minorities located in the same jurisdiction. In order to obtain the full measure of the franchise, local minorities have pursued a strategy of seeking to expand the scope of their conflict with tyrannical local majorities. In E. E. Schattschneider's terms, they "socialized" the conflict[37] by expanding it to the national level where they were able to form a coalition with other minorities and become part of a national majority on the voting rights issue. Congressional enactment and judicial validation of the Voting Rights Act are manifestations of the majority position. In discussing the scope of conflict notion, Schattschneider wrote:

The attempt to control the scope of conflict has a bearing on federal-state-local relations, for one way to restrict the scope of conflict is to localize it, while one way to expand it is to nationalize it. One of the most remarkable developments in recent American politics is the extent to which the federal, state and local governments have become involved in doing the same kinds of things in large areas of public policy, so that it is possible for contestants to move freely from one level of government to another in an attempt to find the level at which they might try most advantageously to get what they want. This development has opened up vast new areas for the politics of scope. It follows that debates about federalism, local self-government, centralization and decentralization are actually controversies about the scale of conflict.[38]

Viewed from the competitive perspective, federalism can be seen to have been a device that facilitated the denial of voting rights to locally situated minorities in the United States. However, federalism has also made it possible for citizens of the United States to bring the weight of the national government to bear in their struggle to overcome the discriminatory actions perpetrated upon them as citizens of constituent states. Until the passage of the 1965 Voting Rights Act, the remedies available (in the 1957, 1960, and 1964 Civil Rights Acts) for guaranteeing the vote against illegal state conduct were primarily judicial remedies and had little impact and effect on black voting rights. Litigation in voting rights cases usually raised a constitutional issue regarding the limits of national government intrusion into the sphere of state authority. The joining of such an issue is quite consistent with the competitive theories of federalism.

The cooperative theories, in contrast, have emphasized the collaborative aspects of federal-state relations. Rather than dwelling on the separateness and independence of the two levels, cooperative theories stress the functional interdependence of national, state, and local government relationships. As depicted by cooperative theories, the dominant feature of American federalism is the inextricable intertwining of functional relationships, which in the language of Morton Grodzins resemble a marble cake[39] rather than a layer cake. American federalism has always had cooperative features, but the increased national government involvement in domestic programs through grants-in-aid to state and local governments often working through *regional* federal-state clearing units is largely a development of the middle decades of this century.

Administrative implementation of the Voting Rights Act is in one sense quite similar to the implementation of other cooperative federalism programs. Local jurisdictions are required to submit proposed voting changes for review and approval by federal officials. Numerous other federal programs require local jurisdictions to submit their plans and proposals for review by federal agencies. In another sense, however, voting rights implementation is unique among federal programs. Local governments generally submit plans to regional federal offices—the Voting Rights Act called for submission to Washington, D.C. In many other policy areas, a financial carrot can either lure or coerce compliance with federal government policies from even the most unwilling subnational partners. In contrast, voting rights policy implementation is fiscally dry—federal officials have no funds to offer or deny as a means to induce policy compliance. An important question to be addressed in the following chapters is, how has the Department of Justice been able to obtain policy compliance without the benefit of the incentives common to the cash-based federal programs? Despite the resistance of die-hard segregationists and the absence of financial incentives of most other federal programs, voting rights policy implementation has tended to be a form of intergovernmental relations and interorganizational communications characterized more by cooperation than conflict.

This chapter has delineated the main provisions of the Voting Rights Act and defined voting rights enforcement as an enterprise in intergovernmental policy implementation. Chapter 2 traces the history of voting rights and places the Act in the context of contemporary civil rights legislation and litigation. Chapter 3 examines the organizational structure and bureaucratic routines of Section 5 implementation. Chapter 4 views the U.S. Supreme Court's impact on voting rights policy. Chapter 5 considers voting rights policy implementation as shared action across levels of government and examines the interactions between Department of Justice officials and representatives from covered jurisdictions, and between Department of Justice officials and representatives of local minority populations. Chapter 6 juxtaposes the assessments of the Department of Justice, the General Accounting Office, the U.S. Commission on Civil Rights, and county attorneys in Georgia and Mississippi regarding the record of compliance achieved in voting rights enforcement. The final chapter offers several conclusions in light of the impending 1982 congressional consideration of the future of the Act.

NOTES

1. 42 U.S.C. 1973, et seq.

2. Carl E. Van Horn and Donald S. Van Meter, "The Implementation of Intergovernmental Policy," in Charles O. Jones and Robert D. Thomas, eds., *Public Policy Making in a Federal System* (Beverly Hills, Calif.: Sage Publications, 1976), p. 46.

3. U.S. Commission on Civil Rights, *Using the Voting Rights Act* (Washington, D.C.: U.S. Government Printing Office, 1976), p. 5.

4. Ibid.

5. Ibid., p. 6.

6. Andrew Dunsire, "Implementation Theory," in *Implementation, Evaluation and Change* (U.K.: The Open University, 1980), pp.5-54.

7. George C. Edwards, III, *Implementing Public Policy* (Washington, D.C.:Congressional Quarterly Press, 1980), p. 1.

8. Donald S. Van Meter and Carl E. Van Horn, "The Policy Implementation Process: A Conceptual Framework," *Administration and Society* 6 (February 1975): 447.

9. Robert T. Nakamura and Frank Smallwood, *The Politics of Policy Implementation* (New York: St. Martin's Press, 1980), p. 1.

10. Lawrence Baum, "Judicial Impact as a Form of Policy Implementation," in John A. Gardiner, ed., *Public Law and Public Policy* (New York: Praeger Publishers, 1977), p. 129.

11. Charles O. Jones, *An Introduction to the Study of Public Policy*, 2nd. edition (North Scituate, Mass.: Duxbury, 1977), pp. 138-40.

12. Eugene Bardach, *The Implementation Game: What Happens After a Bill Becomes a Law* (Cambridge, Mass.: MIT Press, 1977), p. 36.

13. Walter Williams, "Implementation Analysis and Assessment," *Policy Analysis* 1 (Summer 1975): 545.

14. Van Meter and Van Horn,"The Policy Implementation Process," p. 447.

15. Woodrow Wilson, "The Study of Administration," *Political Science Quarterly* 2 (1887): 197-222; Frederick W. Taylor, *The Principles of Scientific Management* (New York: W.W. Norton, 1911). See also Nakamura and Smallwood, *The Politics of Policy Implementation*, chapter 1.

16. Bardach, *The Implementation Game*, p. 37.

17. Ibid., p. 46.

18. Paul Sabatier and Daniel Mazmanian, "The Implementation of Public Policy: A Framework of Analysis," *Policy Studies Journal* 8 (Special Issue no. 2, 1980): 541.

19. Jeffrey L. Pressman and Aaron Wildavsky, *Implementation* (Berkeley, Ca.: University of California Press, 1973); and Martha Derthick, *New Towns In-Town* (Washington, D.C.: The Urban Institute, 1972).

20. Sabatier and Mazmanian, "The Implementation of Public Policy," pp. 541-43.

21. Interview with David Hunter, Staff Attorney, Voting Section, Civil Rights Division, U.S. Department of Justice, Washington, D.C., September 1, 1977.

22. Paul H. Appleby, *Citizens as Sovereigns* (Syracuse, N.Y.: Syracuse University Press, 1962).

23. Robert A. Dahl, *A Preface to Democratic Theory* (Chicago: University of Chicago Press, 1956).

24. Frederick C. Mosher, *Democracy and the Public Service* (New York: Oxford University Press, 1968), p. 3.

25. Emmett S. Redford, *Democracy and the Administrative State* (New York: Oxford University Press, 1969), especially chapters 3 and 5.

26. Francis E. Rourke, *Bureaucracy, Politics and Public Policy*, 2nd edition (Boston: Little, Brown and Co., 1976), p. 13.

27. Ibid., p. 15.

28. Lawrence C. Dodd and Richard L. Schott, *Congress and the Administrative State* (New York: John Wiley and Sons, 1979), pp. 291-93.

29. Howard Ball, *Courts and Politics: The Federal Judicial System* (Englewood Cliffs, N.J.: Prentice-Hall, 1980), pp. 21-23, 28-36.

30. *Allen v. Board of Elections*, 393 U.S. 544 (1969).

31. *Perkins v. Matthews*, 400 U.S. 379; 27 L. Ed 2d 476; 91 S. Ct. 431 (1970); *Richmond v. U.S.*, 45 L. Ed 2d 245 (1975).

32. Stephen L. Wasby, "The Supreme Court's Impact: Some Problems of Conceptualization and Measurement," in Samuel Krislov, et al., eds., *Compliance and the Law: A Multi-Disciplinary Approach* (Beverly Hills, Calif.: Sage Publications, 1972), p. 133. See also, Stephen L. Wasby, *The Impact of the U.S. Supreme Court: Some Perspectives* (Homewood, Ill.: Dorsey Press, 1970), especially pp. 27ff.

33. Baum, "Judicial Impact," p. 129.

34. Ibid.

35. Chester I. Barnard, *The Functions of the Executive* (Cambridge, Mass.: Harvard University Press, 1938), pp. 167-68; and Herbert A. Simon, *Administrative Behavior*, 2nd edition (New York: The Free Press, 1957), p. 131.

36. Richard H. Leach, *American Federalism* (New York: W.W. Norton and Company, 1970), pp. 1-24.

37. E. E. Schattschneider, *The Semi-Sovereign People* (New York: Holt, Rinehart and Winston, 1960), pp. 1-18.

38. Ibid., pp. 10-11.

39. Morton Grodzins, "The Federal System," in *Goals for Americans* (New York: The American Assembly, Columbia University, 1960), p. 265.

PART TWO

THE POLICY MADE AND REDEFINED

2 Evolution of the 1965 Voting Rights Act

INTRODUCTION

The formulation and passage of the 1965 Voting Rights Act was "probably the most radical piece of civil rights legislation since Reconstruction."[1] In order to understand the radical character of the 1965 legislation, it is necessary to examine the circumstances and events that made such dramatic national legislation necessary. Racism in America is a centuries-old dilemma;[2] the Civil War and the passage of the Civil War Amendments to the U.S. Constitution (Thirteenth, Fourteenth, and Fifteenth Amendments) were outcomes of the problem. An understanding of the Voting Rights Act of 1965 must, therefore, begin with the events that occurred immediately after the enactment of these amendments in the years immediately following the conclusion of the Civil War.

PROLOGUE: CIVIL RIGHTS ACTIVITIES TO *BROWN V. BOARD OF EDUCATION*

CIVIL WAR AMENDMENTS, CONGRESSIONAL RESPONSE, AND JUDICIAL REVIEW

In their totality, the Civil War Amendments (Thirteen-Fifteen)[3] conferred on the recently freed black slaves some basic rights: freedom from slavery, citizenship—with its concomitant privileges and immunities, due process of law, and equal protection of the laws—and the right to vote regardless of race, color, or previous condition of servitude. In each amendment, Congress was given the power to enforce the provisions "by appropriate legislation."

The post-war "radical" Reconstruction Congress, in a concerted effort to eradicate all badges of slavery that remained in the South after the Civil War, soon enacted a series of Civil Rights Acts. These acts were, in the eyes of the national legislators, consistent with the command in the Civil War Amendments that Congress could pass appropriate legislation to eradicate the vestiges of the evil of slavery once and for all in America.

This national protection of civil rights of all citizens, in the seven civil rights acts passed by Congress between 1866 and 1875, took the form of anti-peonage provisions; public accommodations protections; voting protections; juror protections against discrimination; contractual protections; protections for selling, leasing, and purchasing of property; and provisions for punishing individuals who conspired or acted "under the color of law" to deprive citizens of their civil rights. In sum, there was a prolonged, directed, clear effort by the Congress to act emphatically upon states and private individuals to ensure the political, legal, and social equality of all citizens.

By 1905, however, this aggressive attempt by the national government to guarantee to all citizens basic civil rights had failed.[4] The effort failed, in great part, because of the interpretation the U.S. Supreme Court gave to the "state action" concept in the Civil War Amendments. Congress, consistent with the notion of constitutionalism, or limited government, has to act in a manner that is consistent with the U.S. Constitution's grants of power and with its restrictions on power. The question that was raised in litigation before the Supreme Court was whether, in passing these various civil rights acts, the Congress had acted constitutionally in light of the words of the Fourteenth Amendment which prohibits "state action" that denied persons privileges and immunities, due process, and the equal protection of the laws.

In the 1883 *Civil Rights Cases*, the U.S. Supreme Court majority concluded that what the Reconstruction Congress attempted to do—regulate and control the actions of private individuals with respect to their actions against the recently freed black citizens—could not constitutionally be done. The Act in question was the 1875 Act that prohibited racial discrimination by owners of places of public accommodations. The Court ruled that the Fourteenth Amendment, upon which the 1875 Act rested, provided for congressional action to correct the effects of any state action that deprived citizens of privileges and immunities, due process, and equal protection of the laws. Until the state has acted in such a manner, congressional activity is inappropriate and unconstitutional. Congress can only deal with unconstitutional state laws or acts done under state authority, *after* the act has taken place. In addition, concluded the Supreme Court, under most circumstances, the national legislature cannot regulate or control the actions of private persons who wrong other persons. "The wrongful act of an individual, unsupported by any such [State] authority, is simply a private wrong. . . . If not sanctioned in some way by the State, or not done under State authority, it is simply a crime of that individual."[5]

This decision of the U.S. Supreme Court, accompanied by the reemergence of a more conservative attitude in the national legislature, greatly narrowed the possibility of federal intervention on behalf of black citizens in America. Congress could only act to provide a remedy when a state or an agent of the state acted so as to interfere with the protected civil rights of persons or citizens.

Other later decisions of the U.S. Supreme Court, especially *Plessy v. Ferguson* (1896),[6] effectively halted the movement—at both the state and national levels—toward racial equality. This 1896 "separate but equal" facilities (in transportation) judgment of the Court soon was used as precedent to legitimize state "Jim Crowism" in the South.[7] At the same time, the 1883 opinion of the Supreme Court effectively removed the national government from the business of protecting civil rights of Americans for 82 years. (It was not until 1957 that Congress passed the first piece of civil rights legislation since the 1875 Civil Rights Act.) American blacks in the twentieth century were thus confronted with the twin spectres of (1) official, legitimate state racial segregation of the races in every area of social interaction, and (2) a handcuffing of the national government's power to direct the society toward racial integration.

SMITH V. ALLWRIGHT (1944) AND
BROWN V. BOARD OF EDUCATION (1954/1955)

Scholars debate the date of the beginning of the end of the long, dark night of racial oppression in America. Some claim that the 1944 "white primary" case, *Smith v. Allwright*, was the "initial political mobilization of Negroes in the 20th century south";[8] others maintain that the school integration case, *Brown v. Board of Education* was the "beginning of a social revolution."[9] Both opinions were critically important to the black community in its struggle to achieve political and social equality in a society that had officially sanctioned a separate-but-equal environment since 1896 and had not permitted direct action by the national government on behalf of black citizens.

Smith v. Allwright involved the "white-primary," an effort to limit black political participation. Southern states, in order to disenfranchise blacks, determined that the state political party nominating process was a private activity and that party officials could prohibit blacks from participation in the primary election. In this 1944 opinion, in which the practice was challenged as being in violation of the U.S. Constitution, the Supreme Court stated that

> it may now be taken as a postulate that the right to vote in such a primary for the nomination of candidates without discrimination by the State, like the right to vote in a general election, is a right secured by the Constitution. . . . We think that this statutory system for the selection of party nominees for inclusion on the general election ballot makes the party which is required to follow these legislative directions an agency for the state in so far as it determines the participants in a primary election.[10]

As a consequence of this ruling, southern state leaders began the search for a legal substitute that would restrict the voting rights of blacks. Until the 1954 *Brown* decision, however, there was very little concerted effort for this substitute that would deny blacks the vote in the South.[11] Indeed, there was in some southern states a slow growth of black voter registration and voting. All this changed when *Brown v. Board of Education*[12] was decided in 1954.

The *Brown* decision in May, 1954—known as "Black Monday" in some sections of the South—sent major tremors throughout the South. (*Brown* was followed by various activities, sponsored by the NAACP and the Student Nonviolent Coordinating Committee [SNCC], that began to develop a consciousness of purpose on the part of black citizens. These activities included voter registration drives, economic boycotts, sit-ins, and freedom rides.) Extensive efforts by white segregationists were begun almost immediately to block blacks from achieving civil rights after the opinion was read by Chief Justice Earl Warren, and after the Montgomery, Alabama, boycotts in 1955, led by Dr.Martin Luther King, Jr.

In *Brown,* the U.S.Supreme Court unanimously concluded that the *Plessy v. Ferguson* "separate but equal" doctrine had no relevancy to the issue of state-ordered segregation of educational programs. The question raised was whether the segregation of children by race in public schools deprives minority children of equal educational opportunities. The answer by a unanimous court: "We believe that it does."

We conclude that in the field of public education the doctrine of "separate but equal" has no place. Separate educational facilities are inherently unequal. Therefore we hold that the plaintiffs and others similarly situated for whom the actions have been brought are, by reason of the segregation complained of, deprived of the equal protection of the laws guaranteed by the Fourteenth Amendment.[13]

Immediately on the heels of the 1954 *Brown* decision, the 1955 *Brown II* judgment,[14] and black protest actions, southern segregationists intensified their efforts to blunt these hesitant thrusts by blacks against the pervasive pattern of white racism. There soon developed in the South, especially in the most repressive of these states—Louisiana and Mississippi—several strategies for delaying, avoiding, and evading federal court orders (and the U.S. Constitution) that called for the integration of schools.[15] In the area of voting rights of blacks, the development of discriminatory actions, such as literacy tests, racial gerrymandering, at-large elections, reregistration drives (that effectively purged blacks from the election rolls), threats, and actual violence, soon became common tactics that effectively denied blacks the right to vote.

In response to these at times violent efforts to subdue blacks who were demanding their constitutional rights, there soon grew a national legislative concern for some type of federal action that would assist the blacks in their quest for political and social equality.

NATIONAL LEGISLATIVE ACTIVITY IN CIVIL RIGHTS

THE LITIGATIVE PERIOD, 1957-1964

The 1965 Voting Rights Act was the continuation—and the radical conclusion—of a haphazard civil rights policy developed by the mid-twentieth-century Congress in response to violent events that were taking place in the South in the 1960s as a result of the white segregationists' response to black boycotts, sit-ins, voter registration drives, litigation, freedom rides and freedom summers, and Supreme Court decisions. Until 1957, because of Supreme Court decisions in the 1880s, the national government could do little to prevent discrimination by states with respect to voting rights.

Both the 1957 and the 1960 Civil Rights Acts reflected a national commitment to the traditional Fourteenth/Fifteenth Amendment litigative strategy to combat voter discrimination in the South. This strategy placed "much faith in the federal courts' ability to rectify racial discrimination in the electoral process."[16] Given the precedential strength of the *Civil Rights Cases* with respect to limits on the congressional power to enforce the Fifteenth Amendment,[17] and given a reluctant Republican president and a congressional branch with Democrats in the majority but controlled by southern Democrats who stood as a block against such national action, the litigative strategy was the only tactic that could get through the Congress at that time.

The litigative approach was a slow and cumbersome tactic; both the 1957 and 1960 Acts allowed the federal government to go to Court on behalf of blacks who had been disenfranchised. The only other remedies for citizens who alleged a deprivation of constitutionally protected rights were civil actions against those who were responsible for voting discrimination (Section 1983 of 42 U.S. Code. Section 1986 provided for suits for damages in cases of a conspiracy to deprive people of their constitutional rights.) To suggest that these remedies were not employed by blacks—because of economic reprisals and basic fear of physical harm—would be a dramatic understatement. These remedies had never been used since Congress passed the legislation in 1866.

What became available for blacks in 1957 was a fairly weak civil rights statute. The 1957 Act contained five major sections. (1) Special three-judge federal district courts could be convened; they were given jurisdiction to hear civil rights cases taken out of state courts by the U.S. Department of Justice without having to exhaust state remedies. (2) Federal judges were empowered to hold persons in civil and criminal contempt if court orders involving voting rights were not carried out by defendants. (3) The Act authorized the appointment of an Assistant Attorney General for Civil Rights, which led to the changing of the Civil Rights Unit in Justice to a Division. (An immediate benefit was that the civil rights staff increased its attorney force almost 100 percent; it went from 8 to 14 attorneys in 1958.)[18] (4) The Attorney General was empowered to file suits in federal district court seeking injunctive relief against violations of the Fifteenth Amendment. (5) The U.S. Commission on Civil Rights was created to monitor voting activities in the nation, especially in the South, and to render annual reports on the condition of civil rights in America.

Given the lengthy legal hearings and all the other time-consuming delays and evasions, all legal but certainly not within the spirit of the law, only four cases were heard and decided in three years, and not a single black voter was registered as a result of the passage of the 1957 Act.[19] The 1960 Civil Rights Act attempted to close some loopholes in the 1957 legislation (although all of its teeth were removed during floor fights in Congress).[20]

Title III of the 1960 Act declared that local voting records were public and had to be preserved for a period of almost two years following any general or special election. Title VI of the 1960 Act authorized a federal district court judge, after noting a "pattern or practice" of voting discrimination, to issue registration orders and allow federal voting registrars to replace state officials.

These remedial measures did little to improve the voting situation in the South because the primary initiator was still the black citizen, who had to initiate these legal actions in a fundamentally hostile environment, and on whose shoulders was the burden of proof placed by the federal law.[21] In 1963, the U.S. Commission on Civil Rights reported:

The Commission now believes that the only effective method of guaranteeing the vote for all Americans is the enactment by Congress of some form of uniform voter qualification standards. The Commission further believes that the right to vote must, in many instances, be safeguarded and assured by the federal government. Adequate legislation must include both standards and implementation.

This report underlined the inadequacy of the litigative strategy and also the unwillingness of the national political leadership to act definitively on behalf of black Americans. During the Eisenhower and into the Kennedy administrations (1952-1960; 1961-1963), no civil rights program was generated in advance of racial crisis in the South. "I did not lie awake at night worrying about the problems of Negroes," said Attorney General Robert Kennedy.[22] While he and others might have been emotionally involved in the drama surrounding individual blacks in their struggles for political equality, he had higher priorities, such as his "war" on organized crime, for the U.S. Department of Justice in 1961-1963.

In addition, the views on federalism held by both Republican and Democratic Attorney Generals, Herbert Brownell (R) and Robert Kennedy (D), limited the Department of Justice's options. Burke Marshall, an Assistant Attorney General/Civil Rights, in the Kennedy Administration stated: "We must realize the constitutional rights of Negroes in states where they are denied but we must do so with the smallest possible federal intrusion into the conduct of state affairs."[23]

The attitude in the Department of Justice was that the Civil Rights Division's primary task was to cope with eruptions of violence that might occur in Mississippi, Alabama, or Louisiana. These were viewed as random, discontinuous by-products of a society that was painfully, and very slowly, evolving toward complete racial harmony.[24] Short of the traditional litigational efforts under existing law, there would and should not be a federal "presence" in the South.

The most visible and significant federal government activities, prior to 1965, were in actuality *reactive* actions; that is, crisis control and violence avoidance attempted through litigative efforts and informal contacts and bargaining sessions with local and state powerholders that focused specifically on getting blacks registered. It was a "forgo" enforcement strategy of civil rights policy: forgo comprehensive legislation, forgo a national presence, and forgo strong executive leadership to put down the massive resistance by southern whites toward demands by blacks for voting rights.[25] Nicholas Katzenbach summed up the attitude well when he said that Robert Kennedy's voting rights philosophy was that "you can't solve all the South's problems for it" and that his, Katzenbach's, own philosophy paralleling Kennedy's, was to "avoid *at all costs* an occupation of the South" by federal troops, lawyers, registrars, and marshals.[26]

The Lyndon Baines Johnson Administration, 1963-1969, would have continued this litigative, low-profile strategy except for the outbreak of horrible violence during the freedom summer riots in Birmingham, Alabama, in 1963 and the violence and murder that took place during the summer of 1964 in Philadelphia, Mississippi. These events galvanized civil rights forces, angered public opinion, and even prodded conservative Republicans such as U.S. Senator Everett Dirksen (R-Ill.) to join the coalition resulting in the passage of the 1964 Civil Rights Act.[27] It was, as U.S. Senator Paul Douglas (D-Ill.) bitterly remarked, "a sorrowful mockery of our principles that it required the Birmingham, Alabama bombings and the Philadelphia, Mississippi murders to pass the Civil Rights Act of 1964."[28]

The Civil Rights Act of 1964 did attempt to touch upon the continuing voting discrimination problems in the South. Title I did attempt to have three-judge federal district courts hear cases more rapidly and did allow for temporary voting registrars. However, the major thrust of the 1964 legislation was in the area of public accommodations and equal employment opportunities. By the summer of 1964, with three civil rights bills enacted, one could conclude that these acts had failed miserably in their purpose, that is, registration and voting participation of large numbers of blacks in the South.

The failure, beyond the reluctance of the federal executive and the Congress to go beyond "forgo" strategies, lay in the litigative process itself. The voting rights policy, as developed in 1957, 1960, and 1964, relied on jurisprudential performance of federal district court judges in the South. The reliance was misplaced: there was a basic nonperformance on the part of many southern federal district court judges.[29] Furthermore, it became evident that the judicial process "lacked the coercive capability necessary for ensuring meaningful progress in the elimination of racial discrimination in voting."[30]

Immediately after the November, 1964, election results were in, President Lyndon B. Johnson instructed his Attorney General, Nicholas Katzenbach, to "write the god-damnedest, toughest voting rights act that you can devise."[31] The shift from the litigative/court strategy to direct aggressive national executive action on behalf of blacks thus began quietly in November, 1964. The events that took place in Selma, Alabama, between January and April, 1965, were not so quiet. As Senator Douglas commented: "It required the atrocities of Selma to invoke the Fifteenth Amendment's instructions"[32] (and legislative passage of the most radical piece of voting rights legislation formulated since Reconstruction times).

THE 1965 VOTING RIGHTS ACT

The formulation and passage of the very radical 1965 Voting Rights Act was "the most surprising event of early 1965."[33] Although President Johnson, in November, 1964, had directed his Attorney General Katzenbach to draft a (preliminary) voting rights proposal that would secure, "once and for all,"[34] equal voting rights for all citizens (a task completed in late December, 1964), the President had not contemplated introducing new civil rights legislation until 1966. Johnson believed that more radical national action had to take place in order to overcome the strength of local racial prejudice in the South. A thoroughly "political" President, Johnson knew that it would be difficult to overcome southern intransigence in Congress and in the region itself; it would also be difficult to get the Department of Justice Civil Rights Division's administrators to go beyond their litigative, passive civil rights strategies and frame of mind. However, Johnson well knew that the 1964 Civil Rights Act would not improve the condition of voting rights for blacks and that a more radical type of legislative surgery on racial discrimination in voting had to be ready when the demands grew for new national voting rights legislation.

Three proposals for a new voting rights act were drawn up by the Department of Justice for Johnson's review in December, 1964. The Department of Justice recommended in order of priority: (1) a constitutional amendment that would outlaw literacy tests; (2) the use of federal marshals in the southern states and local subdivisions to assist actively in the registering of black citizens; and (3) massive federal intervention in the South to register blacks. The two key concerns of the Justice Department administrators who wrote the initial draft were: (1) that some sort of constraint on the use of literacy tests (and other such devices that had dramatically limited the number of black voters) had to occur; and (2) the necessity of a federal presence in the South, United States marshals, to assist blacks in those areas of intense southern racial discrimination.[35]

Johnson's voting rights plan, therefore, called for direct federal intrusion into the deep South in order to register blacks speedily. It was a radical departure from the litigative strategy implanted in the 1957, 1960, and 1964 Civil Rights Acts. Because of its radical character, similar to the Civil Rights Acts passed by Congress after the Civil War, Johnson planned on introducing the voting rights legislation in 1966 at the earliest. He knew that there would be massive southern opposition to a voting rights act that set aside state voting practices and that brought into even the smallest southern communities the dreaded federal marshal who would take a direct hand in the registering of blacks. That the Voting Rights Act was introduced in March, 1965, and was signed into law in August, 1965, has to be attributed to the one major spark that set off a "deep outrage"[36] on the part of leading political leaders and the general public: the events that took place in Selma, Alabama, from January to March, 1965.

Black civil rights leaders had realized the inadequacy of the litigative strategy long before Selma, Alabama, in 1965. The Southern Christian Leadership Council (SCLC) was born in the early days of black protest in the 1950s. Led by Dr. Martin Luther King, Jr., who organized the Montgomery, Alabama, bus boycott of 1955, the SCLC went to Selma, Alabama, with two purposes in mind: (1) a short-range plan for a voter registration drive that would add more blacks to the voter registration lists and (2) the one major goal: a voting rights law with teeth in it that would enable the DOJ to open up the registration books in the deep South.[37] (They chose Selma, Alabama, because the SCLC leaders expected that Sheriff Jim Clark would prove to be a violent law enforcement officer and that this violence against defenseless blacks would incur the wrath of the general public and lead to the demand for more effective voting rights legislation.)

Protest as a strategy of political pressure (on national leaders) that would win equal voting rights for blacks that they had not attained in the federal courts was the path taken by King. It would prove to be a successful strategy, one that led to the introduction of the Voting Rights Act in March, 1965. The victory, however, was a costly one in terms of human punishment and death. Men, women, and children were jailed by Sheriff Clark for marching to protest voting discrimination in Alabama. Shots were fired on various occasions, children were injured, and 1,500 marchers were set upon by state troopers in March, 1965, to prevent them from marching from Selma to Birmingham, Alabama. A white minister, James Reeb, a supporter of equal voting rights for blacks, was beaten to death by white hoodlums.[38]

A profound mood of indignation spread quickly across the nation. Nightly newscasts depicted gruesome scenes of marchers attacked by guard dogs, beaten by policemen, or hosed down with high-pressure streams of water by firemen. As the protests continued followed by southern violence, President Johnson ordered the Department of Justice to draft a voting rights bill quickly, based on the preliminary proposals he had reviewed in December 1964. He specifically wanted the drafters, Harold H. Green, of the Civil Rights Division, and Sol Lindenbaum, Office of Legal Counsel, to focus on federal intervention in areas where blacks had been systematically denied the right to vote.[39]

A draft of the bill was given to Johnson on March 5, 1965. Less than two weeks later, the Reverend Reeb was beaten to death in Selma, Alabama. The trauma of the senseless murder was immediately felt in Washington, D.C. Senator Walter Mondale (D-Minn.) said that "Sunday's outrage in Selma, Alabama makes passage of legislation to guarantee southern Negroes the right to vote an absolute imperative for Congress this year."[40] On March 15, 1965, after conferring with senatorial leaders Mike Mansfield (D) and Everett Dirksen (R), President Johnson addressed both houses of Congress and the entire nation. His speech, the first delivered in person by a President on a domestic matter since 1946, employing the "we shall overcome" motto of the black protester groups, was the "most genuinely moving speech ever made by Johnson"[41] and probably the most radical statement ever made by a President on civil rights.

Every device of which human ingenuity is capable has been used to deny the black citizen his right to vote. It is wrong—deadly wrong—to deny any of your fellow Americans the right to vote in this country....The black American's actions and protests, his courage to risk safety and even to risk his life, have awakened the conscience of this nation. [There must be] no delay, no hesitation, no compromise with our purpose.[42]

The Voting Rights Act that was sent immediately to the Congress contained provisions that would send federal registrars and examiners into the South; it contained certain triggering mechanisms that prohibited literacy tests and other devices from being employed to prevent blacks from voting.

The 1965 legislation was controversial because the President was asking the Congress to employ Section 2 of the Fifteenth Amendment granting Congress the power to enforce it by appropriate legislation.[43] "It would be difficult to exaggerate the germinal importance[44] of this usage of Section 2 to protect voting rights of black citizens. Although the post-Civil War Reconstruction Congress had used this strategy in passing the seven Civil Rights statutes and, in so acting, had established the principle that "civil rights were inherent ingredients of national citizenship and as such were entitled to federal protection. . . accorded in an affirmative fashion,"[45] in 1883 the U.S. Supreme Court, as has already been noted, struck down these early legislative actions.

The Voting Rights proposal attempted to move the voting rights issue off the litigation treadmill by employing the strategy of the Reconstruction Congresses of the 1860s-1870s. The first four sections were written to overcome the immediate dilemma of vote denial. The legislation accomplished this by suspending certain practices and devices—literacy tests, registration procedures, "good moral character" tests, "understanding" tests—from being employed to prevent blacks from registering in the states covered by the Voting Rights legislation.

In addition to these actions directed at local strategies that denied blacks the right to vote, the legislation also attempted to prevent the states from passing new legislation that would abridge or dilute the voting strength of the newly registered blacks in the covered jurisdictions. Section 5 of the proposed legislation called for any state or local voting change proposed after 1965 to be approved by either the U.S. Department of Justice or by the U.S. District Court in the District of Columbia.

As passed by Congress and signed into law by President Johnson, on August 6, 1965, the Voting Rights Act of 1965 (as amended in 1970 and 1975) prohibited the use (through the year 1982) of literacy tests and other devices in those states where less than 50 percent of the voting age population were registered to vote or voted in the November, 1964 elections (see Appendix A: *Voting Rights Act, 1965, as Amended*). Examiners from the Department of Justice and observers from the U.S. Civil Service Commission were to be sent to those southern states that fell within the parameters of Section 4 of the Act to ensure that black citizens would be registered and allowed to vote. (The southern states originally affected by the 1965 Act were: Alabama, Georgia, Louisiana, Mississippi, South Carolina, Virginia, and portions of the state of North Carolina.) Although several tests and devices previously used were suspended (Section 4) because of their discriminatory effect, Section 5 was also enacted to "guard against ingenious actions by those bent on preventing Negroes from voting."[46] It was clearly the intent of the Voting Rights Act of 1965 to end racial discrimination in voting.

Section 5 effectively froze all voting patterns in the covered jurisdictions as of November, 1964, unless the U.S. Attorney General or the U.S. District Court was convinced that the proposed voting change would not dilute black voting strength. It was to be employed to break the cycle of substitution of new discriminatory laws and practices when the old requirements were either suspended or declared unconstitutional. Section 5 of the Act requires the covered states to submit any change in "voting qualifications or prerequisites to voting, or standard, practice or procedures with respect to voting" different from that in effect on November 1, 1964 to either the Department of Justice or the Federal Court for the District of Columbia for "preclearance" before any such change can be enforced. Submissions are to be examined to determine if they have either the purpose or effect of denying or abridging the right to vote on account of race or color. The state may seek a declaratory judgment from the District Court or submit the change to the U.S. Attorney General. If the Attorney General does not formally object within 60 days, the change may be enforced. Even if the Attorney General does object, the state may seek a declaratory judgment from the District Court.

Section 5 was included in the Voting Rights Act because of the "acknowledged and anticipated inability of the Justice Department—given limited resources—to investigate independently all changes with respect to voting enacted by states and subdivisions covered by the Act."[47] Section 5 placed the burden on covered jurisdictions to submit all voting changes for prior approval to either the administrative or judicial branches of the federal government.

The legislation dramatically shifted the burden from the victim of racially discriminatory voting practices to the perpetrator of these practices and brought the discussion of these issues to the Washington, D.C. environment rather than leave these legal issues to be resolved in local, parochial federal district courts in the South. In part, the Act "effectively isolated from contact with the operation of the law those [southern] U.S. District Court judges in whom the Congress had apparently lost faith."[48] Commenting on the 1965 legislation, Attorney General Nicholas Katzenbach stated that "the Act says that we really can no longer rely on good faith. . . . We are not going to be frustrated again by the long and tedious delays and resort to law as a delaying device."[49]

Congress was reaching into what was traditionally "state action" in order to enforce the right to vote guaranteed to all citizens in the Fifteenth Amendment. The Act prohibited certain state actions which were not unconstitutional per se, such as the literacy tests, but which had been applied in a discriminatory manner.* Blacks and other minorities had been prevented from registering and voting in these southern states; the 1965 legislation was an affirmative action by Congress, using its "appropriate legislation" enforcement powers, to eradicate that racial discrimination.

This systematic exclusion of blacks from the electoral process in the South was "a consequence of our federal system. States not only exercise power to determine who can vote in state and local contests, but, in practice, one's participation in federal elections is essentially in the hands of state officials as well."[50] The radical executive and congressional response, suspension of state acts and practices, use of federal examiners and registrars, and approval of all voting changes by judges and attorneys in Washington, D.C., led to the 1966 legal confrontation between Congress and the states.

As passed, the 1965 Voting Rights Act avoided the home state federal judicial process. One of the critically important provisions in the Act, soon to be challenged in federal court, was that which gave the federal executive branch the responsibility for registering unenrolled black voters—a task that had been assigned, in the 1957, 1960, and 1964 Acts, to the federal courts.

---

*The 1970 amendments to the Voting Rights Act prohibited literacy tests nationwide.

IMPLEMENTATION OF THE 1965 VOTING
RIGHTS ACT, 1965-1970

Once President Johnson signed the Voting Rights Act (August 6, 1965), the Department of Justice (DOJ) with uncharacteristic speed moved to implement the first four sections of the Act. As a continuation of the Kennedy administration's strategy of traditional litigation, DOJ lawyers filed suit in the federal courts in Alabama, Mississippi, Texas, and Virginia to eliminate poll taxes (August 7-10, 1965). Similarly, literacy tests were suspended in Alabama, Georgia, Louisiana, Mississippi, North Carolina, and South Carolina (August 7, 1965).[51] [For an example of a typical literacy test, see Appendix B.] On August 9, 1965, Attorney General Katzenbach activated Section 4 by dispatching 45 federal voting examiners—all employees of the U.S. Civil Service Commission— into nine designated counties and parishes in Alabama, Louisiana, and Mississippi, Within three days, 2,881 black citizens had been registered.[52] A basic constitutional question immediately arose: Was the 1965 legislation, by invading the domain of the state authority to establish voting prerequisites, an infringement of the "reserved powers" that traditionally belonged to the states by virtue of the Tenth Amendment? Under the 1965 Act, federal machinery for voter registration had replaced state machinery. Did the Congress have the power to act legitimately in this manner to remedy consequences of unconstitutional state actions? The Act raised in a fundamental way the issue of intergovernmental relations in civil rights matters.

Southern state constitutional challenges to the 1965 Voting Rights Act were immediately forthcoming. Louisiana, Mississippi, and Alabama state courts issued injunctions that forbade local election officials from entering on their voting rolls the names of those persons registered by the federal examiners who had been called into registration duties by the 1965 legislation. The U.S. Attorney General responded by asking the U.S. Supreme Court to invoke its original jurisdiction to hear the case.

At the same time, South Carolina sought injunctive relief against enforcement of the Act by also asking the Supreme Court to invoke its original jurisdiction. The Supreme Court heard the South Carolina suit, and the other states joined in the argumentation by filing amicus curiae briefs in the case of *South Carolina v. Katzenbach*. This set the stage for judicial involvement in this watershed intergovernmental relations dispute. "The most pressing constitutional questions today [1965] are probably those raised by the Voting Rights Act of 1965,"[53] wrote one major constitutional scholar. He was probably correct for *South Carolina v. Katzenbach* and *Katzenbach v. Morgan*[54] were two of the major civil rights decisions of the 1960s because of the radical character of the challenged national legislation and because of how the Supreme Court responded to the legislation.

South Carolina's challenge reflected the federalism dilemma that had always been present in the civil rights struggle in America. In violation of the Tenth Amendment, alleged the State's attorney in his briefs, Congress had created a mechanism for national intrusion into State activities. The Voting Rights Act, especially Section 5,[55] enabled the national government, *if* the action by Congress was legitimized by the federal courts and *if* it was aggressively enforced by the federal bureaucrats, to review and then to approve or disapprove *all* voting changes proposed by these states *before* the changes could be implemented. This was the radical character of the voting rights legislation; a federal *imprimatur*—judicial or administrative—had to be affixed to all voting decisions before any state covered by the 1965 legislation could act. Until such judgment was made, the state could not enforce legislation or administer regulations that concerned voting.

This extraordinary legislative remedy for the problem of racially discriminatory voting policies in southern states was thought to be blatantly unconstitutional by the southern states. Their major argument, voiced by South Carolina in the litigation, was that the "power of enforcement," the Fifteenth Amendment, is confined to preventing or redressing illegal conduct; Congress could not use the "appropriate legislation" section as a positive source of authority to enact prophylactic measures that were designed to enhance black voting strength.[56]

Congress could only respond to illegal state actions; it did not have the constitutional power to intrude into state affairs in order to enhance the opportunities for blacks to register and vote. To intrude into the local affairs of states, as the 1965 legislation enabled the central government to do, was to violate the federal idea and the notion of "reserved powers" of the states that were protected by the Tenth Amendment.

The Attorney General's brief maintained that, pursuant to provisions of the Fifteenth Amendment, the national government had the constitutional right and obligation to enact the 1965 legislation to protect the voting rights of citizens. His argument was that:

Section 2 [of the Fifteenth Amendment] gives Congress the same broad discretion in enacting measures reasonably adapted to preventing abridgement of the right to vote by reason of race or color as the necessary and proper clause confers upon Congress in regulating local activities where appropriate for protecting interstate commerce. Congress is not confined to dealing with discrimination in voting but might prohibit any conduct which created a danger of discrimination.[57]

The "germinal" idea contained in the legislation passed by Congress was that the national government "has the power to deal with conduct...*within the reserved powers* of the states where the measure is a means of securing the state's performance of its constitutional duties."[58] Congress, in order to guarantee meaningfully to citizens that their fundamental constitutional rights would be protected, must enter into the reserved powers area of those states who were acting in a racially discriminatory manner.

The government's argument, echoing Chief Justice Marshall's views in *McCulloch v. Maryland* (1819), was that Section 2 of the Fifteenth Amendment enabled the Congress to use *any necessary and proper rational means* possible to implement the substance of the Amendment positively. The federal government, they concluded, has the power to reach any state action that is found to discriminate or to perpetuate discrimination. If the end is legitimate, guaranteeing the voting rights of all citizens, then Congress can use the "appropriate legislation" provision to enact legislation whose purpose is to achieve that end.[59]

South Carolina had asked the Supreme Court to issue a declaratory judgment voiding the provisions of the Voting Rights Act that enabled the federal government to intrude into the affairs of the states. The state asked for a ruling that would enjoin Attorney General Katzenbach from carrying out these provisions (Sections 4 and 5 in particular). The Supreme Court, in a nearly unanimous vote, denied the South Carolina request. Chief Justice Earl Warren wrote the opinion for the court in which he said that the Act was "an appropriate means for carrying out Congress' constitutional responsibilities and are consonant with all other provisions of the Constitution." After examining the nature of the civil rights controversy in the federal system, that is, the history of "nearly a century of widespread" racial discrimination in voting in the South, accompanied by the ineffectiveness of prior congressional remedies, Warren concluded that "the portions of the Voting Rights Act properly before us are the valid means for carrying out the commands of the Fifteenth Amendment.... As against the reserved powers of the states, Congress may use *any rational means* to effectuate the constitutional prohibitions of racial discrimination in voting."[60]

Justice Hugo Black wrote a separate concurring and dissenting opinion. While the Alabama-born jurist agreed with Warren's opinion sustaining the power of the Congress under Section 2 of the Fifteenth Amendment to suspend literacy tests and other devices or procedures that effectively disenfranchised citizens, he dissented from the ruling that Section 5 of the 1965 legislation was constitutional.

Black believed that the preclearance provisions in that section were unconstitutional for two reasons: (1) To have a court rule on a state law involving a voting change before it was implemented would be for the court to render an advisory opinion. However, the Constitution gave to federal courts jurisdiction to hear only concrete cases and controversies. Furthermore, if the Congress has in mind a judicial review of these kinds of issues, "at least a trial in this court would treat the states with the dignity to which they should be entitled as constituent members of our Federal Union." (2) The "more basic objection" of Justice Black to Section 5 rested on the issue of federalism and intergovernmental relations in a federal system:

Section Five, by providing that some of the states cannot pass state laws or adopt state constitutional amendments without first being compelled to *beg* federal authorities to approve their policies, so distorts our constitutional structure of government as to render any distinction drawn in the Constitution between state and federal power almost meaningless. . . . If all the provisions of our Constitution which limit the power of the Federal government and reserve other power to the states are to mean anything, they mean at least that the States have power to pass laws and amend their constitutions without first sending their officials hundreds of miles away to *beg* federal authorities to approve them. . . . I cannot help but believe that the inevitable effect of any such law which forces any one of the states to *entreat* federal authorities in far away places for approval of local laws before they can become effective is to create the impression that the state or states treated in this way are little more than *conquered provinces.*[61]

The Court majority had concluded that "exceptional conditions can justify legislative measures not otherwise appropriate," and that Section 5 was a legitimate effort to prevent the entire electoral system of these states from being subverted by the white southern politicians. Justice Black decried the loose constitutional interpretation accepted by the Court majority. If federalism meant anything, argued Justice Black, it meant that states had to use powers *reserved* to them *prior* to any federal review of their constitutionality. It remained to be seen whether or not the southern states would become conquered provinces.

The "federal presence" in the deep South after 1965 was neither massive nor totally successful. One scholar recently observed:

If properly enforced, the provision to allow federal examiners to register black voters could have changed the political climate quite dramatically, particularly in those counties and municipalities where blacks comprise the majority. There were 102 such counties and 407 majority black municipalities when the act was passed. However the Department of Justice (DOJ) developed a most conservative strategy for implementation of the examiner provisions. The selection of counties to receive examiners was done in a way to convey maximum symbolic assurance to supporters of the act and at the same time DOJ conducted behind the scene talks with Southern officials to assure them that federal activity would be restrained.[62]

Federal examiners worked in 32 counties during 1965, an additional 15 counties were visited in 1966, and 13 more counties were added in 1967, bringing the total to 60.[63] Unfortunately, in the covered states there were still 185 counties that had not been entered by federal examiners (including Sunflower County, Mississippi, the home of U.S. Senator James Eastland and Fannie Lou Hamer, a noted civil rights activist who led the black struggle in Mississippi to gain a voice in state Democratic politics).[64] In approximately 2½ years, federal examiners helped with the registration of 150,345 new black voters in the five deep South states.[65] Most of the numerical increase in black registration (approximately 1.5 million by 1968) was accomplished through the struggles of civil rights groups such as the Congress on Racial Equality (CORE), SNCC, NAACP, and the Voter Education Project. Voluntary compliance by many local registrars also facilitated this doubling of the southern black electorate. However, "practically all of federal examining activity occurred during the first two years of the act."[66]

These statistics confirm that the leadership of the Justice Department did not seek to impose a viable federal presence in the South with the deployment of an army of federal examiners, lawyers, and observers. Instead, DOJ's goal was to ensure that every citizen register according to normal and fair local procedures and that the great bulk of this work had to be done by local civil rights organizations. It was these groups, insisted Katzenbach, who would have the hard task of doing the routine, drudging labor of establishing viable political organizations and fostering the growth of black political power.[67]

This reluctance on the part of federal bureaucrats is self-evident in a memorandum, dated January 19, 1967, from John Doar to Attorney General Ramsey Clark. Doar wrote that "a political organization at the local level is needed and the designation of examiners alone and the subsequent registration of Negro-electorate by the federal government cannot achieve this."[68] In sum, the DOJ position was that, in the long run, blacks would be better off not relying on federal action to increase black political participation. Federal action would only reinforce the caste system in the South.[69]

According to Civil Rights Division (CRD) lawyers, the political dynamics of the 1965-1969 period dictated that the Department's major thrust had to be the registration of blacks. An "essential judgment was made that registration was necessary" to break down the southern legal blockade aimed at preventing black voting.[70] James Turner, then a staff attorney in CRD, estimated that the Division's manpower of 40 lawyers was committed about 90 percent of the time to Section 4 enforcement and the remaining 10 percent was devoted to all other civil rights problems in the southern section.[71] Consequently, even though the Voting Rights Act armed DOJ with an extraordinarily broad and powerful legal weapon, the basic policy of DOJ was to operate as quietly as possible to obtain voluntary compliance with only one section of the 1965 VRA. Even after *South Carolina v. Katzenbach* and in the face of a deliberate campaign of legal delays, DOJ attorneys continued to treat southern officials "as men who might be convinced of their error."[72]

Because the Voting Rights Act represented "a substantial departure from the ordinary concepts of federalism," the intergovernmental dimensions of voting rights enforcement posed a serious dilemma for CRD. Frederick Wirt, in a study of the impact on one Mississippi county, describes the quandary in this fashion:

...[federalism] is a system devised for a multi-faceted people upon which federal law had to impose some unity. Federal officials have to develop methods of adjusting their centralizing authority to the conflicting demands of a decentralized nation. If they pushed too hard, reasoned CRD, the South would create greater problems of enforcement, spiraling downward with diminishing compliance.[73]

Basically, CRD was caught in the middle: on one side stood state and county officials who despised the federal presence in their jurisdictions and on the other side stood the civil rights workers who demanded action under the new law (as well as the Constitution) rather than simply "presence" and half-hearted attempts to persuade the "racists" to alter local laws so that blacks could exercise their rightful democratic franchise.[74] A sign on the office wall of Assistant Attorney General for Civil Rights Burke Marshall summed up the national government's dilemma best: "Blessed are the peacemakers—for they shall catch hell from both sides."

By the end of the 1960s, CRD considered its enfranchisement task substantially complete "both by means of federal registration efforts and by the impetus that federal registration had given to local registrars to go ahead and register people."[75] Meanwhile, despite the increasing legal ingenuity of the covered jurisdictions to dilute and minimize the impact of the growing black electorate, Section 5 lay dormant. The Johnson Administration had developed no guidelines or procedures for implementing Section 5. "The failure of DOJ to operationalize Section 5 during the first six years was especially troublesome inasmuch as some states had demonstrated their intentions to circumvent VRA by initiating discriminatory changes even while Congress was debating the bill."[76] The next step, given the growing interest in Section 5 of the Voting Rights Act, was the development by the DOJ of guidelines, so that the Section could be implemented. Passage of the 1965 VRA and implementation of the voter registration segments were now past history. Future developments in American society respecting protection of voting rights rested with the development of Section 5 guidelines.

NOTES

1. Lawrence Tribe, *American Constitutional Law* (New York: Foundation Press, 1978), p. 263.

2. See generally, Gunnar Myrdal, *An American Dilemma*, 2 vols. (New York: McGraw-Hill, 1964).

3. ARTICLE XIII

SECTION 1. Neither slavery nor involuntary servitude, except as a punishment for crime whereof the party shall have been duly convicted, shall exist within the United States, or any place subject to their jurisdiction.

SECTION 2. Congress shall have power to enforce this article by appropriate legislation.

ARTICLE XIV

SECTION 1. All persons born or naturalized in the United States, and subject to the jurisdiction thereof, are citizens of the United States and of the State wherein they reside. No State shall make or enforce any law which shall abridge the privileges or immunities of citizens of the United States; nor shall any State deprive any person of life, liberty, or property, without due process of law; nor deny any person within its jurisdiction the equal protection of the laws.

* * *

SECTION 5. The Congress shall have power to enforce, by appropriate legislation, the provision of this article.

ARTICLE XV

SECTION 1. The right of citizens of the United States to vote shall not be denied or abridged by the United States or by any State on account of race, color, or previous condition of servitude.

SECTION 2. The Congress shall have the power to enforce this article by appropriate legislation.

4. Eugene Greshman, "The Unhappy History of Civil Rights Legislation," *Michigan Law Review* 50, 4 (1952): 1323.

5. 109 U.S. 3 (1883).

6. 163 U.S. 537 (1896).

7. See C. Van Woodward, *The Strange Career of Jim Crow* (New York: Oxford University Press, 1957).

8. David J. Garrow, *Protest at Selma: Martin Luther King, Jr. and the Voting Rights of 1965* (New Haven: Yale University Press, 1978), pp. 8-10.

9. Lois B. Moreland, *White Racism and the Law* (Columbus, Ohio: Charles E. Merrill Co., 1970), p. 9.

10. 327 U.S. 649 (1944).

11. Garrow, *Protest at Selma*, pp. 9-10.

12. 347 U.S. 483 (1954).

13. See S. Sidney Ulmer, "Earl Warren and the Brown Decision," *Journal of Politics* 33, 1971.

14. The Court developed the implementation rule for school integration in 1955: integrate "with all deliberate speed." In 1969 after 15 years of evasion of the *Brown* mandate, the Supreme Court in *Alexander v. Holmes County*, 1969 ruled that the new implementation rule was to be: "integrate now." The "all deliberate speed" rule had been used to delay integration.

15. See generally, Jack W. Peltasen, *58 Lonely Men* (Chicago: University of Chicago Press, 1970).

16. Garrow, *Protest at Selma*, p. 5.

17. Congress could only pass legislation in response to state laws that abridged constitutional protections. "It is State action of a particular character that is prohibited....Individual invasion of individual rights is not the subject matter of the 14th Amendment.... [Congress] can provide modes of relief against State legislation...." *The Civil Rights Cases*, 109 U.S. 3 (1883).

18. Jay A. Sigler, *American Rights Policies* (Homewood, Ill.: Dorsey Press, 1975), p. 258.

19. Garrow, *Protest at Selma*, pp. 14-15.

20. Rowland Evans and Robert Novak, *LBJ: The Exercise of Power* (New York: New American Library, 1966).

21. Jonathan Casper, *The Politics of Civil Liberties* (New York: Harper and Row, 1972), chapter 3.

22. Victor S. Navasky, *Kennedy Justice* (New York: Atheneum, 1971), p. 109.

23. Garrow, *Protest at Selma*, pp. 21-22.

24. Navasky, *Kennedy Justice*.

25. Ibid., p. 110.

26. Howell Raines, *My Soul is Rested* (New York: Bantam Books, 1978), p. 372.

27. Steven F. Lawson, *Black Ballots: Voting Rights in the South, 1944-1969* (New York: Columbia University Press, 1976), p. 309.

28. Ibid., pp. 348-49.

29. Garrow, *Protest at Selma*, pp. 28-29; see also Kenneth Vines, "Federal District Judges and Race Relations Cases in the South," *Journal of Politics* 26 (1964).

30. Garrow, *Protest at Selma*, p. 30.

31. Raines, *My Soul is Rested*, p. 371; see also Lyndon Baines Johnson, *Vantage Point* (New York: Holt, Rinehart, and Winston, 1971), p. 161.

32. Interview with James P. Turner, Deputy Assistant Attorney General, Civil Rights Division, U.S. Department of Justice, September 2, 1977, Washington, D.C.

33. Evans and Novak, *LBJ*, p. 493.

34. Johnson, *Vantage Point*.

35. Garrow, *Protest at Selma*, pp. 36-41 passim.

36. Johnson, *Vantage Point*, p. 162.

37. Garrow, *Protest at Selma*, p.2.

38. See generally, Garrow, *Protest at Selma*, and Raines, *My Soul is Rested*.

39. Evans and Novak, *LBJ*, p. 494.

40. Garrow, *Protest at Selma*, p. 82.

41. Evans and Novak, *LBJ*, p. 497.

42. Garrow, *Protest at Selma*, p. 107.

43. The Fifteenth Amendment, in its entirety, states that:"Section 1. The right of citizens of the U.S. to vote shall not be denied or abridged by the U.S. or by any state on account of race, color, or previous condition of servitude. Section 2. The Congress shall have power to enforce this article by appropriate legislation."

44. Archibald Cox, "Foreword: Constitutional Adjudication and the Promotion of Human Rights," *Harvard Law Review* 80, no. 1 (November 1966):91; 102.

45. Greshman, "Unhappy History," p. 1323.

46. *Allen v. Board of Elections*, 393 U.S. 544 (1968).

47. *Perkins v. Matthews*, 400 U.S. 379; 27 L. Ed 2d 476; 91 S Ct. 431 (1970) at 391.

48. Note, "Federal Protection of Negro Voting Rights," *Virginia Law Review* 51, no. 6 (October 1965):1051; 1197.

49. Ibid., p. 1196.

50. Lucius Barker and Twiley Barker, Jr., eds., *Civil Liberties and the Constitution*, 3rd edition (Englewood Cliffs, N.J.: Prentice-Hall, 1978), p. 265.

51. Henry J. Abraham, *Freedom and the Court: Civil Rights and Liberties in the United States*, 2nd edition (New York: Oxford University Press, 1972), p. 339.

52. James C. Harvey, *Black Civil Rights During the Johnson Administration* (Jackson: University and College Press of Mississippi, 1973), pp. 156-57.

53. Archibald Cox, "Constitutionality of Proposed Voting Rights Act of 1965,"*Houston Law Review* 3, no. 1 (November 1965):1.

54. *Katzenbach v. Morgan*, 384 U.S. 641 (1966), involved a provision (Section 4e) of the 1965 Voting Rights Act which enabled individuals who had received at least a sixth grade education in Puerto Rico to vote even though the person could not read or write English. Morgan, a registered voter in New York City, sought an injunction that would prevent hundreds of thousands of city residents from Puerto Rico from voting by enjoining the U.S. Attorney General from applying the 1965 Act. The U.S. District Court judge ruled that the provision "usurped the tenth amendment" police powers of New York. The Attorney General appealed to the U.S. Supreme Court. His argument was that the provision was a proper usage of the "appropriate legislation" power contained in the 14th Amendment. A 7-2 court majority, in an opinion written by Justice William J. Brennan, upheld the provision's goal and purpose. Brennan noted that the draftsman of the enforcement sections of those Civil War Amendments "sought to grant to Congress . . . the same broad powers expressed in the Necessary and Proper Clause, Article 1, Section 8, Clause 18." The provision which guarantees the vote to educated Puerto Ricans who lived in New York City, must "be regarded as an enactment to enforce the Equal Protection Clause." As in *South Carolina*, the court majority in *Morgan* validated the effort by Congress to enforce the substantive guarantees of the Civil War Amendments *even though* these efforts obviously infringed upon the reserved powers of the states. The dissenting opinion in *Morgan*, written by Justice Harlan, and joined by Justice Stewart, argued that "federal authority, legislative no less than judicial, does not intrude *unless* there has been a *denial* by State action of

Fourteenth Amendment limitations. . . [to validate Section 4e] seems to me tantamount to allowing the Fourteenth Amendment to *swallow* the State's constitutionally ordained primary authority in this field." And, if the Congress can interpose in this area of state responsibility, "I see no reason why it could not substitute its judgment for that of the States in other fields of their exclusive primary competence as well."

55. Section 5 required the covered jurisdictions to submit any change in "voting qualifications or prerequisites to voting, or standard, practice, or procedures with respect to voting" different from those in effect on November 1, 1964, to either the U.S. Department of Justice or to the U.S. District Court, in Washington, D.C., for either preclearance or U.S. District Court issuance of a declaratory judgment indicating that the proposed voting change did not have either the purpose or effect of denying or abridging the right to vote on account of race or color.

56. Cox, "Foreword: Constitutional Adjudication," pp. 100-1.

57. Ibid., p. 102.

58. Ibid., p. 103.

59. Note, "Voting Rights Act of 1965," *University of Texas Law Review* 44, 7 (July 1966):1411; 1414. See also, Note, "Federal Protection," p. 1207.

60. *South Carolina v. Katzenbach*, 383 U.S. 301 (1966), pp. 305, 324, 328-29.

61. Ibid., p. 359.

62. Mack H. Jones, "The 1965 Voting Rights Act and Political Symbolism," Paper presented at the 1979 Annual Meeting of the Southern Political Science Association, Gatlinburg, Tenn., November 1-3, 1979, p. 5.

63. *South Carolina v. Katzenbach*, p. 162.

64. U.S. Commission on Civil Rights, *Political Participation* (Washington, D.C.: U.S. Government Printing Office, 1968), pp. 171-79.

65. Ibid., p. 223.

66. Jones, "1965 Voting Rights Act," p. 6.

67. Lawson, *Black Ballots*.

68. U.S. Commission, *Political Participation*, p. 156.

69. Jones, "1965 Voting Rights Act," p. 7.

70. Turner interview.

71. Ibid. In describing his philosophy about voting rights enforcement, Nicholas Katzenbach has said: "I think I was more conscious of, one, the constitutional issues and, secondly, the philosophy that Bob Kennedy had had and that I had, and that was you didn't solve all the South's problems for it." Quoted in Raines, *My Soul is Rested*, p. 372.

72. Frederick M. Wirt, *Politics of Southern Equality* (Chicago: Aldine Publishing Co., 1970), p. 82.

73. Ibid.

74. Raines, *My Soul is Rested*, p. 250.

75. Interview with Gerald Jones, Chief, Voting Section, Civil Rights Division, U.S. Department of Justice, September 2, 1977, Washington, D.C.

76. Jones, "1965 Voting Rights Act," p. 8.

3 Administrative Implementation: Organizational Structure and Bureaucratic Routines

INTRODUCTION

The passage of the Voting Rights Act of 1965 represented both an affirmation of principles and a statement of objectives regarding abhorrent practices of racial discrimination in voting in the United States. As is the case in most public policy situations, the policy formulators (Congress and the President) had delineated a policy objective, but it remained for the policy refiners (the Supreme Court and the bureaucracy) and the policy implementers (the bureaucracy) to develop the guidelines for compliance with the Act. Before examining the bureaucratic routines of voting rights policy implementation, it is important to consider the events leading to the development of procedures for the administration of Section 5.[1]

TOWARD THE DEVELOPMENT OF SECTION 5 PROCEDURES

Section 5 effectively froze all voting patterns in the covered jurisdictions as of November, 1964, unless the U.S. Attorney General or the U.S. District Court was convinced that the proposed voting change would not dilute black voting strength. The Section was to be employed to break the cycle of substitution of new discriminatory laws and practices when the old requirements were either suspended or declared unconstitutional. Procedurally, the Congress intended to have the U.S. District

Court in Washington, D.C., examine all voting change proposals before they were implemented and to issue a declaratory judgment if the change was not discriminatory in purpose or effect. In the legislative process, however, the Department of Justice was added, almost as an afterthought, as a less expensive and less onerous method of obtaining federal approval of "simple" voting changes "susceptible" to ready and quick appraisal.[2] In the haste to bring the legislation to the public as soon as possible after the events of Selma, the Congress kept both avenues to preclearance open but did not clearly delineate the responsibilities and differences between the kinds of submissions that ought to go to the District Court and those that should be submitted to the Attorney General.[3]

Given the policy position of nonconfrontation discussed in Chapter 2, the small number of CRD attorneys assigned to voting rights, and the CRD's commitment to Section 4 enforcement, very few Section 5 submissions were forthcoming from local jurisdictions. The DOJ had no attorney handling these submissions on a regular basis, and there were no guidelines for internal and external assistance. By 1969, however, events within DOJ and elsewhere led to the next generation of civil rights dilemmas: how to make sure that these newly enfranchised black voters would not lose their vote and how to prevent the dilution of this emergent political force. Because Section 5 was the legislative antidote to dilution, its enforcement now took center stage.

In 1966, the Supreme Court, in *South Carolina v. Katzenbach*, judged Section 5 to be constitutional. While admitting that the Voting Rights Act was an "uncommon exercise of congressional power," Chief Justice Earl Warren (reviewing the history of racial turbulence in the South) concluded that "exceptional conditions can justify legislative measures not otherwise appropriate."[4] The test used to measure the constitutionality of Section 5 was the one Chief Justice Marshall had used in 1819: "Let the end be legitimate,...then all means...consistent with the letter and spirit of the Constitution are constitutional." Three years later, in the opinion that combined three Mississippi cases with a Virginia case, the Supreme Court defined the scope of Section 5.

Private litigants in these two southern states had challenged the enforceability of state election laws and procedures. After dealing with a complex jurisdictional question (whether a private individual had the standing to invoke the jurisdiction of a three-judge district court in a Section 5 suit), the Supreme Court turned to the substantive question of whether the new laws in these states were subject to the approval requirements of Section 5 of the Voting Rights Act. The Virginia case involved a bulletin issued to local election judges to aid illiterate voters. This type of notice, the Court said, was subject to Section 5 approval. The three Mississippi cases involved 1966 Amendments to Section 2870 of the Mississippi Code, 1942, which changed the method of voting for county supervisors from district to at-large, made the office of county superintendent of schools an appointive one in some counties, and increased the requirements of an independent candidate to gain a position on a general election ballot.[5]

The Supreme Court, asked if these changes fell within the parameters of Section 5, concluded that "the Voting Rights Act was aimed to the subtle, as well as the obvious, state regulations which have the effect of denying citizens their right to vote because of their race."[6] The Court concluded that Section 5 ought to be construed liberally and that lower courts would not be able to restrict the limit of the Section 5 protection.

In *Allen v. State Board of Elections*, the Court also addressed the issue of preclearance submission procedures. Appellees had contended that since no formal preclearance submissions were required by the Attorney General, their Section 5 obligations were fulfilled whenever the Attorney General became aware of state enactments. After taking notice of the absence of formal procedures, the Court stated that the Voting Rights Act "required that the State in some unambiguous and recordable manner submit any legislation or regulation...directly to the Attorney General with a request for his consideration...."[7]

Allen, along with *Perkins v. Matthews*,[8] had a significant effect on the evolving implementation process. The Court outlined at least seven basic types of voting changes subject to Section 5 preclearance:

(1) redistricting;
(2) annexation;
(3) polling places;
(4) precinct changes;

(5) reregistration procedures;
(6) incorporations; and
(7) changes in election laws such as filing fees, at-large elections, etc.

The Supreme Court's conclusion, that the scope of Section 5 was broad enough to encompass every action that affected the state or local electoral system in the covered jurisdictions, came at the time of great stress for the civil rights movement. While *Allen* was followed by an increase in the number of preclearances filed with the Department of Justice in 1969, the Department of Justice was under the direction of a new (Republican) President, Richard M. Nixon. Nixon had run on a platform that called for the withdrawal of even the smallest federal "presence" in the South in the area of civil rights.

The Nixon Administration threatened "even the easygoing enforcement of the Voting Rights Act's key provisions because [the Act gave] great discretionary power and authority to the Attorney General."[9] This attack on the Voting Rights Act was a part of the "southern strategy," whereby the new administration would weaken or eviscerate various civil rights and social service measures that had been enacted under the leadership of Democratic presidents.

Nixon and his close friend and advisor (the new Attorney General of the United States), John N. Mitchell, believed that the Voting Rights Act had to be dramatically revised. Nixon was also very concerned about the personnel in the Department of Justice's Civil Rights Division. As he wrote years later, Nixon was "determined to ensure that the young liberal lawyers in the CRD would be prevented from running wild through the South enforcing compliance with extreme or punitive requirements they had formulated in Washington, D.C."[10] The Nixon strategy was to try to kill the Voting Rights Act when it came up for renewal in 1970. Additionally, the Nixon Justice Department greatly weakened the Section 5 enforcement process by objecting to submitted voting changes only when the Civil Rights Division attorneys saw in the proposed change a clear case of racial discrimination. "The Department's actual practices removed the burden on the submitting jurisdiction by requiring that either the department or interested private parties develop evidence that the proposed change would be iniquitous to blacks."[11]

Despite the antipathy of the new administration (and, in part, because of it), there were a number of events that, collectively, led the CRD to construct a strategy and elaborate guidelines with respect to Section 5 implementation. These legal, administrative, and political forces had the cumulative effect of raising Section 5 to the "highest priority of the Voting Section of the Civil Rights Division."[12]

These were (in addition to the 1969 *Allen* opinion):

(1) reorganization of the Civil Rights Division during 1969, the first year of the Nixon Administration;
(2) the passage of the 1970 Amendments to the Voting Rights Act and defeat of the Nixon proposals for eliminating Section 5;
(3) the growing strength of civil rights groups in the South;
(4) pressure for submission guidelines from conservative white leaders in the South; and
(5) legislative oversight committee criticism.

NIXON ADMINISTRATION REORGANIZATION OF THE CIVIL RIGHTS DIVISION

In the early days of the Nixon Administration, in line with the President's dislike of the young liberal attorneys running around in the DOJ, a change took place in the organization of the Civil Rights Division. In October, 1969, the Division was reorganized along functional rather than geographic lines. As a consequence of the 1969 reorganization, a reshuffling occured in CRD. "People were given the opportunity to make a choice and then these were submitted to the Assistant Attorney General's Office and then on the basis of those selections, assignments were made."[13] Some desired to get out of the education area and into voting. Others wanted to continue in voting, and asked to remain.

Whatever the real reasons for the reorganization—greater political control of the sections or a more effective utilization of legal skills—its effect was to establish a cadre of line attorneys, 13 in all, who were strongly committed to the enforcement of voting rights laws. These Voting Section lawyers became *the* Section 5 experts and, with the addition of paralegal analysts in the next few years, initiated a concerted campaign to implement Section 5. However absent other events, the reorganization alone would not have accounted for the dramatic increase in the number of submissions received by DOJ after 1970.

CONGRESSIONAL EXTENSION OF THE VOTING RIGHTS ACT AND DEFEAT OF THE NIXON ADMINISTRATION PROPOSALS

Congressional debates in 1969 and 1970 on the question of extending the VRA clearly indicated that Attorney General John Mitchell seriously questioned the workability of Section 5. During the summer of 1969, he appeared before the House Judiciary Committee to argue against the extension of the Act in its original shape and scope. Not prepared to support "regional legislation" and opposed to an outright extension of the Act as well as its enforcement, Mitchell suggested that: (1) preclearance procedures under Section 5 be abandoned as unnecessary, and (2) the Act be amended so that CRD's Voting Section be required to monitor voting changes nationally and, if discriminatory voting changes were discovered, the DOJ should go to District Court and seek the traditional relief. "In contrast to the 1965 Act, our proposal leaves the decisions to the Court where in our opinion it belongs; it properly places the burden of proof on the Government and not on the states,...it is not necessary any more to discriminate against these southern states."[14]

Furthermore, Mitchell's position with respect to voting changes did not include either redistricting or annexation plans. There was an instant response to Administration thinking. Representative William McCullough, ranking Republican member of the House Judiciary Committee, was so outraged by Mitchell's suggestions that he countered: "The proposal sweeps broadly into those areas where the need is least, and retreats from those areas where the need is the greatest. The Administration has created a remedy for which there is no wrong and leaves grievous wrongs without adequate remedy."[15]

In the ensuing months, the Nixon Administration, having alienated the civil rights forces with these potential modifications, proceeded to alienate the southern forces by not supporting the proposals in the Congress. Finally, Congress passed the 1970 Amendments to the 1965 Voting Rights Act. The legislation extended the Act for an additional five-year period, ended the use of literacy tests nationally, lowered the voting age in federal elections, and standardized residency requirements. Congressional insistence on retaining the preclearance procedures signaled "a strong mandate to us in the CRD to improve the enforcement of Section 5."[16]

Oregon v. Mitchell was the judgment of the Supreme Court that examined the 1970 amendments to the 1965 Voting Rights Act. These amendments continued the provisions in the 1965 legislation and also lowered the voting age to 18 for federal and state elections by using the "appropriate legislation" enforcement clauses of the Fourteenth and Fifteenth Amendments. In a decision that had no clear-cut majority, the Court ruled that Congress did not have the power to lower the voting age for state elections.[17] Congress, however, immediately adopted the Twenty-Sixth Amendment to reverse the justices on the issue of voting age in state elections.[18]

By the end of 1971, after five years of judicial review of the 1965 Voting Rights Act (in *South Carolina, Morgan, Allen, Perkins, Oregon,* and others), the U.S. Supreme Court had substantially validated the radical legislation of the Congress and had accepted the radical idea that Congress could give meaning to the substantive words of the Civil War Amendments and then positively act to enforce these perceptions by enacting prophylactic legislation that adversely impacted on the "reserved powers" of the states.

As a consequence of judicial validation of the Voting Rights Act, the Tenth Amendment was, once again, perceived by southerners as having been eviscerated by the U.S. Congress and by the U.S. Supreme Court. Arguments made by advocates of the "reserved powers" of the states were rejected by the Supreme Court majorities in favor of the view that congressional power to enact legislation to enforce the Fourteenth and Fifteenth Amendments was not to be restrained by the Tenth Amendment.

Whether these judgments by the Supreme Court involving Section 5 would actually lead to legislative supremacy, to the "swallowing" of the states by the national government, to the states becoming "conquered provinces" that would have to "beg" federal authorities for permission to function, was to be left up to the federal administrators who would have to develop and implement these validated provisions of the Voting Rights Act. All the court opinions through 1971 validated in no uncertain terms the possibility of major federal inroads into the traditional "police powers" of the states.

DEVELOPMENT OF CIVIL RIGHTS ORGANIZATIONAL VIABILITY

Still another element in the unfolding 1969-1971 Section 5 enforcement scenario was the growing strength of the civil rights organizations in the Deep South. David Norman, a former DOJ official in the Nixon Administration, has commented that a growing force pushing Voting Rights Act enforcement came from the civil rights groups as they became adept at using Section 5.[19]

Recognition of the importance of the Section and the subsequent reporting of violations by civil rights groups had the effect of putting additional pressure on the CRD just as they were gearing up for intensive work with Section 5. One reason for the CRD/Voting Section's hesitancy was uncertainty over the scope and dimensions of Section 5. Attorney General Mitchell had excluded annexation and redistricting from coverage; he also suggested that the burden of proof fall upon the govenment with respect to demonstrating discrimination. The staff attorneys in the Voting Section believed that Section 5 covered annexation and redistricting but were constrained by the policy makers in DOJ. This impasse was cleared up in 1969 when the Supreme Court announced the *Allen* case.

PRESSURE FOR SUBMISSION GUIDELINES FROM CONSERVATIVE WHITE LEADERS IN THE SOUTH

As these political, legal, and administrative events increased the pressure on the covered jurisdictions to submit voting changes to the federal government in Washington, D.C., the local units and their representatives in Congress began to insist on some set of firm guidelines from the Department of Justice. The strongest demands for regulations came from conservative southern lawyers who had to comply with the Act but did not know how to comply because there were no preclearance procedures in existence. Complaints were made "at the highest level in the Nixon Administration" about the lack of specific guidelines.[20]

IMPACT OF CONGRESSIONAL CIVIL RIGHTS OVERSIGHT COMMITTEES

A few months before the Department of Justice's Civil Rights Division announced its preliminary guidelines in the *Federal Register*, Representative Don Edward's (D-Cal.) Civil Rights Oversight Committee of the House Judiciary Committee held hearings on the enforcement of the 1965 Voting Rights Act by the Department of Justice. These meetings were extremely critical of the way in which Justice had enforced the Voting Rights Act.

Edwards himself began the sessions by noting that reregistration of all voters was underway in several dozen black counties, and that the department had displayed almost no interest in considering whether any of these reregistrations could work to dilute black voting strength. Furthermore, a number of these counties conducting reregistration had not even submitted their plans for doing so to Justice, and the department, lacking any system for detecting the illegal implementation of unsubmitted changes, had failed to take any action to insure compliance with section 5 by those subdivisions prior to the implementation of the reregistration plans.[21]

In response, the Nixon Justice Department attorneys present assured the legislators that they were in the process of adopting a set of guidelines to administer the requirements of Section 5 of the Voting Rights Act.

The development of these regulations took place under trying circumstances. Section 5 had not been implemented at all by the Department of Justice during the Johnson years, 1965-1968, because of the policy judgment, made in 1965, that registration was the first priority of the Civil Rights Division in Justice. By the time Richard Nixon took office in 1969, there was a growing demand that Justice seriously work to implement Section 5 of the Voting Rights Act. Supreme Court opinions, especially *Allen*, led to increased filings by southern jurisdictions, but the submitters did not have any guidance. Within two years, however, the attorneys in the Civil Rights Division, confronted with hard, painful cross pressures (from an angry Nixon and Mitchell who wanted to see the Voting Rights Act die, from the Supreme Court, civil rights groups, and legislators in Congress who were extremely critical of the lack of formal rules to implement Section 5, and from southern whites who were under pressure from local civil rights organizations to submit voting changes), were forced to promulgate rules for the implementation of Section 5.

The initial phase of implementing the Voting Rights Act, that of using federal marshals and examiners to register blacks in the South, had come to an end in the late 1960s. The second phase, the first years of the Nixon Administration, 1969-1971, characterized by dilatory tactics and largely unsuccessful efforts to kill the Voting Rights Act itself, had come to a close with the announcement of the regulations in September 1971. The implementation of voting rights protection was thus to enter a new phase in its short, checkered history.

IMPLEMENTATION PRACTICES AND PROCEDURES

The organizational structure and the bureaucratic routines of an organization charged with responsibility for policy implementation can have a significant influence on the manner in which policy objectives are accomplished. Responsibility for Section 5 implementation rests with the lawyer-bureaucrats working in the Voting Section of the Civil Rights Division at the Department of

Justice. The central concern of the remainder of this chapter is to examine how organizational arrangements and bureaucratic procedures have affected the manner in which the Voting Section has been able to achieve compliance with the requirements of the 1965 Voting Rights Act.

THE DEPARTMENT OF JUSTICE: ORGANIZATION AND PERSONNEL

Although the Department of Justice was founded in 1870 and the office of Attorney General is as old as the Constitution itself, the Civil Rights Division was not established until 1957, and the Voting Section did not emerge until 1969 (Figure 3.1). The Civil Rights Division was established in 1957 after the passage of the Civil Rights Act of that year. The CRD has primary responsibility for the enforcement of the Civil Rights Acts of 1957, 1960, 1964, and 1968, as well as the Voting Rights Act of 1965, and it reports to an Associate Attorney General who has responsibility for supervision and coordination of civil rights matters in the department. From 1957 until 1969, the CRD was organized into sections corresponding to geographic regions.

Each of the sections handled the full range of civil rights matters within a particular geographic area. In 1969, it was reorganized along function lines with Section 5 enforcement responsibility falling to the Voting Section (Figure 3.2).

However, voting rights enforcement is not strictly speaking the responsibility of the Voting Section; it is the task of a cadre of lawyers and paraprofessionals working in the Section. At least two characteristics of those personnel are worth noting before turning to a consideration of the administrative processing of preclearance submissions.

During the 1960s, the Civil Rights Division devoted approximately 90 percent of its time to Section 4 (voter registration) enforcement. For Division personnel, this often meant civil rights experience in the field as part of the Department of Justice's voter registration supervision activities. As one Voting Section official put it: "Right after the Act was passed, there was a large focus on trying to get blacks registered, and then through the voting

Figure 3.1
U.S. Department of Justice

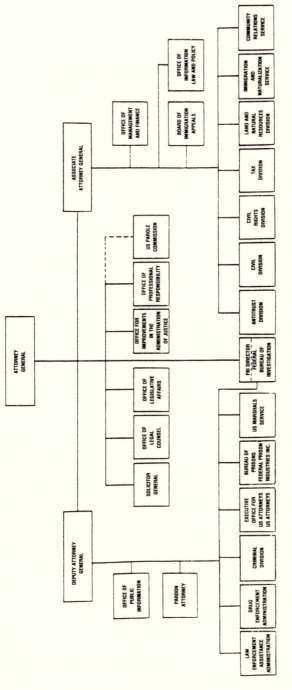

Source: U.S. Department of Justice, Office of the Attorney General, *The Annual Report of the Attorney General of the United States 1979*, (Washington, D.C.: U.S. Government Printing Office, 1979), p. iv.

Figure 3.2
Civil Rights Division

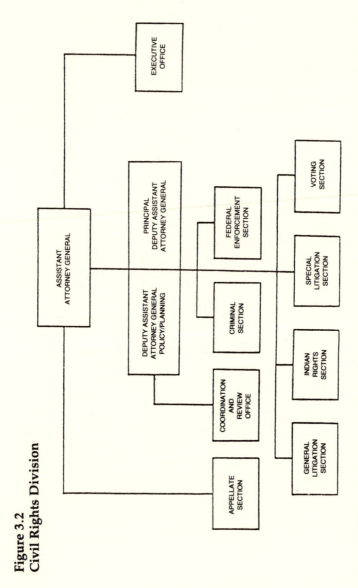

Source: U.S. Department of Justice, Office of the Attorney General, *The Annual Report of the Attorney General of the United States 1979*, (Washington, D.C.: U.S. Government Printing Office, 1979), p. 112.

process. That is where the manpower went in those sections; going into areas, finding out what the problems were, and determining whether or not they should be designated for Federal Examiners."[22] In the early 1970s, some of the lawyer-bureaucrats who were handling preclearance submissions were, therefore, individuals with prior civil rights field experience and familiarity with local situations. In recent years, however, the Voting Section has been staffed with individuals who usually do not have direct knowledge of local situations. As a result, they have had to rely more heavily on whatever information local officials are willing to submit. This change in the nature of CRD personnel is one important factor shaping the interaction between Justice Department administrators and officials from covered jurisdictions.

A second important personnel characteristic is the training and background of Department of Justice personnel. As Richard Stillman has reminded us, Department of Justice staff members tend to be legal specialists rather than policy generalists.[23] He has argued that "the narrow legal technical orientation gained from . . . case method training makes lawyers particularly unfit to address broad policy issues of large public agencies, particularly of the Department of Justice.[24] Although the question of fitness to address broad policy issues is not our concern here, it does appear that the legal training of Justice Department lawyers has oriented them in the direction of preferring case-by-case solutions to problems. Compromise and bargaining are perceived to be normal and appropriate techniques for achieving acceptable issue resolutions. The lawyer's orientation to problem solving is, therefore, a second important factor structuring the interaction between Justice Department administrators and officials from covered jurisdictions. When Department of Justice lawyer-bureaucrats interact with lawyers representing the covered jurisdictions, the preclearance process becomes essentially a lawyer's game.

ADMINISTRATIVE PROCESSING OF PRECLEARANCE SUBMISSIONS

Although a few jurisdictions made preclearance submissions during the late 1960s (from 1965 to 1969, a total of 323 voting changes were submitted), Section 5 enforcement lay virtually dormant until the turn of the decade. The few early submissions to the Department of Justice were voluntary and done with very little understanding of exactly what Section 5 entailed. The Justice Department had not paid much attention to Section 5 enforcement, choosing instead to concentrate its efforts and manpower on achieving the voter registration objectives embodied in Section 4. Commenting on this lack of attention to Section 5, the Head of the Voting Section noted:

By the end of the decade that job [voter registration] had been largely accomplished, both by means of Federal registration and by the impetus that Federal registration had given to local registrars to go ahead and register people, then the focus turned to Section 5. This is an area of the Voting Rights Act we had not given much attention to up to this point.[25]

After the events of 1969-1971 which led the Civil Rights Division to turn its attention to Section 5 enforcement, and the subsequent development and promulgation of administrative regulations[26] in September of 1971, the number of voting changes submitted for preclearance increased dramatically (from 255 in 1970 to over 1,000 in 1971). In 1976, local jurisdictions submitted 7,470 voting "changes" to the Department of Justice.[27] In each year since 1977, between 4,000 and 5,000 voting related changes have been submitted. (See Appendices C and D). A single submission from a covered jurisdiction often contains multiple changes like moving six polling places or 67 annexations. Each change has to be researched and analyzed as to the likelihood that it is discriminatory. Primary resonsibility for processing the daily load of approximately 20 changes rests with the attorneys and paralegal staff of the Civil Rights Division's Voting Section.

The Voting Section is divided for operational purposes into the Submission Unit and the Litigative Staff, as illustrated in Table 3.1.

Before the 1975 amendments, Department of Justice attorneys reviewed voting changes with assistance from five paraprofessionals who were paired with attorneys to serve as "law clerks." With the anticipated growth in submissions resulting from the new minor-

Table 3.1
Voting Section Professional and Paraprofessional Staffing
as of July 1977

<table>
<tr><td colspan="2" align="center">*CHIEF*</td></tr>
<tr><td colspan="2" align="center">Deputy Chief[a]</td></tr>
<tr>
<td align="center">SUBMISSION UNIT
1 Senior Attorney Advisor[b]
1 Paraprofessional Director
11 Paraprofessionals</td>
<td align="center">LITIGATIVE STAFF
1 Assistant for Litigation
13 Attorneys
2 Paraprofessionals</td>
</tr>
</table>

[a]Responsible for administration of the Voting Section and election coverage activity.
[b]Also performs litigative activity.

Source: U.S. Comptroller General, General Accounting Office, *Voting Rights Act—Enforcement Needs Strengthening*, February 6, 1978, Appendix 6.

ity language provisions, six more paraprofessionals were added as part of a February, 1976, reorganization.[28] After a period of training by Voting Section attorneys, the research analysts (the preferred title of the paraprofessionals) assumed principal responsibility for examination of voting changes.[29] The position of paraprofessional was developed at the Civil Rights Division prior to the passage of the Voting Rights Act as the following description by the Chief of the Voting Section indicates:

It has an interesting history to it because the Civil Rights Division practically created the position which is now developed into the paralegal specialist. During the early days of the sixties, when we in the division were largely involved in developing those big voting cases prior to the Voting Rights Act, it meant going into counties and plowing into all of those registration records and trying to decipher this application as opposed to that one—why this guy was registered and this one wasn't, that kind of thing. John Boyd was here at the time. He came up with the idea of why should a lawyer have to sit down and go through all of those records? Why don't we use non-legal people with a good, practical, analytical mind [sic] to do that, and we did. It started out just using the secretaries to do that kind of thing and then we brought in people, college grads usually, right out of school and eager to get involved. We assigned them to doing that kind of work and called them research analysts. That kind of took on and we spread it into other areas in the civil rights field after we got into the functional areas. After we created the Voting Section in 1969, I started pushing the idea that what we needed to do is get more research analysts into analyzing these submissions because most of it is factual—that is, gathering facts and making an analysis of a local factual-type situation.[30]

The Section 5 unit's paraprofessionals and their director come from a diverse background. Presently, some are law students, others are simply college graduates who qualified for this GS 5-10 level job, and others have been clerical employees elsewhere in the Department. In commenting on the prime talent he looks for in a candidate, the attorney responsible for the Submission Unit stated:

Just the ability to speak to people in Mississippi or Alabama or Georgia, blacks and whites. Just an intelligent person who can learn just what we are looking for. Just willing to deal with people a bit resourcefully. . . . Writing ability is very important because they have a lot of letters to write.[31]

No explicit training manual for the analysts exists; instead the training is essentially an on-the-job process.[32]

Because the Voting Rights Act insists that submissions be acted upon within a 60-day time limit, the Submission Unit must gather, analyze, and verify the necessary evidence and then make a decision with speed uncharacteristic of adjudicatory proceedings. They cannot delay. Failure to review a submission in 60 days results in its preclearance, even if the proposed change is discriminatory.

In addition to the time factor, Voting Section personnel encounter another difficulty during the processing of preclearance submissions. The Voting Section is mandated to issue a federal imprimatur for all changes in electoral qualifications, practices, or procedures in all of the covered jurisdictions. Jurisdictions covering the original 1965 Act include approximately 550 counties and several thousand cities, towns, villages, and other special districts. From the viewpoint of the Voting Section, the logistics of enforcement pose a nearly insurmountable task because the relatively small staff of the Submission Unit located in Washington, D.C., must monitor the actions of elected officials (in often isolated communities) throughout the Deep South without the aid of their own field personnel.

Given the volume of changes, the shortage of personnel, and the urgency of time, the preclearance process has not surprisingly evolved as a series of routinized tasks and discretionary judgments. Table 3.2 illustrates the process.[33]

Table 3.2
Voting Change Preclearance Process

PHASE ONE: INITIAL PROCESSING

1. Letter from submitting authority passes through DOJ mail sort and arrives at Section 5 office.

DAY 1

(60-day
time limit
begins here)

2. Paraprofessional staff member logs submission in triplicate on an information card which serves as:
   (a) a label for the submission file to be maintained,
   (b) input data for computer listings,
   (c) a control card for compliance follow-up.

3. To complete the information card, the para-professional:
   (a) notes type of change(s) in the submission,
   (b) assigns each change in the submission an identification number (change number),
   (c) dates receipt of submission by Section 5 office,
   (d) estimates review completion date,
   (e) describes submitting jurisdiction, and
   (f) lists name of the paraprofessional assigned to analyze the submission.

4. Paraprofessional director reads letter from submitting authority and assigns the submission to a paraprofessional giving consideration to the

Table 3.2 continued

geographic origin and complexity of the change and to the experience of the paraprofessional. (Some letters received by the Section 5 office are not submissions, but rather requests for information and receive appropriate response from the paraprofessional director at this point.)

PHASE TWO: CASE ANALYSIS BY
PARAPROFESSIONAL
1. Previous record is checked for information, for example:
    (a) name(s) of city attorney,
    (b) form of government,
    (c) population characteristics.

2. If no previous file exists, new record is developed.

3. Demographic and legal information about the proposed voting change is obtained, for example:
    (a) nature of the area annexed,
    (b) location and number of new polling places,
    (c) existence of petitions to annex.

4. Contacts are made with minorities in affected area and officials of the submitting authority.

5. On the basis of this research, the paraprofessional recommends one of the following courses of action:
    (a) the submission cannot be reviewed under Section 5 at the time,
    (b) additional information should be requested from the submitting authority,
    (c) no objection should be interposed, or
    (d) an objection should be interposed.

PHASE THREE: FINAL DECISION

DAY 45
1. Paraprofessional director makes a procedural review of the case analysis.

DAYS 45
to 60
2. Legal review and decision are made by Senior Attorney, Section 5 Office.

Table 3.2 continued

    3. If decision is either "no objection" or "change
      cannot be reviewed under section 5 at the time,"
      then a standard letter is returned to the submitting
      authority.
               END OF PRECLEARANCE PROCESS.

    4. If decision is to "object", then
        (a) Section 5 Attorney prepares letter of
            objection,
        (b) Chief, Voting Section, reviews letter of
            objection,
        (c) Deputy Assistant Attorney General, Civil
            Rights Division, reviews letter of objection,
        (d) Assistant Attorney General, Civil Rights
            Division, reviews and signs letter of
            objection,

DAY 60   (e) Letter of objection mailed to submitting
            authority.
               END OF PRECLEARANCE PROCESS.
               LITIGATION STAFF INVOLVED.

*PHASE FOUR: FOLLOW-UP ON REQUEST FOR
ADDITIONAL INFORMATION*
    1. If submitting authority complies, then preclearance
      begins again at Day 1.

DAY 90   2. If 30 days elapse without receipt of additonal information,
      Section 5 office initiates a memo requesting a FBI
      investigation.

    3. Memo is reviewed by Chief, Observer Program.

    4. FBI visits submitting authority.

    5. Usually, submitting authority mails requested
      information.
               PRECLEARANCE PROCESS BEGINS
                        AGAIN AT DAY 1

Designed to satisfy the recordkeeping requirements of Section 51.26 of the Act, the initial preclearance phase simply creates the necessary documentation for subsequent decisions. In contrast, the second phase of the preclearance process is pivotal because the paralegal research analysts make the initial (and normally upheld) determinations with respect to whether or not the proposed change has a discriminatory purpose or effect. Their casework includes not only gathering and analyzing sufficient information about the submission, but also includes the critical decision on the action to be followed by the Voting Section.

A perusal of the steps comprising phase two discloses a rather ordinary and straightforward approach to processing submissions. Underlying these standard operating procedures are three points of decision, which entail substantial discretion. First, the preparation and analysis of the demographic and legal information about each change is in the hands of paraprofessionals who possess neither demographic/statistical skills nor legal training. Since Section 51.10 mandates that the covered jurisdictions transmit all relevant materials including census data, there is room for differences of opinion about the quality of the submitted data, as well as the distinct possibility of data manipulation. In many cases, this issue does not pose a serious problem. In some of the more extreme situations, however, the absence of analytic abilities within the Submission Unit has led to the underestimation of the minority population.[34]

The second major point of administrative discretion develops out of the standard procedure "to telephone minority persons in the locality to see if the voting change is going to bother them.[35] The number of local minority contacts made per case depends, as one paraprofessional put it, "on the type of change—the more significant the change, the more contacts required."[36] Research analysts in the Voting Section select these "contacts" from an inhouse file of minority political leaders and other individuals considered knowledgeable about race relations in a given locality. Supplementing the documents from the submitting authority, contacts with local white officials are also normally made and received. From this brief description, it becomes obvious that the procedures used by paraprofessionals place them in an adjudicatory role.

This judgment takes tangible form in the recommendation about the case. While the paraprofessional can choose one of four options, it is the decision to object or not to object that is crucial to all parties. This choice, although ostensibly based on detailed information, confronts a fundamental substantive problem in the preclearance process: under what circumstances and given what characteristics will a voting change be objected to by the Department of Justice? Put another way, what is the "operational definition" of discriminatory purpose or effect as discussed in Section 5?[37]

In essence, the determination of discrimination has become routinized through the adoption of some elementary decision rules. The research analysts are trained to spot "red flags" or "suspicious type changes."[38] These include at-large elections, reductions in the number of polling places, changes in the location of polling places, and redistricting. Proposed changes such as these examples alert the paralegals to investigate the motive behind the change and the potential impact of the change. Investigating motivation and impact in often isolated localities throughout the South and Southwest without a field staff puts a premium on the telephone calls to on-site persons. Yet, even after a number of contacts and extensive documentation, the operationalization of discrimination ultimately becomes "situational." In the words of the Director of the paraprofessional staff, "one looks at the circumstances of the change: the area, the people affected, what's going to hurt the people."[39]

The final phase within the 60-day time limit is the most hectic, with letters usually being mailed at the last possible moment. Casework on a proposed change must reach the paraprofessional director's desk no later than Day 45 for procedural review. Legal review and final recommendation by the Submission Unit Attorney is the last step. Describing this process, the Submission Unit Staff Attorney said:

I want them [paraprofessionals] to do all the research on it and let the decision be made at a higher level than it is actually done. If they recommend objection and we are not objecting, we can just change it. If they recommend a no objection, and haven't done the homework on it, it's likely to go out that way. . .I might not catch it, or it just might not be visible to me while I'm checking. It's better that they make mistakes, instead of doing too much.[40]

Because the review and signature steps in regard to interposing an "objection" will catch almost all errors, the chance of mistake is more likely in the finding of "no objection."

When the decision is to seek additional information from the submitting authority, a subsequent procedure is followed. If the local officials respond promptly, they merely go back to Day 1 and begin preclearance over again. However, if they delay more than 30 days, the Section 5 office initiates a memo, which brings the FBI to their community. The almost automatic nature of phase four comes out in this description by the Voting Section's Chief:

If they are out thirty days or more, we will send the FBI out to meet with the official and find out what the problem is. Usually that has the best result, when the FBI goes out and visits. We are getting a lot more of the submissions completed now than we once did.[41]

Use of the FBI in this fashion is seen as a free resource by the Voting Section and serves as part of their surrogate field staff. Although Voting Section personnel believe that use of the FBI "is fairly effective in stimulating a response,"[42] the 1978 Government Accounting Office report on voting rights enforcement suggests that local officials do not necessarily tremble and quiver before the federal "muscle." Some jurisdictions have not responded in over two years after receipt of a request for additional information about a proposed voting change.[43] Even more damaging, the proposed changes are often implemented and elections conducted without completion of the preclearance process.

THE CONSEQUENCES OF ADMINISTRATIVE PRACTICES AND PROCEDURES

What becomes clear from the previous discussion is that in operationalizing "discriminatory purpose or effect," Department of Justice officials have evolved some elementary decision rules which they call upon when confronted with a new submission. However, these are essentially cognitive decision rules that individual research analysts have come to learn from experience, rather than formal standards that delineate objectional kinds of voting changes. To be sure, 28 CFR 51 informs covered jurisdictions about the requirement to submit voting changes for preclearance; it tells them about the kinds of changes that must be submitted and about the types of supporting evidence required; but it does not (and probably cannot) provide much information about the criteria Department of Justice officials will be applying in making a decision as to whether or not to enter an objection (see Section 51.19). Two important consequences flow from this situation: (1) covered jurisdictions may be at least partially in the dark as to what counts as evidence on nondiscrimination, particularly when they have not had previous experience with the preclearance process; and (2) in the absence of standards that identify in advance the acceptability of certain kinds of voting changes, decisions regarding the acceptability of submitted changes are frequently a matter of negotiation between local officials and the Voting Section.

Since the burden of proof under Section 5 is on the submitting authority, it is important for covered jurisdictions to know what counts as evidence of nondiscrimination. Kenneth Culp Davis has argued [44] that in addition to other safeguards (for example, judicial review), administrative actions should also be subject to predetermined or prospective rules which are known in advance to the affected parties. The Department of Justice has, of course, made some effort to inform covered jurisdictions about the requirements of Section 5. After 28 CFR 51 was published, Voting Section attorneys traveled to some jurisdictions to meet with local officials. By 1973, information packets (containing the Amended 1965 Act, the 1971 Procedures for Administration of the Act, and a request to send all preclearances to either the Department of Justice or to submit them to the District Court for a declaratory judgment) were sent to all covered jurisdictions.

It should also be noted that covered jurisdictions are not entirely without guidance as to the operational standard for determining "discriminatory purpose or effect." In its 1976 opinion in the New Orleans redistricting case, *Beer v. U.S.*,[45] the Supreme Court articulated a standard that has come to be generally regarded as a benchmark. In the opinion written by Justice Stewart, the Court held that the purpose of Section 5 "has always been to insure that no voting procedure changes would be made that would lead to a retrogression in the position of racial minorities with respect to their effective exercise of the electoral franchise." This means that a change that results in an improvement of the position of minority voters is not likely to be objected to even if a better condition could have been achieved. As an attorney in the Submission Unit put it, "If a change makes something better, we're not supposed to object even if it is still not very good."[46]

Attorneys in the Voting Section believe that over 90 percent of all voting changes are reported to the Attorney General, and that those that remain unreported are probably the least dangerous types of change with respect to diluting the black vote.[47] Of those reported, approximately 95 percent are precleared. A major factor in the high preclearance rate is the process of informal discussion—advisement, assistance, and negotiation—between local government officials and Department of Justice officials. If there is a possibility of a Department of Justice objection, local officials often try to elicit from the Voting Section what they would minimally have to do to pass the preclearance test.[48]

The Voting Section apparently does not want to interfere excessively in local policy-making processes and prefers to work with local officials in the covered jurisdictions (when asked) in a cooperative manner. This posture is illustrated by the following comment by the attorney in charge of preclearance submissions in the Voting Section:

[Local jurisdictions] want guidelines, they want to know what we are going to look for. They're going to revise their city charter and the city attorney will call me up to ask...and this is a widespread type of request.... They have a job to do and they want to get our clearance...we'll do what we can for them...we try to make things go smoothly for them so they can hold elections.[49]

There can be little doubt that the strategy of negotiating over the difficult parts of potentially objectionable preclearance submissions has facilitated the task of obtaining procedural compliance with Section 5 of the Voting Rights Act. That is a very positive accomplishment. However, this strategy—no matter what its virtues—is problematical in two important ways. First, it may produce substantive compliance at very marginal levels of acceptability. The negotiation process can produce "no objection" whenever the affected black population is not harmed by proposed voting changes, although their relative voting strength may not have been substantially improved. It may permit an unconstitutional scheme to be replaced with a less obnoxious, but possibly still somewhat discriminatory procedure. Second, a negotiation strategy is not very helpful in providing guidance as to what counts as evidence of nondiscrimination. As Lowi has noted, "there is an implicit rule in every bargained or adjudicated case, but it cannot be known to the bargainer until he knows the outcome, and its later application must be deciphered by lawyers representing potential cases."[50] These are significant compliance problems that result from a policy implementation process that relies heavily on negotiated preclearances.

This individualized approach to obtaining compliance partially achieves the substantive objectives of the Voting Rights Act. Yet, the preclearance process transpires in the absence of specified decision criteria that are well known in advance to those who have the obligation to comply with Section 5. For Department of Justice decision makers, the problem is perhaps less severe since the experience of past decisions provides guides, or rules of thumb, for their future decisions. However, local jurisdictions, which are much less frequently involved and not themselves parties to past decisions involving other jurisdictions, are not much better off in terms of knowing "what counts" as the result of this implementation approach. It is doubtful that Department of Justice officials could ever formulate a complete set of decision criteria setting down exactly what counts as evidence of nondiscrimination—the nature of the subject militates against very precise standards. Perhaps, however, they can do better than they are now doing. If local jurisdictions are required to comply with federal regulations, they are entitled to have some guidance as to the decision criteria by which their preclearance submissions will be judged. (Hypothetical example cases drawn up with real situations in mind are a possible alternative to rules enunciating general principles.)[51]

In perspective, however, the more serious of the two concerns may be that negotiation results in missed opportunities. Some voting changes are no doubt precleared that are free of all visible traces of racial discrimination—optimal preclearances. However, changes may also be precleared that only result in less discrimination than was present in the prior condition—suboptimal preclearances. Critics of the Department of Justice have argued that the all-too-frequent selection of suboptimal preclearances rather than optimal ones amounts to missed opportunities on the part of federal voting rights officials. In rebuttal, Department of Justice officials point out that to do otherwise may very well result in less Section 5 compliance than presently achieved. A closer examination of this defense will be considered in Chapter 6.

Implicit in the foregoing discussion of administrative practices and procedures is the notion that voting rights policy implementation is an interactive process between those who interpret and apply the policy and those who are afffected by it. Success in implementing voting rights policy has necessitated shared action across levels of government in a federal system where local responses to national government initiatives are not always automatic.

From the viewpoint of local governments upon which the burden of submission falls, the matter of compliance has seemed from the outset to reflect the agony Justice Black expressed in *South Carolina v. Katzenbach*[52] about local officials having to entreat distant federal bureaucrats. In the face of continuing resistance both locally and in Washington to the Act, the Civil Rights Division has had to devise a strategy of enforcement that would obtain compliance without turning the covered jurisdictions into "conquered provinces." From the viewpoint of civil rights leaders who are trying to consolidate their newly won electoral gains, anything less than vigorous enforcement by the Department of Justice is often perceived as a return to the "forgo" strategy.[53]

The lawyer-bureaucrats at the Department of Justice have had to deal with the administrative dilemma of implementing national instructions in a constitutional system that permits subnational units a considerable degree of flexibility in determining the manner and the degree to which they will comply with those instructions. Nevertheless, the Voting Section claims that the vast majority of all voting changes are reported to the Attorney General. Given the original massive resistance to voting rights policy, the number of covered jurisdictions now submitting successfully precleared voting changes indeed seems remarkable.

We have examined the making and the refining of voting rights policy by legislators, judges, and the bureaucrats in the Department of Justice; the next facet of this examination of the 1965 Voting Rights policy is the implementation of that policy in a federal context in which federal courts on occasion determine some of the parameters of implementation. Part Three, *The Policy Implemented*, will examine the impact the U.S. Supreme Court has had on the implementation of the Voting Rights policy (Chapter 4) and will then examine the basic intergovernmental dimensions of voting rights enforcement (Chapter 5).

NOTES

1. 28 CFR 51.

2. John J. Roman, "Section Five of the VRA: The Formation of an Extraordinary Federal Remedy," *American University Law Review* 22, 2 (1972): 124.

3. Ibid., pp. 124-26.

4. *South Carolina v. Katzenbach*, 383 U.S. 301 (1966) at 334.

5. *Allen v. State Board of Elections*, 393 U.S. 547 (1969).

6. Ibid., p. 567.

7. Ibid., p. 571.

8. *Perkins v. Matthews*, 400 U.S. 379; 27 L. Ed 2d 476; 91 S Ct. 431 (1970) at 391. *Perkins* dealt with voting booth changes in Canton, Mississippi, as well as annexation of land and changes from ward to at-large elections. The Court said that these were voting changes subject to preclearance under Section Five. In *United States v. Georgia*, 1973, the Supreme Court stated, again, that redistricting was a voting change subject to Section Five preclearance.

9. David J. Garrow, *Protest at Selma: Martin Luther King, Jr. and the Voting Rights Act of 1965* (New Haven: Yale University Press, 1978), p. 194.

10. Richard M. Nixon, *RN: The Memoirs of Richard Nixon* (New York: Grosset and Dunlap, 1978), p. 440.

11. Garrow, *Protest at Selma*, p. 198.

12. J. Stanley Pottinger, Assistant Attorney General, Civil Rights Division, U.S. Department of Justice, *Statement on Extension of the Voting Rights Act*, Subcommittee on Civil Rights and Constitutional Rights, House Judiciary Committee, March 5, 1975, p. 11.

13. Interview with Gerald Jones, Chief, Voting Section, Civil Rights Division, U.S. Department of Justice, September 2, 1977, Washington, D.C.

14. David Hunter, *The Shameful Blight* (Washington, D.C.: Washington Research Project, 1972), pp. 137-38. Also, see Garrow, *Protest at Selma*.

15. Richard Harris, *Justice: The Crisis of Law, Order and Freedom in America* (New York: E. P. Dutton, 1970), p. 203.

16. Pottinger, *Statement on Extension*.

17. There were five opinions written in *Oregon v. Mitchell*, 400 U.S. 112; 27 L. Ed 2d 272; 91 S Ct. 269 (1970). Four justices believed the Congress had the power to lower the voting age in both federal and state elections; four other justices believed that Congress did not have this power at all. Justice Black believed that Congress could lower the voting age in federal elections but not in state elections. The other eight justices rejected that position; however, Black's position became the court's judgment simply because he was the fifth vote. "Quite remarkably, Justice Black therefore announced the Court's judgment but did so 'in an opinion expressing [only] his own view of the cases'," Lawrence Tribe, *American Constitutional Law* (New York: Foundation Press, 1978), p. 167, fn. 27.

18. Adopted in 1971, the 26th Amendment guarantees that "the rights of citizens of the United States, who are eighteen years of age or older, to vote shall not be denied or abridged by the United States or any state on account of age."

19. Interview with David Norman, former Deputy Attorney General, Civil Rights Division, U.S. Department of Justice, October 3, 1977, Washington, D.C.

20. Ibid.

21. Garrow, *Protest at Selma*, pp. 198-99.

22. Jones interview.

23. Richard H. Stillman, II, "The Bureaucracy Problem at DOJ," *Public Administration Review* 36 (July/August 1976): 436.

24. Ibid., p. 434.

25. Jones interview.

26. 36 FR 18186.

27. In 1975 Congress amended the Voting Rights Act to strengthen the Fourteenth Amendment voting rights of citizens with a limited knowledge of English. As a result the entire state of Texas was covered by the Act. Starting in late 1975, a large number of voting changes from Texas began to be received.

28. U.S. Comptroller General, General Accounting Office, *Voting Rights Act—Enforcement Needs Strengthening*, February 6, 1978, p. 11.

29. Interview with David Hunter, Staff Attorney, Voting Section, Civil Rights Division, U.S. Department of Justice, September 1, 1977, Washington, D.C.

30. Jones interview.

31. Hunter interview. With the new 1975 minority language provisions, a few paraprofessionals have been hired for their bilingual skills.

32. Interview with Janet Blizzard, Voting Section Paralegal Supervisor, Civil Rights Division, U.S. Department of Justice, September 2, 1977, Washington, D.C.

33. The voting change preclearance process as outlined here has been reconstructed from our interviews of officials in the Civil Rights Division and the Voting Section and from the information contained in the February, 1978 GAO report on voting rights enforcement.

34. Hunter interview.

35. Ibid.

36. Interview with Liz Dunagin, Research Analyst, Civil Rights Division, U.S. Department of Justice, September 2, 1977, Washington, D.C.

37. The problem of defining discrimination has provoked controversy within the Civil Rights Division which manifests itself in two distinct perspectives. For more detail, see H. Ball, D. Krane, and T. Lauth, "Judicial Impact on the Enforcement of Voting Rights Policy By Attorneys in the Department of Justice," paper presented at the 1977 annual meeting of the Southern Political Science Association, New Orleans, November 3-5, 1977.

38. Hunter interview.

39. Blizzard interview.

40. Hunter interview.

41. Jones interview.

42. Hunter interview.

43. U.S. Comptroller General, *Voting Rights Act*.

44. Kenneth Culp Davis, *Discretionary Justice: A Preliminary Inquiry* (Baton Rouge: Louisiana State University Press, 1969).

45. *Beer v. U.S.*, 425 U.S. 130; 47 L. Ed 2d 629; 96 S Ct. 1357 (1976).

46. Hunter interview.

47. It should be noted that the 1978 GAO Report placed the submission rate somewhat lower. U.S. Comptroller General, *Voting Rights Act*, pp. 10-20.

48. Hunter interview.

49. Hunter interview.

50. Theodore J. Lowi, *The End of Liberalism: Ideology, Policy, and the Crisis of Public Authority* (New York: W. W. Norton and Company, 1969), p. 300.

51. Davis, *Discretionary Justice*, pp. 59-63; and Lowi, *End of Liberalism*, p. 300.

52. 383 U.S. 301 (1966) at 361.

53. James Harvey, *Black Civil Rights During the Johnson Administration* (Jackson: University and College Press of Mississippi, 1973), pp. 162-67.

PART THREE

THE POLICY IMPLEMENTED

4 The Burger Court's Impact on Voting Rights Implementation

THE SUPREME COURT AS UMPIRE: VOTING RIGHTS CASES OF THE 1970s

Although the Civil Rights Division prefers to negotiate rather than adjudicate Section 5 determinations, eventually enforcement necessitates complete follow-through with threatened legal action. Entry into the federal judicial system, however, is not without risk. Because federal courts make policy as well as enforce norms, the CRD's decision to sue becomes a calculated gamble that the courts will refrain from significantly modifying agency policy. That is, as umpires in the intergovernmental system, federal justices not only can declare a particular administrative action fair or foul, but the federal justices also can alter the rules by which the game is played.[1]

Under the leadership of Chief Justice Earl Warren, the Supreme Court in the late 1960s broadly interpreted the parameters of the Voting Rights Act. In legitimizing national legislation that invaded the turf of the states and local jurisdictions affected by the Act, the justices created the opportunity for DOJ to administer the law, subject only to DOJ self-imposed constraints and practical political limitations. With respect to the meaning of Section 5 of the Voting Rights Act, the majority's *dicta* in *South Carolina* was clear: "suspension of all new voting regulations pending review by federal authorities to determine whether their use would *perpetuate* voting discrimination."[2] However, there were no cases that came to the Court during Warren's tenure as Chief Justice that would have allowed the Supreme Court to fashion that *dicta* into a rule of law. The reason for this is simple: the CRD did not begin to implement Section 5 until the early 1970s—after Warren had stepped down and at a time when a new court majority on the issues of the meaning of Section 5 and the nature of federalism had coalesced.

What the Warren Court stated in *dicta* about Section 5 was certainly pleasing to civil rights advocates. The *dicta* had clearly emphasized the prophylactic character of Section 5: *any* voting change in any covered electoral system that would have the effect or purpose of *continuing* the vestiges of racial discrimination was not to be permitted. As was pointed out in the preceding chapters, however, the Voting Section attorneys, confronted with the basic (political) intergovernmental relations dilemma, chose not to interpret the meaning of Section 5 in quite that liberal a fashion. In 1975 and 1976, in the *Richmond* and *Beer* decisions, a much different Supreme Court, ignoring the *dicta* in *South Carolina*, severely narrowed the meaning of Section 5 and, in so adjudicating, validated the CRD interpretation of the meaning of discriminatory purpose and effect. In *Beer v. United States*, the point of law was created in which the Court majority stated that the purpose of Section 5 was "to insure that there would be no changes made in voting procedures which would lead to a *retrogression* in the position of racial minorities with respect to their effective exercise of the electoral franchise."[3]

What the Burger Court majority stated was that every action was relative in the area of vote dilution and discrimination. A covered jurisdiction that had a horrible history of racial discrimination in voting could effectively perpetuate that discrimination by implementing a voting change that was not retrogressive, that is, that showed only the slightest improvement over its past discriminatory pattern. The two important cases in 1975 and 1976 that developed this standard were *Richmond v. United States*, 1975, and *Beer v. United States*, 1976. Both decisions validated the CRD procedures developed for implementing Section 5 of the Voting Rights Act.

THE BURGER COURT'S IMPACT ON THE DEFINITION OF DISCRIMINATION

RICHMOND V. UNITED STATES

In this 1975 majority opinion written by Justice Bryan White, the Burger Court said that the Voting Rights Act does not prohibit cities with past records of racial discrimination, which are covered under Section 5 of the Voting Rights Act, from annexing territory with a relatively low black population. Southern cities can modify their racial composition to favor white voters by annexing predominantly white suburbs so long as the move has: (1) some legitimate governmental motive, such as economic gains for the municipality, and (2) blacks enjoy a proportionate share of the political power in the enlarged city.

Richmond v. United States involved an annexation of land adjacent to Richmond, Virginia, that decreased black population from 52% to 42%. An earlier annexation, with at-large elections for the enlargd area, had been rejected by the District Court in Washington, D.C., and by the DOJ in 1971. In a round of informal bargaining and negotiations that commenced following the objection, the city officials and the Department of Justice arrived at an arrangement by which the annexation would not be objected to if the city went to ward elections. The plan outlined a nine-ward city in which four were predominantly white, four were predominantly black, and one was 3/5 white and 2/5 black. A separate suit, brought in federal district court, ruled that the original, pre-bargaining plan diluted the voting strength of the black population and, therefore, had the purpose and effect of denying the black voters their Fifteenth Amendment rights. The city and the DOJ then asked the U.S. District Court to issue a consent judgment validating the plan that had been worked out by them. The District Court refused to issue the consent judgment because the court felt that the new plan perpetuated racial discrimination in Richmond. Together, the city and the DOJ appealed the judgment to the Supreme Court. On appeal to the Supreme Court, the question raised was: did the annexation plan have either the purpose or effect of denying or abridging the right to vote?

Justice White for the Supreme Court majority of five answered the question. If the annexation could be sustained on sound, objectively verifiable, legitimate economic and/or administrative grounds *and* if the ward system as developed by the city in consultation with the DOJ fairly reflected the strength of the black community after the annexation, then the annexation does not, in its purpose or effect, dilute black voting strength.[4] Congress did not intend to have blacks assigned a proportion of the electoral process regardless of legitimate annexations, stated White. So long as there is no "under valuation" of black voting strength in the new city and so long as there will be no under-representation, then the annexation may stand.[5]

Justice William Brennan, Jr., joined by fellow judicial liberals Thurgood Marshall and William O. Douglas, bitterly dissented. The new standard developed by the Burger Court would allow plans to be approved that would have a flagrantly discriminatory purpose. There was a significant dilution of black voting strength in Richmond, Virginia, but because the city was allowed to develop an after-the-fact economic justification for what was, in Brennan's mind, a classic example of racial gerrymandering, the annexation was valid.

Richmond was a clear victory for the DOJ Voting Section attorneys and for the bargaining-compromise pattern of intergovernmental relations developed by these federal bureaucrats. Working together, the city officials and the federal regulators had worked out an agreement that might have pleased municipal managers but greatly displeased civil rights supporters. And the message was fairly clear to those city managers who were not overly enthusiastic about the Voting Rights Act: dilution of black voting strength was possible through annexation *if* the manager and his city attorneys, working with the DOJ, could develop a nonracial, that is, economic, administrative, etc., justification for the enlargement of a city that might be approaching a situation where a black voting majority could materialize.

BEER V. UNITED STATES

This 1976 opinion of the Supreme Court concerned a redistricting plan for New Orleans, Louisiana, that had been objected to by the

DOJ. In *Beer v. United States*, the Court, in a majority opinion written by Justice Potter Stewart, stated that the purpose of Section 5 "has always been to insure that no voting procedure changes would be made that would [worsen or] lead to a *retrogression* in the position of racial minorities with respect to their effective exercise of the electoral franchise."[6] The New Orleans redistricting was done in such a way that it gave black residents of the city the opportunity to select one and possibly two black representatives to sit on the city council composed of seven members—two at-large candidates and five from councilmanic districts. Both the DOJ and the D.C. District Court ruled that the plan would have the purpose or effect of diluting the black voting strength in the city. The objections had been made because it was thought New Orleans obviously discriminated in the drawing of Council District lines. (The lines were drawn north to south while black population concentrations went from east to west.)

The Supreme Court, however, stated that so long as the reapportionment enhances the position of racial minorities, it can hardly have the effect of diluting their voting strength. Furthermore, so long as the dilution of the black vote was less onerous than the voting conditions that confronted minorities before the change, then the DOJ could not object. "We conclude that such ameliorative new legislative apportionment cannot violate Sec. 5 unless the new apportionment itself so discriminates on the basis of race or color as to violate the Constitution."[7]

For the Burger Court majority, the New Orleans plan was not retrogressive but ameliorative. For the dissenters, the New Orleans plan perpetuated voting discrimination in that city, and the Court placed its imprimatur on that dilution of black voting strength. For the Burger Court, what was important in the New Orleans case was that black representation on the city council would increase 100 percent—from none to one—even though the black population in the city was over 45 percent. Gerrymandering and at-large representation was not to be objected to if there was some amelioration of past racial discrimination, stated the Burger Court majority. The impact of *Beer*, according to one observer, "will result in fewer redistricting plans being denied Section Five clearance in the future."[8]

For civil rights advocates, the response has to be ironically to go into federal district courts in southern states and appeal these actions on "Equal Protection" grounds. What *Beer* means for the DOJ is that any voting change that comes to the DOJ for examination, so long as there is no retrogression and regardless of the dilution effect, has to be precleared. The *Richmond* and *Beer* decisions affirm the enforcement strategy of the CRD and represent a defeat for negotiation by preclearances based on a principle of proportional representation. To a large extent then, these two cases reflect the DOJ's position on Section 5 determinations and likewise explain why the DOJ attorney in charge of the Voting Section can claim that *Beer* "really hasn't made that much impact."[9]

THE BURGER COURT'S IMPACT ON ENFORCEMENT MECHANICS

Between 1971 and 1980, the Burger Court announced a number of decisions that affected the mechanics of Section 5 compliance. These decisions of the Supreme Court focused primarily on the following issues:

(1) when are Section 5 submissions not required, including (a) traditional Fourteenth and Fifteenth Amendment reapportionment cases in federal courts, and (b) exemptions from coverage of Section 5;

(2) who can use the "bail out" provision in Section 4(a) of the Voting Rights Act to avoid the Section 5 preclearance procedure;

(3) what should the time frame be for DOJ consideraion of Section 5 submissions;

(4) what should federal District Court activities and preclearance procedures be; and

(5) should there be judicial review of a DOJ decision not to object to voting changes submitted under Section 5?

WHEN ARE SECTION 5 SUBMISSIONS NOT REQUIRED?

TRADITIONAL CIVIL RIGHTS LITIGATION IN FEDERAL COURTS AND SECTION 5

In the first opinion of the Supreme Court that narrowed the scope of earlier Court decisions in the area of Section 5 litigation, the Court, in *Connor v. Johnson*, reasoned that if individuals brought traditional Fourteenth and Fifteenth Amendment "one man, one vote" reapportionment conflicts into the U.S. District Courts in the covered jurisdictions, and if the District Court rules on the question of malapportionment, then that decision was not subject to preclearance procedures outlined in Section 5 of the Voting Rights Act of 1965. "A decree of the United States District Court is not within reach of Section 5 of the Act," concluded the Court.[10]*

In *East Carroll Parish School Board v. Marshall*, a 1976 opinion of the Supreme Court, the Justices reaffirmed the *Connor* view that reapportionment plans could be insulated from Section 5 preclearance procedures if the District Court heard the case before the covered jurisdiction submitted the change to the Justice Department or the U.S. District Court in the District of Columbia, in accordance with Section 5. The interesting aspect of this brief *per curiam* order was that the Court reached out in a footnote (6) to reject a Department of Justice amicus curiae brief that argued in favor of Section 5 review of reapportionment proposals in covered jurisdictions. "Although the issue was not raised by petitioner nor did the respondent file a cross petition, in any event, we agree...that Court ordered plans resulting from equitable jurisdiction over adversary proceedings are not controlled by Section Five."[11] If a Court orders a reapportionment based on "one man, one vote," there is no preclearance. However, if the covered jurisdiction apportions itself without judicial instructions, then it must submit that voting change for Section 5 preclearance. By way of *dicta* then, the Court affirmed its position in *Connor*.[12]

What the impact will be of such a judgment is hard to determine. Concerned civil rights activists consider the *Connor* precedent to be the most serious gap in Section 5 coverage and its

---

*The subsequent history of *Connor v. Johnson*, (all told involving eight appearances before the U.S. S. Ct.), *Connor v. Finch* (1976), and finally, *Connor v. Coleman* (1979) points out that when a state, Mississippi, *subsequent* to traditional litigation, passes a voting change (reapportionment statute), enacted during the continuing earlier litigation, that statute is subject to Section 5 preclearance. In *Connor v. Waller* (1975), the Court held that the Mississippi legislature reapportionment acts would "not now and will not be effective as laws until and unless cleared pursuant to Section 5 of the Voting Rights Act."

existence leaves open the possibility of an end run on Section 5. On the other hand, the Voting Section lawyers did not show much concern over this situation. All of them we have spoken to about enforcement dilemmas suggest that the traditional litigation (that is, initiated by private parties arguing Fourteenth and Fifteenth Amendment violations in the U.S. District Courts) serves the same purpose: eradication of inequity in voting. According to the DOJ's summary data on the number and type of reported voting changes (see Appendix D), annexation submissions are frequently presented and screened by the CRD (21 percent of all changes reported). In contrast, redistricting changes account for only 3 percent of the submissions. If there is a conspiracy in the covered jurisdictions to use the local federal courts to evade equitable resolution of the voting problem (assuming that the strategy would be successful), this has not been observed by researchers in the field and by the Voting Section attorneys.[13]

EXEMPTIONS FROM COVERAGE OF SECTION 5

A procedural question arose in the federal courts in the late 1970s that greatly concerned the staffers in the Voting Section of the DOJ. The question involved the interpretation of a most important definitional clause in the Voting Rights Act involving the question of exemption from Section 5 coverage, as extended to "states and political subdivisions" in those covered jurisdictions. Section 14 (c) (2) of the Voting Rights Act defined "political subdivision" as follows:

the term "political subdivision" shall mean any county or parish, except that where registration for voting is not conducted under the supervision of a county or parish, the term shall include any other subdivision of a State *which conducts registration for voting*.

The City of Sheffield, Alabama, sought to change a voting procedure. The city had never conducted a voter registration drive because, under Alabama law, voter registration is conducted by county boards whose members are appointed by state officials. Sheffield held a referendum to decide whether to change from a commissioner form of city government to a mayor-council form. It passed and the DOJ notified the city officials that while the holding of a referendum was legitimate, any such contemplated change in the city government had to be precleared by either the DOJ or the District Court in the District of Columbia.

The city ignored the guidelines and scheduled the council election. The DOJ went into federal court in Alabama in order to enforce the Section 5 commands by preventing the election. The federal judge refused to issue a temporary restraining order and the election was held. After the election, a three-judge U.S. federal district court, hearing full arguments on the merits, dismissed the DOJ suit. It held that the 1965 Voting Rights Act's Section 14 (c) (2) exempted Sheffield from coverage because, since the city did not conduct voter registration, it was not a "State or political subdivision." The case was appealed to the U.S. Supreme Court. Prior to the Supreme Court's decision in this case, one apprehensive DOJ manager stated that should the Court affirm the lower court's ruling, the Voting Section "might just as well pack it in."[14]

In a controversial decision, the Supreme Court voted 6-3 to reverse the decision of the lower court, thereby extending the scope of Section 5 of the Voting Rights Act to cities and other subdivisions (in covered jurisdictions) even though they might not conduct voter registration business. Justice William Brennan Jr., stated that Section 5 was intended by the Congress to apply to *all entities* having power over any aspect of the electoral process within a covered jurisdiction.[15] Therefore, Sheffield, Alabama, was required to obtain preclearance of a voting change even though it did not conduct voter registration.

The language, structure, history, and purposes of the Act persuade us that Section 5, like the constitutional provisions it is designed to implement, applies to all entities having power over any aspect of the electoral process within designated jurisdictions, not only to counties or to whatever units of state government perform the function of registering voters. . . . Because Section 5 embodies a [legislative] judgment that voting changes occurring outside the registration process have the potential to discriminate in voting on the basis of race, it would be irrational for Section 5 coverage to turn on whether the political unit enacting or administering the change itself registers voters. [To allow the lower federal ruling to stand would see local pressure at work to limit the political power of minorities.]...The clear consequence of this lower court interpretation would be to nullify Section 5 and the Act in a large number of its potential applications. *The terms of the Act do not require such an absurd result.*[16]

Concluding that the legislative history of Section 5 "leaves little doubt" that Congress viewed Section 5 territorially and "includes political units like Sheffield whether or not they conduct voter registration," the Supreme Court reversed the judgment of the U.S. District Court.[17]

Three judges dissented. Justice Stevens wrote the opinion in dissent, joined by Chief Justice Burger and Justice Rehnquist. For Stevens, the definition of "political subdivision" in Section 14 (c) (2) was clear and unambiguous. It *was* intended to limit the reach of the Voting Rights Act, and it should be construed as exempting a city such as Sheffield, which did not register voters, from the preclearance requirements of Section 5. An action of a city should not be regarded as the action of a state or political subdivision. The dissenters were obviously concerned about impact of this case on the sovereignty of the states. *Sheffield* "is a significant and undesirable encroachment on state sovereignty," wrote Stevens.[18] For that and other reasons, the three judges thought that the lower court ruling should have been affirmed. *Sheffield*, however, is still the law of the land; it has not been modified and has been the basis for DOJ preclearance activity since 1978.

WHO CAN USE THE "BAIL OUT PROVISIONS" [SECTION 4 (A)] OF THE VOTING RIGHTS ACT TO AVOID SECTION 5 PRECLEARANCE PROCESSES?

The City of Rome, Georgia, after many years of nonaction, submitted a series of voting changes to the DOJ for Section 5 preclearance. The DOJ objected to many of the changes on the grounds that they would deprive the black population in Rome (about 24 pecent) of the opportunity to elect black candidates. The city attorney then went into federal court in the District of Columbia seeking a declaratory judgment under the Voting Rights Act that would nullify the DOJ's objection. Beyond the city's attack on the constitutionality of the Act itself, the Rome attorney argued that the city could bail out of the coverage of the Voting Rights Act by proving that no test or device had been used in Rome, Georgia, for the past 17 years for the purpose or with the effect of denying or abridging the right to vote on account of race or color.[19]

The lower federal court, in a summary judgment, ruled in favor of the DOJ. A city cannot bail out of coverage under the Act through the declaratory judgment route; there is no independent piecemeal bail out. A *state* may seek a declaratory judgment in order to bail out; a political subdivision cannot so act. The city immediately appealed to the U.S. Supreme Court and, in the spring of 1980, the Court, by a 6-3 vote, affirmed the judgment of the lower federal court.

Writing for the six-man majority, Justice Thurgood Marshall stated that:

The city comes within the Act because it is part of a covered state. Under the plain language of the statute, then, it appears that any bail out action to exempt the city must be filed by, and seek to exempt all of, the state of Georgia. . . . When an entire state is covered, it is irrelevant whether political units of it might otherwise come under Section 5 as "political subdivisions." . . . Our conclusion is that, under the express statutory language, the city is not a political subdivision" for purposes of Section 4 (a) "bail out."[20]

The majority found support for this view in statements made in legislative committees that examined the 1965 proposed legislation: "subdivisions within a state covered by the formula are not afforded the opportunity for separate exemption."[21]

Consistent with the 1965 *South Carolina* opinion, the 1980 majority did not find any conflict between the Voting Rights Act and the nature of the enforcement provisions in the Fifteenth Amendment. Nor did Marshall accept the notion that principles of federalism were being violated by the Voting Rights Act. The Eleventh Amendment and the principle of state sovereignty are generally limited by the enforement provisions of the Fifteenth Amendment's fifth section. The Fifteenth Amendment, stated the majority, "supercedes contrary exertions of state power." The Court concluded that, substantively and procedurally, the lower court ruling should be affirmed and that the City of Rome, Georgia, or any other city in a covered jurisdiction could not bail out of coverage under the Voting Rights Act by itself.[22]

The three dissenters, Justices Powell, Rehnquist, and Stewart, challenged the majority ruling on a number of grounds. Justice Powell noted what he believed was the inconsistency between *Sheffield* and *Rome*. In the former case, political sudivisions—cities— are "state" for preclearance purposes, whereas the 1980 opinion stated that, for bail out purposes, cities cannot be considered "political subdivisions." He and the other dissenters challenged the inconsistency in blunt terms.

The court construes the identical words [State and political subdivisions] to have one meaning in one situation and a wholly different sense when applied in another context. Such a protean construction reduces the statute to irrationality.[23]

The other major objection to the majority opinion was the per- ceived impact the judgment would have on the federal-state relationships. Local control of the mechanics of state government will be destroyed by this federal encroachment, they warned. Rehnquist's concluding remarks summed up this substantive perception of the dissenters.

To permit congressional power to prohibit the conduct challenged in this case requires state and local governments to cede far more of their powers to the federal government than the Civil War amendments ever envisioned;...the intrusion is all the more offensive to our constitu- tional system when it is recognized the only values fostered are debat- able assumptions about political theory which should properly be left to the local democratic processes.[24]

WHAT SHOULD THE TIME FRAME BE FOR DOJ CONSIDERATION OF SECTION 5 SUBMISSIONS?

Georgia v. United States, 1973, was the opinion that validated the Department of Justice's regulation that provided that the manda- tory 60-day period of Section 5 for considerations of original submissions "is tolled whenever the Attorney General finds it necessary to request additional information from the submitting jurisdiction. Under the regulation, the 60-day period commences anew when the jurisdiction in question furnishes the requested information to the Attorney General."[25] The Supreme Court upheld the regulation, holding that it was "wholly reasonable and consistent with the Voting Rights Act."[26]

WHAT SHOULD DISTRICT COURT ACTIVITIES AND SECTION FIVE PRECLEARANCE PROCEDURES BE?

In *Perkins v. Matthews*, 1971, the Supreme Court placed limits on the determinations that U.S. District Court judges could make with respect to Section 5. The Justices stated that a U.S. District Court judge could only rule that a voting change did or did not fall within the parameters of Section 5. After making that decision, the lower court could not then rule on the question of discriminatory purpose or effect because that was the statutory responsibility of either the District Court in the District of Columbia or the DOJ.[27] In a 1977 opinion, *United States v. Board of Supervisors of Warren County, Mississippi*, the Court reaffirmed the *Perkins* ruling.[28]

Board of Supervisors is an interesting case because its facts illuminate the informal bargaining process that takes place between the DOJ and local officials in covered jurisdictions. The DOJ had objected to a 1970 redistricting of Warren County. After the county officials had submitted two plans to CRD lawyers for their review and comments and the DOJ had indicated reservations about the validity of the plans before they were formally submitted, the United States District Court, Southern District/Mississippi, ordered one of the two county plans to be enforced. The Supreme Court reversed and remanded, stating in a short *per curiam* note that the District Court inquiry in this litigation was limited solely to the question of whether the voting change is subject to Section 5 preclearance.[29]

SHOULD THERE BE JUDICIAL REVIEW OF DECISIONS NOT TO OBJECT?

In another recent case, *Morris v. Greshette*, 1976, the Supreme Court ruled that a Department of Justice decision not to object to a voting change submitted under Section 5 was not subject to judicial review. This opinion, too, did not cause undue disturbance within the Department of Justice and the attorneys we spoke to about this question did not seem to think there would be any significant change in their activities.[30] Given our understanding of the informal bargaining that precedes the formal submission and the very small number of objections, this opinion should elicit concern from civil rights activists and members of the United States Commission of Civil Rights.

Two dissenters on the Supreme Court, Justices Thurgood Marshall and William J. Brennan, Jr., voiced their apprehension about the possibility that an Attorney General in the Department of Justice could subvert the Section 5 preclearance procedures in return for a state's electoral votes.[31] Given the negotiations through which the Justice Department lawyers presently interact with the officials in the covered jurisdictions, that fear is not totally misplaced. The point is that the DOJ policymakers have always been aware of political realities and that this opinion probably will not have a significant impact on the Voting Section's bargaining approach to enforcement. It certainly has had an impact on civil rights organizations who have objected to the less-than-rigorous enforcement of Section 5. This judgment of the Supreme Court effectively cuts off legal challenges to decisions not to object that might be filed by adversely affected parties.

THE SUPREME COURT'S CONDITIONING IMPACT

Any assessment of DOJ's enforcement of Section 5 must consider the intervening actions of the Supreme Court. A Court opinion is an obvious conditioning factor and, at times, is a critical causal influence on the direction of public policy. From the description of events surrounding the Court's role in voting rights policy, two periods of judicial involvement and two types of judicial impact can be identified. In both situations, it is important to observe the operation of other political forces that also shaped the character of Section 5 policy and its implementation.

In the 1966-1971 period, the Supreme Court exercised its most dramatic impact on voting rights policy. If the Supreme Court had upheld the Tenth Amendment position of the southern states, the Voting Rights Act would have been eviscerated and voter registration drives would have been halted in their tracks. Given the bloody battles still in progress and the Court's natural tendency to watch the prevailing political winds,[32] the *South Carolina* decision was hardly surprising. A second critical juncture for the Act came in 1969 as the CRD began shifting its resources from Section 4 to Section 5 enforcement. Recall that within the DOJ, and especially in CRD, this time frame was marked by political turmoil, reorganization, and uncertainty. Presidential directives and senior DOJ policymakers were at odds with CRD staff attorneys over the parameters, procedures, and problems involved in seeking compliance with Section 5. The internal battles between Attorney General Mitchell and the staff attorneys sympathetic to the civil rights movement also had parallels in the declining public opinion support for continued progress toward racial equality.[33] Thus, *Allen v. State*, 1969, which clarified the administrative confusion and controversy over the sweep of Section 5 coverage, was an equally crucial decision—in effect, it stymied the "southern strategy" in voting rights policy. Even the *Allen* ruling, however, was still not sufficient to energize Section 5 implementation. With the Act's renewal scheduled for 1970, CRD leadership stalled on writing preclearance guidelines until the outcome in Congress was evident.

On the other hand, the Burger Court has narrowed the expansive coverage of Section 5, as defined in *Allen v. State*. In contrast to the Warren Court's decisions on the legitimacy of the preclearance remedy, the voting rights cases of the 1970s have centered on the mechanics of enforcement. While the Court has played a negligible role in directing the bureaucratic workings of the Voting Section staff, the cumulative effect of cases like *Perkins* and *Connor* on civil rights groups has been negative. Neither ruling forced the CRD to abandon its enforcement-through-bargaining strategy. Instead, the opinions have strengthened the hand of the covered jurisdiction by reducing the chances of an election overturn (*Perkins*) and by enhancing the district court route as an alternative to the Attorney General's preclearance (*Connor*).[34] Certainly, the Court appears satisfied with the general contours of the compliance process—that is, an enforcement system that uses highly routinized procedures for normal submissions and that relies on informal negotiations and not heavy-handed criminal penalties in stubborn cases. Just as certainly, the Burger Court has acted to protect the local jurisdictions from what it perceives as an overwhelming federal demand.[35] The affirmation of CRD's legal-technical methods and especially the encouragement of more district court determinations move the Section 5 process a step back toward the old pre-1965 litigative mode.

The Supreme Court has not been a singular effector of change in the area of voting rights; instead, it has been a catalyst. Because its opinions supported the momentum of voting rights policy as the policy moved from legislative formulation to administrative refinement, the Court is best seen through its interactive effects with the administrative and political dynamics of the interpreting and implementing units. By its broad definition of Section 5 coverage, the Warren Court acted in consonance with the political decision of the President and the Congress. The intermittent voting rights cases through the 1970s attest to the Burger Court's willingness to take cues from DOJ policy makers as well as from the President and his national constituency. By this interpretation, we do not suggest that the Court acted merely in an ancillary fashion, nor do we suggest that the Court could go it alone. Rather the Supreme Court's influence depends on the situation in which it finds itself—the standing case, the available remedies, the particular administrative agency, and the political climate. In a phrase, the Supreme Court exercises "situational impact." Too often in analyses of voting rights policy, or other policies for that matter, the Supreme Court's ruling is portrayed as the breakpoint for a given course of action. Such myopia misses the larger political background and stream of decisions and events, before and after, which also condition the fate of policy options.

In order to better understand the reasons why local jurisdictions tend to submit voting changes rather than refuse to comply, why the Department of Justice prefers to work out acceptable solutions to potentially objectionable preclearance submissions (in line with Supreme Court parameters described in this chapter) rather than formally objecting to local actions, and how the Court judgments have blended into the mainstream of voting rights implementation, it is important to view this implementation dilemma from the "federalism" perspective. Chapter 5 will present an examination of the intergovernmental dimensions of voting rights enforcement.

NOTES

1. Howard Ball, *Courts and Politics: The Federal Judicial System* (Englewood Cliffs, N.J.: Prentice-Hall, 1980), pp. 21-53.

2. 383 U.S. 301 (1966).

3. *Beer v. U.S.*, 96 S Ct. 1357 (1976).

4. *Richmond v. U.S.*, 45 L. Ed 245 (1975).

5. Ibid.

6. 96 S Ct. 1361 (1976).

7. Ibid. at 1363.

8. Richard L. Engstrom, "Racial Discrimination in the Electoral Process: The Voting Rights Act and the Vote Dilution Issue," in Robert P. Steed, Lawrence W. Moreland, and Tod A. Baker, eds., *Party Politics in the South* (New York: Praeger Publishers, 1980), p. 209.

9. Interview with General Jones, Chief, Voting Section, Civil Rights Division, U.S. Department of Justice, September 2, 1977, Washington, D.C.

10. *Connor v. Johnson*, 402 U.S. 691 (1972) at 697.

11. 96 S Ct. at 1085 (1976).

12. Ibid.

13. Interview with David Hunter, Staff Attorney, Voting Section, Civil Rights Division, U.S. Department of Justice, September 1, 1977, Washington, D.C.; also see J. Stanley Pottinger, Assistant Attorney General, Civil Rights Division, U.S. Department of Justice, *Statement on Extension of the Voting Rights Act*, Subcommittee on Civil Rights and Constitutional Rights, House Judiciary Committee, March 5, 1975, p. 11.

14. Interview with James P. Turner, Deputy Assistant Attorney General, Civil Rights Division, U.S. Department of Justice, September 2, 1977, Washington, D.C.

15. *U.S. v. Sheffield Board of Commissioners*, 55 L. Ed 2d 148 (1978) at 158.

16. Ibid. at 163.

17. Ibid. at 162.

18. Ibid. at 172-173.

19. *City of Rome v. U.S.*, 64 L. Ed 2d 119 (1979).

20. Ibid. at 131.

21. Ibid., fn 2, at pp. 131-132.

22. Ibid. at 146.

23. Ibid. at 153.

24. Ibid. at 168.

25. *Georgia v. United States*, 36 L. Ed 2d 472 (1973).

26. Ibid.

27. *Perkins v. Matthews*, 400 U.S. 379 (1971).

28. *United States v. Board of Supervisors of Warren County, Miss.*, 51 L. Ed 2d 106 (1976).

29. Ibid. at 108.

30. *Morris v. Greshette*, 53 L. Ed 2d 506 (1976).

31. Ibid. at 521.

32. Richard Funston, "The Supreme Court and Critical Elections," *American Political Science Review* 69, 3 (September, 1975):795-811.

33. James C. Harvey, *Black Civil Rights During the Johnson Administration* (Jackson: University and College Press of Mississippi, 1973), p. 41.

34. With the appointment by President Carter of more black judges to the federal courts, the possibility exists that the *Connors* route around Section 5 may become less appealing.

35. See, for example, *National League of Cities, et al. v. Usery*, 96 S Ct. 2465 (1976).

5 Intergovernmental Dimensions of Voting Rights Enforcement

INTRODUCTION

Organizational arrangements for implementing national policy in the American federal system must be designed to operate under conditions of "chaos, fragmentation, and dispersal of power [which] characterize the multiplicity of governments at the national, state, and local levels."[1] Procedural and structural changes not only must contend with the administrative and geographic realities of federalism but must also cope with the more fundamental political tension between national control and local autonomy. The remedy most frequently prescribed to relieve this powerful contradictory tension is the antidote of coordination.[2] Because "action in the American federal state is not automatic,"[3] federalism can be made to work only if the national government can establish a framework of communication and understanding between the various public entities so that a "working partnership" prevails.[4]

The radical character of voting rights policy directly contradicted the usual pattern of American federalism.[5] Instead of the more typical cooperative, mutually beneficial arrangements between "working partners," voting rights implementation had to be initiated in an atmosphere of "conflict between federal and state actors predicated on a complete absence of any similarity in approach to programs and an absence of respect and confidence in the governmental efforts each put[s] forward."[6] State and local officials in the covered jurisdictions strongly disagreed with the legitimacy and the substance of the 1965 Act because it violated their sense of "state action." Behind the rhetoric of state sovereignty lay the fear that vigorous enforcement of the Voting Rights Act would unbalance local political alignments and would result in a massive redistribution of economic and political resources to the black community.[7] In this highly charged context, the basic strategic goal of DOJ was "aimed at establishing a mutually acceptable set of objectives and values and accommodating these to the solution of the problems of different political constituencies."[8]

In order to elicit compliance, the Voting Section had to overcome its inherent administrative weaknesses and had to build working relationships with southern election officials and southern civil rights leaders. Ultimately, to prevent the racial conflict from swamping its limited regulatory capacities, the only feasible approach to enforcement rested on the ability and ingenuity of the CRD attorneys to bring together the local contenders and to strike a bargained voting change between the two sides, which could then be "precleared" by the Attorney General. Despite its poverty of compliance-inducing resources, the Voting Section has been able to develop and implement such a bargaining strategy.

COMMUNICATION BETWEEN D.C. AND DIXIE

When the 1971 voting rights regulations were announced in *The Federal Register,* the CRD had to make up for time lost during the first six years of the Section 5 lifespan. In a sense, the attorneys in the Voting Section found themselves playing a game of "catch up ball" with local election officials who had been using the time to devise ways to circumvent the Voting Rights Act. At first, the VS/CRD staff traveled to the covered jurisdictions and met with local officials on a case-by-case basis. However, as the number of submissions multiplied fivefold, from 255 in 1970 to 1,118 in 1971, and the number of available personnel remained constant, a more efficient means of spreading the word became a necessity. In 1973, the Voting Section composed information packets, which were mailed to the legal officers of the covered jurisdictions. As indicated in chapter 3, these packets contained a copy of the amended 1965 Voting Rights Act, the 1971 regulations, and a request to send all preclearances to the DOJ or to submit them to the U.S. District Court in Washington, D.C. for a declaratory judgment.

The importance of these initial campaigns to educate subnational officials should not be overlooked. Dissemination of the September, 1971, regulations meant that now all parties concerned with vote dilution had a common language and a common set of procedural steps to follow. For example, the terms *voting*, *changes affecting voting*, and *submission* were defined for the first time. Similarly, the content of submissions, the form of communications from local groups, and the basic appeal routes were specified. Such elementary steps often seem rather simple when compared to grander events like a pivotal Supreme Court case (for example, *Allen v. State*) or a long-running enforcement struggle (such as DOJ's nine-year battle with Warren County, Miss.); but without a standard linguistic code and standard operational procedures, neither the negotiations necessary for inducing compliance nor the procedural fairness necessary for ensuring obedience can be achieved.

Linguistic and procedural consistency is a vital part of policy implementation,[9] but establishing and maintaining the required consistency in a federal framework is no easy matter. Sheldon Edner explains that the language of a public official is a function of the official's jurisdiction: "Because they serve different constituencies, these governments [in a federal system] speak the language of their constituencies, languages which may or may not share similar meanings and definitions of issues."[10] Language differences derive from more than a jurisdiction's place in the intergovernmental maze (for example, federalese versus localese); more directly, language patterns reflect the cultural, economic, and political differences that underlie and give dynamics to American federalism.[11] Similar observations can be made about procedures. In fact, the extension of civil liberties, including voting rights, in the United States has evolved out of a constant struggle to replace localized procedures with more standard, national ones. The point to be emphasized here is basic: a standard language and standard operating procedures function as two pillars supporting the framework of intergovernmental bridges.

Following the transmission of information about the new Section 5 rules, the CRD bureaucrats had to organize the return communication flow from the covered jurisdictions. The rising flood of preclearance submissions (which now averages 19 voting change requests per business day) presented the Voting Section with three different tasks: (1) advising local attorneys on the nuances of Section 5 regulations, (2) validating the data contained in the submission documents, and (3) prompting actions from recalcitrant covered jurisdictions. Given its lack of field personnel, the Voting Section needed to devise a modus operandi that would permit the in-house staff to accomplish all of these objectives.

Part of the shift to increased DOJ emphasis on Section 5 implementation resulted in the utilization of paralegal research assistants. The effects of the increased use of research analysts were immediate: (1) the paralegals with their director and staff attorney could concentrate on processing the preclearance submissions, and (2) most of the Voting Section's attorneys were freed for litigative activity arising primarily out of the objections interposed by the Attorney General.

The larger adaptation made by the Voting Section as it changed from case-by-case processing of submissions by the staff attorneys to a more functionally specialized system was a significant, though not readily discernible, shift in its relation with the concerned parties in the covered jurisdictions. In the pre-1971 period, CRD attorneys were, in effect, de facto members of the civil rights movement. Although the CRD preferred a low profile, their work brought them into intimate contact with southern election officials and local movement leadership. CRD actions and decisions were grounded in personal knowledge of the participants and their local community. As the federal forces withdrew from the field and the Voting Section inherited the principal responsibility for consolidating the voting rights revolution, actions and decisions on preclearance submissions became increasingly impersonal and routinized, as one would expect.

Even more critical, a separation of the participants has occurred. In its efforts to manage the large volume of preclearance submissions, the Voting Section has developed a two-track system of communication with the covered jurisdictions. The parallel streams of information are not formal channels; rather the two routes have evolved from the Submission Unit's division of labor and sequence of work. One track connects the Submission Unit, usually its staff attorney, with the covered jurisdiction's attorney. The other track connects the Submission Unit, usually one of the research analysts, with the covered jurisdiction's minority leadership. One should not presume that local election officials and minority leaders are in communication with each other. Quite the contrary. Numerous cases exist where voting changes are submitted (and cleared) without the knowledge of local blacks.[12] The pattern of intergovernmental interaction that has emerged since 1971 consists of two mutually exclusive (one is tempted to say segregated) channels of communication between Washington and the covered jurisdictions.

The communication track between local attorneys and the Submission Unit carries the bulk of the intergovernmental implementation of Section 5. The principal traffic, of course, consists of the submission letters and accompanying documents. As David Hunter, Submission Unit attorney, observes: "The main source of submissions are just ones that jurisdictions voluntarily make."[13] Although the Section 5 regulations do not specifically mention census data or maps, the typical submission includes demographic and geographic materials. It is also common for covered jurisdictions to supplement the required copy of the new ordinance or regulation with voter register data, reports from consultants, and statements by local citizens groups. The Voting Section maintains an essentially passive posture toward the initiation of preclearance requests and "just about never" sends a staff member out to a local jurisdiction to collect additional data on a submission once it has been received.[14]

To focus only on the legally required flow of information would miss a substantial portion of the message traffic in this channel between the Submission Unit and the covered jurisdictions. Local city or county attorneys often write or telephone the Submission Unit staff attorney in order to obtain advice as to whether a proposed voting change would pass muster when formally submitted. Guiding the legal representatives of covered jurisdictions through the details of the preclearance requirements has become the chief task of the Submission Unit's attorney. This pre-submission counseling of the regulated communities has meant that almost all submissions receive the preclearance stamp of approval; that is, the sticking points are often resolved before the formal preclearance request is mailed to the Justice Department. As one local attorney in a Mississippi town that has benefited from this type of advice told us: "It's easier to work with them [the Voting Section staff] than with the electric power company."

If ensuring an easy flow of voting change requests is the purpose of the first link between the Voting Section and the covered jurisdictions, then validating the quality of the information contained in the individual submissions is the objective of the second link. A major source of energy activating this alternate channel has been private civil rights groups who became sophisticated about Section 5 potential and began to complain to the Department of Justice about voting changes. To compensate for its lack of field staff (and the 60-day time limit), the Voting Section has institutionalized as part of its standard operating procedures the input of local civil rights groups and individuals. A permanent registry of minority elected officials, minority group leaders, and other informed citizens is maintained by the Voting Section for use by the staff attorneys and paralegal research analysts. These "contacts" [black and white] include school teachers, ministers, social workers, community activists, and university professors who are familiar with the black community in their area. The number of local minority contacts made per submission varies directly with the scope and complexity of the proposed change. This pool of informants provides information not normally incorporated in the jurisdiction's submission papers and helps evaluate the discriminatory impact of the proposed change.

The Voting Section further supplements this minority contact channel with the publication of a weekly listing of submissions, available to anyone upon request (see Figure 5.1). The weekly listing does not necesarily go to the same set of individuals and groups that the Submission Unit relies on as its primary contacts in the minority population. Although the weekly list is intended to elicit local opinion as to the effect of a proposed voting change, the sparse information on the weekly list (date, type of change, and

Figure 5.1 U.S DOJ Voting Change Submission Lists*

U.S. Department of Justice

Washington, D.C. 20530

DJ 166-012-3

November 24, 1981

N O T I C E

      The following submissions to the Attorney General pursuant to Section 5 of the Voting Rights Act were received through November 20, 1981. The Attorney General has sixty days from the date of receipt to respond to each submission. In order to assure that comments and information from interested parties may be considered in reaching our determination, such comments and information should be received by this Department no later than thirty days from the date of this notice.

11/4   Keller Independent School District (Tarrant County), Texas
        Polling place

11/5   Richland County, South Carolina
        Additional registration hours

11/9   Grant Road Public Utility District (Harris County), Texas
        Maintenance tax election; polling place; absentee voting location; bilingual procedures; annexation

        Houston County, Georgia
        Additional registration location; addditional hours

11/11   Refugio County, Texas
        Redistricting
        Expedited Consideration Requested

11/12   Bosque County, Texas
        Redistricting (commissioner and justice of the peace precincts)

        Dalworthington Gardens (Tarrant County), Texas
        Method of election--from elected marshall to appointed police chief

*This is a replica of selections from the November 24, 1981 weekly list of submissions issued by the U.S. Department of Justice.

Figure 5.1 continued.

11/13   Crowley (Acadia Parish), Louisiana
Act No. 161, S.B. No. 230 (1981)--method of electing
aldermembers
Additional Information Received

Fort Mill School District No. 4 (York County), South
Carolina
Act No. R196 (1981)--revised the method of election and
terms of office of members of the board of trustees;
election date
Additional Information Received

Linden-Kildare Consolidated Independent School District
(Cass County), Texas
Bond election
Expedited Consideration Requested

Houston (Harris County), Texas
Consolidations of voting precincts
Expedited Consideration Requested

Kermit (Winkler County), Texas
Annexation

Rockingham County, Virginia
Relocation of registrar's office
Expedited Consideration Requested

11/14   Georgetown County, South Carolina
Act No. R251 (1981)--relating to voting precincts
and polling places
Additional Information Received

Brown County, Texas
Redistricting

Wilson County, Texas
Redistricting; two polling places
Additional Information Received

11/16   Safford (Graham County), Arizona
Ordinance No. 253 (1979)--election date

Georgetown County, South Carolina
Act No. R251 (1981)--relating to voting precincts
and polling places
Additional Information Received

Bexar County, Texas
Justice of the peace boundary line changes
Expedited Consideration Requested

El Paso County, Texas
Referendum election--recreation of a Regional Transit
Authority
Additional Information Received

122

Figure 5.1 continued.

11/16 Fredericksburg (Gillespie County), Texas
Referendum election; form of government; increase in
number of councilmembers; staggered terms

Silsbee (Hardin County), Texas
Polling place

Silsbee Independent School District (Hardin County),
Texas
Polling place

South Park Independent School District (Jefferson
County), Texas
Bond election
Expedited Consideration Requested

Kenedy (Karnes County), Texas
Annexation

Madisonville (Madison County), Texas
Annexation

Wilson County, Texas
Redistricting; two polling places
Additional Information Received

Mathews County, Virginia
Method of election--from three single-member districts
to at-large; increase in number of supervisors--from
three to five; staggered terms
Additional Information Received

Pittsylvania County, Virginia
Redistricting; consolidation of two voting precincts;
two voting precinct boundary lines; elimination of
polling place
Additional Information Received

Note: All inquiries regarding submissions should be directed
to the Associate Director of the Section 5 Unit, Margay M.
Williams (202-724-7400).

Gerald W. Jones
Chief, Voting Section

name of jurisdiction) presumes that the individual scanning the list understands the situation from this skeletal description and will either mail or telephone to DOJ an informed opinion about the proposed change.

In effect, this second link serves as the Voting Section's chief instrument for monitoring the behavior of local election officials. Describing his reliance on local "whistleblowers," the Submission Unit's line attorney explains:

It doesn't seem likely that there are a whole lot of very discriminatory changes out there that haven't been submitted. There might be some. . . . If there were real big problems, I think we would have heard about them. . . . If they're really controversial like that, they'll get caught quickly by civil rights groups.[15]

White election officials also attest to the efficacy of this monitoring linkage between the Voting Section and local black communities. One local mayor whose city has experienced substantial contact with the Voting Section expressed the belief that "the blacks have a toll-free line to the Justice Department. . . and some blacks make a career out of informing for the Department of Justice." Although both apprehension and exasperation provoked this remark, it does, however, capture the views of many white election officials throughout the covered jurisdictions.

By building two parallel pipelines to the covered jurisdictions, the Voting Section not only can streamline the flow of submissions, but also can monitor the content of the information flow. These two considerations bear on the basic issue of compliance. Since the Section 5 preclearance procedure is not an immensely popular requirement among southern election officials, the question of why submissions are made needs to be answered. While at this point in the analysis a complete answer cannot be given, nevertheless, the Voting Section's style of intergovernmental communication does have a contributory effect on compliance. The Submission Unit's advice and counseling posture toward local attorneys acts as an inducement to submit. By minimizing the paperwork and procedural hassle, the Voting Section eases the pain of preclearance. On the other hand, by maintaining the permanent registry of local minority contacts, the Voting Section has access to an extensive number of locally based watchdogs who can ensure that local officials will submit voting changes for preclearance. Certainly, many local attorneys make submissions because they know and obey the law, as the Voting Section readily admits:

there is some incentive to make submissions. In the bigger areas, where it's certainly more professionalized, they have city attorneys and they just figure out what the law is and they do it. Even in smaller areas, there is the natural willingness to do what the law requires; even if it is not a law they have chosen themselves.[16]

And, of course, if the local officials choose to ignore the Voting Rights Act or submit biased or misleading information, the Voting Section remains confident in the alertness of minority whistleblowers.

DECISION MAKING IN AN INTERGOVERNMENTAL CONTEXT

No matter how convenient and streamlined the Voting Section makes the submission procedures, the feeling of federal interference into local affairs remains persistent. Although some voting changes provoke little reaction from the minority community, the majority of preclearance requests contain electoral changes with some impact on black voting strength. As the information moves up from the covered jurisdictions to the Submission Unit, it soon becomes evident from the collected data, documents, and opinions that "both sides believe they are right."[17] Consequently, the decision-making steps (see chapter 3) leading to the Attorney General's "stamp of approval" put the Voting Section in an adjudicatory relationship between two parallel political constituencies which are jockeying for an enhanced local position. This conflict waged across governmental planes creates several pressures that condition and shape the Voting Section's preclearance decision.

Even though the Voting Section readily offers pre-submission advice and counseling, its basic enforcement orientation reflects its legislative mandate; that is, "the burden of proof is on them [local election officials] to show us [the DOJ] that a change is not discriminatory."[18] Any voting change submitted for preclearance is considered a new change. This simply means that any submission gives the Voting Section carte blanche to review the jurisdiction's complete set of electoral procedures. Because any significant voting change cannot be evaluated in isolation from the totality of prevailing local practices, DOJ retains the option to initiate a comprehensive investigation of a jurisdiction's record on voting procedures. Second, the possibility that a reported voting change might trigger an in-depth examination of local electoral history goes far toward ensuring the validity of the materials submitted. The Voting Section's *inclusive* methodology for reviewing a voting change as it relates to the broader electoral context clashes with the desire of local attorneys for an *exclusive* review (that is, one strictly limited to the submitted change). As a result of these polar positions, the administrative mechanics of enforcement become one of the main friction points between the Voting Section and the covered jurisdictions. Two sticking points, in particular, generate this friction: (1) the validation of the data submitted and (2) the time required to process submissions.

Since the preclearance decision ultimately turns on the information analyzed by the Submission Unit, it is only natural that the quality of the data accompanying the submissions sometimes causes more than a modest difference of opinion among the three parties to a voting change. The possible points of disagreement are limited only by the ingenuity of the contending attorneys. A review of some typical data-related arguments will demonstrate the complexity of this set of problems. One bedeviling question is the applicable year. Should census and voter registration figures be matched to the date of the proposed change (for example, April, 1979)? Or should a standard year such as 1970 be selected? If a voting change must be reviewed against a larger background, should the Voting Section insist on information beginning in 1964-1965 or even earlier? Given the natural demographic and socioeconomic changes in a local population, which year or years best portray(s) the political character of a community?

A second validity puzzle is the collection of the required information. With the burden of proof on the submitting jurisdiction, the Voting Section relies on the local officials to gather and collect the necessary materials. Should the local officials be required to use only standard census sources provided by the U.S. Bureau of Census or should the locals be allowed to collect and submit their own demographic data? Some communities have hired outside consulting firms to collect the demographic data and other communities have used their own personnel. Since the urge to engage in a "Gomillion-like" gerrymander[19] has not yet died in many covered jurisdictions, the potential for bias exists in data collected by a city engineer or housing officer in a small town in the Georgia-Alabama black belt or Mississippi delta. Once the documents reach the desk of a research analyst in the Submission Unit, how should the data be interpreted by a person who has the responsibility for processing approximately two dozen submissions at any one time? Should the paralegal analyst take the submitted census and voter registration data as well as the maps at face value? Given the press of time, should all information submitted be subjected to rigorous verification? Or should only obvious contradictions and gaps be investigated more fully? The importance of the data validity issue can best be imparted by the views of a staff attorney from the Voting Section.[20]

Q. Would you contact some of the local minority leadership in the instance when the submitting authority is being reluctant to give you a complete package of information?

A. The kind of people we would contact wouldn't have it. They wouldn't know population data. They wouldn't be able to tell us whether they think blacks could win at-large elections, whether there is racial bloc voting, or whether this location for a polling place is convenient. They might have some idea of racial composition, but they are not going to have statistical information. They are not going to have election returns.

Q. Who decides whose population data are correct?

A. To the extent we can, we use the 1970 census. If there have been changes, or if the census isn't broken down enough, then we will try to get more. I guess that is a matter of judgment. They have made estimates, then we have to see what the basis is. One of the things we ask for on estimates is who did them and how they were done.

Q. Do you have instances of jurisdictions hiring planning firms to develop this material? Who mediates the situation when they say ours is correct because it is 1977?

A. Unless we have reason to doubt that, we are likely to take their word for it. For example, in [city, state], we were dealing with their annexation; there was a big problem of statistics. They did a lot of surveys and their people down there had problems with what the city as coming up with when we were getting information. I spent a lot of time going over the statistics, seeing how reasonable they were and discovered, even though I don't know that much about the methodology of statistics that there were things that just didn't make sense. It couldn't all be right. There is a lot of uncertainty out there. Another thing they gave us [sic] we wanted to know the racial composition of the five new districts they had as well as several old districts and they played around with the 1970 census bloc data to come up with estimates of the racial composition. They gave us these estimates for the districts that looked fine, and then just to be neat about it, they added it all up to give us the totals for the city. Well, if they had done it right, it would have come up the same as what the 1970 census had, since they weren't using any updates. They were only 90 people off with all of their roundings through the bloc data and that was fine, except on the racial composition the 1970 census said something like 34%, and this came up with something like 42.8% black.

Q. One of the prime complaints by the black community is that they are underestimated by the U.S. Census.

A. Yes, but both [estimates] were from the census. They were just using the bloc data rather than the house count data. They were trying to come up with these districts based on the blocs and they must of been doing estimates based on the number of units and the racial composition and all that, and somehow that made a 10% difference in the racial composition of the city. That's very suspicious! It's still better than nothing, but I would say in evaluating the racial composition of those districts, it's ± 10% in each one. It's still useful, but we still know that there was some black majority; but say, if one of those came out 55% rather than 80%, that 55% wouldn't tell me much of anything. We do get instances like that.

Q. It sounds like there is a fairly extensive and detailed kind of data analysis that goes on in your office, at least in some cases. The data are generated locally and then you make some analysis and some judgments about their quality.

A. Sometimes where they don't have the data or where we don't think it is any good, we'll object and tell them that they just can't implement their re-districting plan because we are not convinced that they are not discriminating. I don't like to do that because sometimes even though the data aren't any good, the new plan might be better than to make them go back to the old plan which could actually be more discriminatory. We had this case in ——— County earlier this year and there are many questions about the data. . . . we didn't have to object on the annexation. We did for the county supervisors [districts]. That was in litigation for a long time and that was a matter of bad statistics. This went back to 1970 and 1971. They had done the re-districting and the statistics just weren't any good. That ended up in the Supreme Court.

The moral of this short case study seems so elementary— the quality of Section 5 determinations depends on the validity of the census and voter registration data submitted by the covered jurisdictions. Yet, the Voting Section, as already described, does not employ a professional demographer nor provide the paralegal assistants with significant training in demographic and statistical analysis. Several negative consequences follow from the Voting Section's less-than-rigorous methodology. "Guesstimating" the racial composition of districts and wards easily leads to the underestimation of the minority population which, in turn, causes confusion for local officials and minority leaders alike. The absence of clear criteria for verifying submitted materials can spark court fights which can be deliberately protracted to delay electoral reform. With limited resources, the CRD can challenge only the most obvious attempts at statistical manipulation. This leaves the Voting Section with two unattractive options: (1) in most cases, it can accept the accuracy of the materials prepared by the covered jurisdictions, or (2) when something looks "very suspicious," it can negotiate with the submitting jurisdiction.

In its efforts to obtain unbiased data about the local political context, the Voting Section is not at the absolute mercy of the covered jurisdictions. Local officials frequently express frustration over the Submission Unit's manipulation of the 60-day time limit. If the Submission Unit determines the evidence supporting a preclearance request is insufficient or biased, the 60-day clock can be stopped and reset to Day 1 after receipt of new and acceptable evidence. In effect, the legislatively mandated guarantee against undue delay by the Attorney General has been converted by CRD into a trump card for use in negotiations with local officials.

Local officials themselves are not without countermeasures to CRD's threat to restart the 60-day clock. Anthony Downs, with his "Law of Counter-Control," reminds us every action taken by a superior to control subordinates engenders a reaction to evade or counteract the control.[21] Attorneys from the covered jurisdictions, as might be expected, have discovered that submitting a preclearance request shortly before the date of a local election (say 60 days before) puts pressure on the Submission Unit to process the proposed voting change without restarting the clock. Consequently, the Voting Section finds itself in a many-sided quandry: that is, it can halt the local election, thereby upsetting the normal operation of democracy in local government; it can process the submission, thereby risking a decision based on biased information; or, it can stop the clock, thereby encouraging the jurisdiction to proceed with the election. Examples of all three choices can be found in the Voting Section's files of Section 5 dispositions.

Why should the Voting Section find itself in this quandary? After all, the Submission Unit also relies on the local black community to point out inaccuracy and inconsistency in the submitted documents. However, closer examination of politics in southern jurisdictions reveals a serious weakness in the Voting Section's dependence on civil rights groups as a surrogate field staff. Reliance on local citizens— black and white—to monitor violations assumes that the citizens are sufficiently knowledgeable and motivated to act. Even well-organized groups, let alone individuals, encounter trouble in penetrating the closed-door machinations of some southern election commissions. The frequent use of executive sessions, the lack of publicity about submissions, and the common failure of election officers to communicate with local minority leaders restrict the ability of local blacks to raise objections to a proposed voting change. Compounding these obstacles to effective whistleblowing is the difficulty of developing viable census and registration statistics as a check on those submitted by the local jurisdiction. Not only is time, money, and expertise in scarce supply for minority leaders, but more damaging, some of the basic data may be unavailable. It is not unheard of to find that officials responsible for election statistics do not maintain accurate or complete records. For example, no complete number for registered voters can be obtained in some southern counties and, therefore, no complete count can be obtained for the whole state.

As a final fallback procedure to ferret out information, the Voting Section occasionally utilizes the assistance of the Federal Bureau of Investigation. The typical request for FBI help originates in a memorandum from the Assistant Attorney General (CRD) asking the Director of the FBI to "please conduct an investigation to determine: (1) whether the subject voting change has been implemented [used or enforced]; and (2) when the requested additional information regarding the change will be submitted." (See Appendix E for a copy of a complete memo.) While the Voting Section treats the FBI as a "free resource," the staff has mixed feelings about use of the FBI.

We also use the FBI when we have not had a response to a letter asking for more information, or when we haven't had a response to a letter asking for a submission, we'll ask the FBI to investigate to find out what is going on. This is fairly effective in stimulating a response. I have the feeling that people are kind of frightened of the FBI coming out to see them. I don't really think that's a good idea.[22]

Usually, an FBI visit is a reminder and a prod to local officials to complete the information necessary for a submission.

We don't ask the FBI to get the information. If local officials try to give it to the FBI, it wouldn't count as a submission. . . . We don't ask the FBI to get the information, but to find out when it is likely to come. Chances are that it comes more quickly than it would have otherwise.[23]

Although the Voting Section personnel believe that the use of the FBI "is fairly effective in stimulating a response [from the local level]," a recent Government Accounting Office (GAO) report suggests that local officials sometimes become more resistant when federal muscle is applied.[24] According to the GAO, some jurisdictions have not responded in over two years after a receipt of a request for additional information about a proposed voting change.

The enforcement mechanics of Section 5 trap the Voting Section in a powerful vise of cross-pressure from minority leaders and white election officials. From one side, the legitimate interests of the black community in the validity of information supporting preclearance reports pressure the Submission Unit to exercise great care in processing proposed voting changes. From the other side, the reaction of white constituencies force local election officials to pressure the Submission Unit for expeditious and timely Section 5 decisions. Despite the Voting Section's efforts to balance the preclearance requirements of Section 5 with a relatively convenient submission procedure, the federal and racial conflicts inherent in voting rights policy lead to the "defensive politics" characteristic of all policy implementation. Where resistance to black political progress is encountered, the validation of evidence in support of preclearance submissions becomes an elaborate series of moves and countermoves. The repertoire of defensive games played by local officials includes "not our problem," "their fault," "massive resistance," "tenacity," "tokenism," and simple delay.[25] Even the use of minority whistleblowers and FBI visits do not always overcome the unwillingness of resistant jurisdictions. To cope with the friction of enforcement, the DOJ prefers to induce cooperation through negotiation rather than resort to direct coercion.

While the extraction of accurate statistics from covered jurisdictions provokes one class of intergovernmental conflicts over voting rights policy, the preclearance decision itself triggers another set of disputes. Once the documents reporting a voting change have entered and completed the Submission Unit's processing routines (as illustrated in Table 3.2), the Chief of the Voting Section mails a letter to the local governmental unit notifying it that the U.S. Attorney General either "does not interpose any objection" or "interposes an objection" to the proposed change in voting procedure (for examples typical of letters sent to the covered jurisdictions, see Appendix F). The effective enforcement of the 1965 Voting Rights Act rests on the substantive meaning of "discriminatory purpose or effect" as translated into operational practice by the Voting Section's staff. The guiding criteria for Section 5 determinations have emerged out of the in-house dialogue between two groups of CRD staff, each proposing a different answer to the question of the proper definition of discrimination. For purposes of identification, we have labeled these two contrasting viewpoints as the pragmatic/bargaining approach and the normative/principle approach.

The pragmatic posture holds that a voting change should fail to gain preclearance under Section 5 if: (1) the purpose of the voting change is obviously discriminatory, (2) if the effect is obviously discriminatory, or (3) if there is a retrogression of black voting strength after the voting change. These three conditions have been converted into the elementary decision rules utilized by the research analysts. Their pattern of work, which relies on the spotting of "suspicious type changes" or "red flags," involves a comparison of the proposed new electoral practice with the existing voting practice. If the new procedure is less discriminatory than the old procedure, then the recommendation will be for preclearance. An example of the pragmatic approach in action comes from these comments by the Chief of the Voting Section describing the CRD's reasoning about the now-classic Richmond, Virginia case.

... The context then is that you have a situation where the annexation was made purposely to eliminate or at least delete the black threat in the political sense. The only way that they could really do that effectively was because they were using the at-large election system, which means that the majority can control the whole representative body. In the meantime, the change that had occurred was that the city had changed from that system of election and they had gone to the district system. The plan really gave blacks a realistic opportunity of, if not controlling the city government, at least having substantial representation on that body. The court is saying that in the context of what the city now has done, you can look to see whether or not there was besides a racial purpose some other legitimate purpose for the making of the annexation and retaining it at the present time.

Q. What strategy did you have when the case was remanded?

A. Where that case finally came out was really the very same we said in our initial letter of objection. We said we objected to that annexation in context of that at-large election. We even cited the indication that it was purposely done. We said that we would reconsider should the city choose to go to a better drawn system of singular districts. The city wouldn't do that initially, they wanted to fight it. It got involved with people wanting the annexation and went through this long, involved process and it comes out right where we suggested in the first place.

Q. Did Richmond go to wards before or after the opinion?

A. Before the opinion. During the pending of that law suit *Petersburg* came along and they saw the handwriting on the wall and decided we would go singular district; by that time the other parties involved in the law suit would not consent to that resolution, so it got prolonged.

Q. *Richmond* is a case where a municipality changes an election pattern. What about a situation where it doesn't? Given what the Supreme Court has said, doesn't that have an adverse impact on voting rights? That is, where once a city had an at-large system, the Supreme Court said that an annexation is legitimate even though the city hasn't changed the electoral process.

A. *Petersburg* said that. In *Richmond*, the Court affirmed *Petersburg*. *Petersburg* was a situation where there was no question but the legitimacy and the necessity for that annexation. Blacks were just as much in favor of the annexation as were the whites because the city had to expand. It was again the system of election. In the Supreme Court's decision, *Petersburg* even recognized the fact that everybody had no question about the validity of the annexation, however, when the effect of the annexation would be to dilute the minority voting, then the jurisdiction is under obligation to take whatever step is necessary to eliminate to the extent possible the dilution involved. They endorsed our suggestion that singular districting would be a way of doing that. The city went to singular districts and went back to court and the court gave them a declaratory judgment. I don't think *Richmond* bothers us when there has been no change in the underlying election system.[26]

This recount of the *Richmond* case illustrates the emphasis of the pragmatic approach on bargaining to achieve a nondiscriminatory result. The pragmatist's basic solution to the cross-pressures from blacks and whites is bargaining aimed at discovering acceptable procedures or arrangements that are less discriminatory than the existing practice or preserve whatever gains in election strength the black community has managed to win. Using these criteria, the Voting Section has precleared over 94% of all submissions.

A small minority of staff attorneys in the Voting Section and many observers outside of the DOJ skeptically discount the agency's claim of near-perfect submission compliance. This group argues that there is another standard that should be utilized, which would enable the Justice Department to object more frequently (assuming that this was the DOJ policy position). This normative/principle posture maintains that the pragmatist's criteria suffers from two fallacies: (1) the demonstration of obvious discrimination in purpose or effect is very difficult, if not impossible, to find on the record of any given case, and (2) the standard of "no retrogression," while laudable, still permits an unconstitutional scheme to be replaced with a less obnoxious, but possibly still discriminatory electoral procedure or practice.

The normative/principle approach to Section 5 determinations views the prevailing pragmatic/bargaining answer as political appeasement to the pressures of local and congressional officials. The normativists see the CRD's bargaining and toleration of minimally acceptable electoral changes as solutions which are not as bad as the prior situation, but which fail to achieve an equitable condition. The present DOJ policy, argue the normativists, makes a trade-off between the *full* political potential of minorities and the maintenance of reasonably smooth-working relationships with the covered jurisdictions. Simply put, the normativists accuse the pragmatists of sacrificing electoral equity on the altar of federalism. The problems of validating data, the difficulties of monitoring covered jurisdictions, and the refusal to impose criminal penalties all disturb the normativists. Their solution is the establishment of a firm principle—representation should be equivalent to population proportion—and the consistent application of the principle. The normativists believe that if a covered jurisdiction could have done better ("better" being defined as a more equitable distribution of political power), then the Attorney General ought to object. This viewpoint, needless to say, has not been the dominant policy mood within the Department of Justice.

Political realities underpin the CRD's pragmatic strategy of bargaining to obtain compliance. As is typical in most federal policies, voting rights enforcement involves governmental units that are not strictly speaking in a superior-subordinate relationship. Thus, while the federal regulations pertaining to Section 5 give local minorities a *de jure* veto over the granting of a preclearance, the DOJ does not want to interfere dramatically in local policy-making processes and, consequently, the Voting Section prefers to work out the new electoral practices with local officials and minority groups (when asked) in a cooperative effort. So long as the CRD, particularly the personnel in the Voting Section, sees no retrogression in a proposed voting change, Division staff will preclear it. By shifting from a strict definition of discrimination—that is, is the new voting practice on its own merits discriminatory?—to a comparative definition—is the new practice less discriminatory than the previous practice?—the CRD reduces the degree of white resistance to electoral change and makes it possible to achieve incremental advances in electoral procedures. Such a posture may not satisfy black demands for proportional representation, but in the minds of CRD policymakers, given their administrative shortcomings, a feasible strategy that facilitates progress is more desirable than a confrontation over principles, which may not be successful.

The upshot of CRD's trade-off has been that a major political and ethical issue, voting rights equality, has been transformed into a technical-legal problem. Although civil rights activists account for much of the energy and visibility of this policy arena, the main players, the rules of combat, and the prize are all elements of the legal order. The preclearance guidelines were written by lawyers in the Voting Section to be employed by the paralegal research analysts and to be complied with by the legal counsels of the covered jurisdictions. Enforcement takes place within a fraternal relationship between professionals, as explained by the Submission Unit staff attorney:

It's generally not an emotional thing. They have their clients and we have our client. Lawyers tend to be fairly friendly usually, even if they're on opposite sides. I'm handling a case now in ——— County and the lawyers on the other side and I get along fine together; we don't have a whole lot in common. It's not like I think they are immoral people because they are defending a jurisdiction that wants to have an at-large election.[27]

To the degree that bargaining between fraternal professionals induces compliance, then it is a reasonable implementation strategy for a fiscally dry, poorly staffed federal agency. However, to the extent that bargaining produces an operational definition of discrimination that distorts the Section 5 remedy, a suboptimal level of electoral opportunity for minorities may well result.

THE INTERPOSITION OF AN OBJECTION

Through 1981, there have been 35,000 changes submitted for preclearance, and only 815, or 2.3 percent, have been objected to by the Attorney General. Voting Section lawyers are convinced that their pragmatic style of informal assistance, discussion, and negotiation goes far to minimize the number of objections interposed. For all of the Voting Section's cajoling and prompting, however, some jurisdictions simply refuse to enact a voting change because they could not arrive at a workable preclearance agreement with the CRD attorneys and/or the local minority population. Because submissions that result in objections are clear violations of the 1965 Act, one would expect the CRD to abandon its advice and counseling approach and adopt a tougher regulatory stance toward diehard jurisdictions. While an intractable case may eventually wind up in a federal court, nevertheless, the Voting Section doggedly pursues its pragmatic course of informal bargaining. Where proposed electoral changes are deemed to be discriminatory, why does the CRD continue its less-than-hardline approach to enforcement? What factors go into objection decisions? How are they resolved? Since the interposition of an objection is an unusual act for CRD, examining these questions also reveals important insights about Section 5 determinations.

Unlike the straightforward preclearance letter that emanates directly from the Voting Section, the in-house routine for processing objections requires several additional steps and considerations. The Chief of the Voting Section describes the flow of paperwork in this fashion.

All objections get as far as me. Most of them get as far as the front office. An objection to a piece of local legislation is usually a matter of sufficient seriousness that we think that everybody should know that we are taking that action, even though we don't see that there is any chance of their differing with our views. . . . As a matter of fact, there has been a slight change now because, before Drew Days came on, when Stan Pottinger was here all of the letters went out over his signature block, but he did not actually sign them. I would sign his signature to some objections if it was a clear case and I did not see that there was any problem. I would sign for Stan and sent it out. Drew wanted it changed so that he would get to sign all of the objections, so that's what we are doing now. He actually gets to sign all of them, although some of them are more or less nothing.[28]

The identification and sequence of "check-off" and signature points in a bureaucratic routine may appear trivial or simply boring in detail, but each action often represents a decision or "nondecision," which conditions the final resolution of the matter at hand. In a given case, who signs off at what level in the Department of Justice may reveal the pivotal basis of an objection decision.

The first and simplest answer to the question "what factors go into a decision to interpose an objection?" is the retrogressive effect of a proposed electoral change. Covered jurisdictions reporting changes that are obvious "red flags" (for example, an unwarranted reduction in the number of polling places or a "Gomillion-like" redistricting) will prompt an objection. O'Connor and Ingersoll, in their study of annexation cases, have shown that DOJ will interpose an objection when the dilution of black voting strength exceeds 3 percent.[29] Similarly, a protracted disagreement over the demographic information contained in a submission ("a matter of bad statistics") will trigger an objection. A less obvious cause for the rejection of a submission is ignorance on the part of local officials. While the Voting Section's assistance and counseling normally remedies ignorance of Section 5 procedures, an occasional case will create a problem.

> . . .as election administrators, they might suspect that if they don't submit, they're going to get into some kind of trouble, even if it [the change] is not discriminatory. There could be a challenge of the election or something will happen, or they'll look bad, like this county attorney in ⸺ County, where he just wasn't aware of the requirement. He was new and was making the submission a week before the election. And having the election called off, he probably looks pretty bad and so do the others there, and he doesn't like that, I'm sure.[30]

Irreconcilable differences between election officials and minority leaders present the CRD with its most troublesome situations. The political maneuvering described in the opening vignette nicely illustrates the problem. Discrimination, to some extent, is in the eye of the beholder and what appears as blatant electoral fraud to one party may be seen as administrative efficiency by another party. Not every decision to object or not to object rests on evidence "beyond the shadow of a doubt"; rather the political context of a given situation will be the overriding factor. In other situations, it is not uncommon for one governmental unit to draft legislation modeled after another jurisdiction's ordinance that has already been approved (either by the Attorney General or the federal courts). This common practice, much to the consternation of local officials, does not guarantee safety from an objection. Cases even exist where the CRD has interposed an objection, but then has had to reverse itself in response to political pressure. Again, the dominant operating style is not dispassionate judgment; instead the basis for interposing an objection also manifests the CRD's commitment to its posture of pragmatic bargaining.

Given the rarity of objections in the overall enforcement of Section 5 requirements, one would expect the Voting Section to maintain careful and continuing scrutiny of each insubordinate jurisdiction. Unfortunately, and rather unexpectedly, the Voting Section staff admit that "there are a lot of them [submissions] that we have objected to and we really don't know what they are doing."[31] This failure to keep a close watch on post-objection actions pinpoints a basic weakness in the CRD's ability to enforce the law. From the perspective of legislative intent, the conduct of a local election in spite of an interposed objection constitutes a serious breach of the 1965 Act. Part of the Voting Section's inability to prevent this type of election derives from the absence of follow-up mechanisms: "One of the things that I have been working on and we haven't yet established is the system to do it routinely, that is, automatic follow-up on our objections to see what is happening."[32] Permitting elections to proceed without the preclearance imprimatur may also be part of the CRD's pragmatic posture.

Q. You raise an objection and yet the covered jurisdiction goes ahead and holds their election; basically, they make the voting change and ignore your efforts. We have noticed that in a lot of places. What can you do?

A. That is a problem and we try to approach it from a very practical standpoint, if it is a situation where there is election machinery already in gear. There have been several cases as a matter of fact that have allowed elections to go ahead when that kind of situation exists. In some instances where the election is already in gear, absentee ballots have already been distributed, we will take the position that the election under no circumstances is a lawful one because it is under a procedure that is really unenforceable. If they go ahead with it anyway, anybody can challenge them on that score. If they go ahead with it with the intention of resolving the problem, and then rerun the election later, and let this newly elected body only serve as a temporary one, if that is the approach they take, we seldom, if ever, attack that. That is a very practical position to take because you are talking about a mechanism that could really foul up all kinds of local government if you take a hard-nose attitude about the objections, that is, they are to stop that procedure and do this. It is often just as much in the interest of voters as it is in the interest of the government because they have certain interests in terms of having a voice even if it is something of a not completely effective voice in saying what is going on, plus the confusion that often evolves from last-minute abortions of elections and that sort of thing is often disheartening to voters, apathy among voters is something that you fight constantly anyway. All in all I think that this is the practical approach.[33]

To a large extent then, the CRD depends on the political interest of local black populations to keep the agency abreast of illegal actions and to pressure local officials into compliance. However, beyond its reliance on local minorities to cry foul, the CRD, as evidenced by this revealing quote, holds to its pragmatic strategy and permits technical violations of the law as part of its negotiated trade-offs. A deal to constitute a "temporary government" to ensure the delivery of normal public goods and services—fire and police protection, sanitation, utilities, etc.—may well be a necessary means to a larger end, but only if one bargain does not lead to another round of negotiations that inordinately prolongs the life of a "temporary" government. Even worse, not challenging an election simply because the electoral process is "in gear" only serves to encourage noncompliance. At some point, local resistance must be met with a federal challenge in order to sustain the credibility of the agency and the national policy.

Court action is always costly and time-consuming, and for the Voting Section represents the failure of its basic compliance strategy. Eventually, after many unsuccessful attempts to strike a deal, the CRD policymakers "have to sue because it is evident in some instances that the local authorities just don't intend to abide by the objections."[34] Going to court is not an easy decision. As long as the CRD can keep negotiations, even if strained, moving ahead, it retains control over the conflict's outcome. Leaving its bureaucratic bailiwick means surrendering some degree of influence to the vagaries of the judicial process. After all, some federal judges in southern districts still oppose federal intervention into local electoral affairs. Because the movement to litigation transforms the agency's relationship with the covered jurisdiction from cooperation to confrontation, the step-up in coercion is not taken lightly by the CRD leadership.

Q. How do you go about determining the suit will be effective because obviously a court case is costly?

A. One judgment we have to make is whether we are likely to win, just what the legal standards are, the courts involved, and all that.

Q. How do you go about making the decision that you are likely to win? Who is involved in making that decision and what things do you look for?

A. Based on the legal research and what the state of the law is and what's likely to happen. When the suit is filed, the final decision now is made by the Assistant Attorney General. Until recently, it went up to the Attorney General, now in most cases it has been sent down to this level [the Civil Rights Division]. Recommendations are made all along the line but the attorney who is developing the suit will write up the complaint and the justification memo and that will be reviewed by usually the attorney in charge of our litigation program, then it will be reviewed by the Chief of the Voting Section, and then it will be reviewed by the Deputy Assistant Attorney General for Civil Rights, and then by the Assistant Attorney General for Civil Rights. So, there are a lot of hurdles to go through to get a suit. I don't think there is any great desire to bring suits that don't have much of a chance, or suits that wouldn't accomplish a whole lot. Still, I'm not sure exactly how we make the judgment here, we're not in this business say just to increase the number of black elected officials or to increase the number of black registered voters. We're here to vindicate the law and the principles involved. It's not a strict cost-benefit analysis. It could be a small area, but an important matter.[35]

From August, 1965, to mid-1980, the Voting Section's Litigative Unit (13 attorneys) was a party to 240 cases, 119 of which the DOJ was the plaintiff. Preclearance actions (73) accounted for about half of the court suits in which DOJ was the plaintiff. In addition, the Justice Department filed 32 amicus curiae briefs in preclearance cases.

The expected payoffs of this litigation are twofold: (1) resolution of the specific disputes with the covered jurisdiction under challenge, and (2) elucidation of precedents that can be generalized. The DOJ's plaintiff actions in support of Section 5 commonly seek injunctive relief, that is, the enjoining or overturning of an election, and such site-specific cases are prosecuted by staff lawyers from the Litigative Unit. The "big" cases involving statewide issues (for example, the reapportionment of Georgia) or broad, fundamental principles (such as the scope of Section 5 coverage) usually are the responsibility of the Assistant Attorney General for Civil Rights, with documentary support from the Voting Section. As a case moves toward the U.S. Supreme Court, the Voting Section's previous positions and views sometimes become modified by higher-level policymakers in Justice.

They are constantly in contact with the Court. They can almost anticipate the views of the positions the various justices will take on a particular question involved in a case. In that respect, they help structure the argument very much. We provide the substance on the merits, but in terms of how it is presented to the courts and what is going to be emphasized and what won't be, they are masters at that. . . . We've sent drafts that reached them, where not only the structure, but the emphasis has been turned completely around, and is successful. We get the end result that we want, but we didn't stress what we wanted. We stressed what we thought would sell to the court.[36]

Whether the lawsuit has local or general impact, the Litigative Unit staff perseveres in their determination to hold informal conversations with the other side. The CRD strives to effect an out-of-court settlement to avoid the cost and delay of litigation—a reasonable estimate for a suit in federal court, complete with appeals to the Supreme Court, is a minimum of three years (and some cases have lasted 15 years). An equally important incentive to rekindle negotiations in the midst of litigation is the retention of control over the final details of the electoral arrangements or new precedents. "Vindication of the law" is important to the CRD's leadership, but so also is the agency's credibility with covered jurisdictions. No one likes to lose a court fight and the best safeguard against a legal setback is an out-of-court settlement.

"CONQUERED PROVINCES" OR COMPROMISED COMPLIANCE

As can be seen from the foregoing, Justice Black's fears appear to have been unfounded—the states have not been treated as "conquered provinces" in the implementation of federal voting rights policy. Both judicial interpretation (for example, *Beer's* no retrogression doctrine) and administrative practices have settled for "no objection" whenever the affected black population is not harmed by proposed voting changes, although the relative voting strength of the black population may not have been substantially improved. Further, the almost unanimous selection by covered jurisdictions of the administrative procedure option (rather than the District Court alternative) when they seek to comply with the preclearance requirement is indicative of their preference for the kinds of outcomes obtainable through the lawyer-bureaucrat bargaining process. These enforcement practices, when coupled with the inability of the Department of Justice to detect many of the unsubmitted voting changes, or to follow up very effectively to make certain that jurisdictions do not implement changes to which the Department had objected,[37] suggest an enforcement pattern in which state and local governments retain a considerable amount of discretion over the manner in which they exercise their reserved power to conduct elections.

The involvement of the national government in an area of policy constitutionally reserved to the states has been acceptable because: (1) the interests of locally situated minorities have been served by the nationalization of the scope of the voting rights conflict; while at the same time, (2) the mode of enforcement resulting in compromised compliance has not fundamentally destroyed state and local election prerogatives.[38]

Historically, the legislative enactment of the 1965 Voting Rights Act (as well as the Civil Rights Acts of 1957, 1960, and 1964) occurred in an environment in which states' rights arguments were pitted against arguments of overriding national purpose. Once in place, the 1965 statute not only forced covered jurisdictions to seek a federal imprimatur for local election procedures, but it also altered the traditional pattern of federal-state-local interaction. In essence, preclearance procedures have "atomized" the relationship between the national government and the subnational units. Because each jurisdiction—be it a municipality, a county, or a state—must report directly to the U.S. Attorney General, Section 5 eliminates any sense of subnational hierarchy. Each subnational unit possesses the same status under the VRA. As a result of this "atomization" of federal layers, a distinct implementation advantage accrues to the federal agent. Since the Voting Section can bypass the state government, it can bring the full "force" of the national government (even if it is only an agency with a staff of about 30 people) to bear on a small-sized, local government. By not having to dissipate its enforcement energies solely on state governments, the Voting Section increases the asymmetry of expertise and power between itself and the local unit. For example, if the Voting Rights Act had made state governments responsible for the actions of their constituent units (as in many other federal policies), then the Voting Section would have to wrestle with each covered state's Attorney General and his or her large and well-funded staff, rather than with the single local attorney who is typically hired on a case-by-case basis.

There can be little doubt that this strategy of negotiating over the different parts of potentially objectionable preclearance submissions has eased the task of obtaining Section 5 compliance. CRD's policy of gradualism, by forgoing immediate proportional representation for black populations, transformed a highly hostile confrontation into a usually cooperative venture. Caught between the pressure for voting rights progress and the defense of the status quo, the decision to adopt the bargaining-compromise pattern of enforcement was probably the most feasible approach for "keeping the peace" among the contending parties, given the paucity of resources available to CRD and the shifting political signals from top DOJ policymakers. However, this enforcement strategy depends on some troublesome elements.

One negative output of the Voting Section's role as "peacekeeper" is the administrative enlargement of the legislation's consumers. Typically, a cozy relationship between regulator and regulated develops over time and, when coupled to appropriate congressional committees, becomes an exclusive policy "subgovernment."[39] While the statutory language clearly designated disenfranchised minorities as the clients of DOJ, the actual practice of negotiated compliance that has developed since 1971 has raised local officials in the covered jurisdictions to an equal "clientele" status. "Parity" for the covered jurisdictions can be attributed in part to the Voting Section's real interest in maintaining the normal functioning of local political processes and in part to judicial pronouncements about the scope of the VRA. This is illustrated in the Submission Unit staff attorney's comment, quoted previously, that local officials "have a job to do and they want to get our clearance. . . . we try to make things go smoothly for them so they can hold elections."[40] The serious consequences of according "client status" to southern election officials appears in cases: (1) where objections have been interposed and the election still proceeds, and (2) where officials elected prior to a preclearance submission remain frozen in office for many years because of the protracted negotiations.

Giving equal client status to southern election officials runs directly counter to the intent of Section 5 "to shift the advantage of time and inertia from the perpetrators of the evil to its victims."[41] This solicitude for the "smooth" operation of electoral calendars in the covered jurisdictions, supported by Supreme Court opinions, while in keeping with traditional notions of cooperative American federalism, constitutes a trade-off between vigorous enforcement of Section 5 and the continuance of amicable relationships with local officials.

In a very real sense, filing the preclearance request becomes an almost politically painless exercise for the covered jurisdictions because many local attorneys realize the regulations afford sub-stantial leeway in regard to voting changes. Despite the "alienness" of the DOJ bureaucrats, local officials can exploit the CRD's willingness to engage in traditional courthouse hallway discus-sions whenever a minority challenge is voiced. It is convenient to go through with the submission to avoid the cost of having a losing candidate (black or white) "blow the whistle" on the local jurisdiction for failing to report the voting change to the Depart-ment of Justice. The "lawyers' game," then, makes the statute enforceable by shifting the mode of compliance from a general-ized solution based on firm principle to a site-specific settlement devised in localized negotiations.

NOTES

1. Morton Grodzins and Daniel Elazar, "Centralization and Decen-tralization in the American Federal System,"in Robert A. Goldwin, ed., *A Nation of States: Essays on the American Federal System*, 2nd edition (Chicago: Rand McNally, 1974).

2. James L. Sundquist and David W. Davis, *Making Federalism Work: A Study of Program Coordination at the Community Level* (Washington, D.C.: The Brookings Institution, 1969).

3. Richard H. Leach, *American Federalism* (New York: W.W. Norton, 1970), p. 60.

4. Daniel J. Elazar, *American Federalism: A View from the States*, 2nd edition (New York: Thomas Y. Crowell, 1972), pp. 47-55.

5. In an informative article examining the minority language provi-sions of the 1975 extension of the Voting Rights Act, Cotrell and Stevens offer an intriguing discussion of shifts in the nature of American federal-ism that can be attributed to the Act. Charles Cotrell and R. Michael Stevens, "The 1975 Voting Rights Act and San Antonio, Texas: Toward a Federal Guarantee of a Republican Form of Local Government," *Publius: The Journal of Federalism* 8, 1 (Winter 1978); 79-99.

6. Sheldon M. Edner, "Intergovernmental Policy Development: The Importance of Problem Definition," in Charles O. Jones and Robert D. Thomas, eds., *Public Policy Making in a Federal System* (Beverly Hills, Calif.: Sage Publications, 1976), p. 158.

7. See Howell Raines, *My Soul is Rested: Movement Days in the Deep South Remembered* (New York: Bantam Books, 1978), pp.325-26 for inter-views with white citizens active in the resistance to civil rights programs.

8. Edner, "Intergovernmental Policy," p. 156.

9. Kenneth Culp Davis, *Discretionary Justice: A Preliminary Inquiry* (Baton Rouge: Louisiana State University Press, 1969); D. S. Van Meter and C. E. Van Horn, "The Policy Implementation Process: A Conceptual Framework," *Administration and Society* 6, 4 (February 1975), pp. 445-88.

10. Sheldon M. Edner, "The Blind Men and the Elephant: How do Intergovernmental Actors Compensate for Their Handicap or is There a Cure for Hereditary Blindness," a paper presented at the annual meeting of the American Political Science Association, Washington, D.C., September 1-4, 1977.

11. Elazar, *American Federalism*, pp. 84-126.

12. David H. Hunter, *The Shameful Blight: The Survival of Racial Discrimination in Voting in the South* (Washington, D.C.: The Washington Research Project, 1972); U.S. Commission on Civil Rights, *The Voting Rights Act: Ten Years After* (Washington, D.C., 1975).

13. Interview with David Hunter, Staff Attorney, Voting Section, Civil Rights Division, U.S. Department of Justice, September 1, 1977, Washington, D.C. It should be noted, however, that the telephoned requests for DOJ advice (from local officials), is often the cover for elaborate negotiations that are followed by the formal submission: "In the course of meetings and telephone conversations with Justice Department officials [the staff attorney] got the feeling that 65 percent would be probably an approved figure," *United Jewish Organizations v. Carey*, 51 L. Ed 2d 229 (1977), at 237.

14. Hunter interview.

15. Ibid.

16. Ibid.

17. Interview with Kay Butler, Staff Attorney, Litigative Unit, Voting Section Civil Rights Division, U.S. Department of Justice, October 3, 1977, Mississippi State.

18. Hunter interview.

19. *Gomillion v. Lightfoot* 364 U.S. 339 (1960).

20. Hunter interview.

21. Anthony Downs, *Inside Bureaucracy* (Boston: Little, Brown and Co., 1967), p. 147.

22. Hunter interview.

23. Ibid.

24. U.S. Comptroller General, U.S. General Accounting Office, *Voting Rights Act—Enforcement Needs Strengthening* (Washington, D.C.; February 6, 1978).

25. Eugene Bardach, *The Implementation Game: What Happens After a Bill Becomes a Law* (Cambridge, Mass.: The MIT Press, 1977), pp. 98-177.

26. Interview with Gerald Jones, Chief, Voting Section, Civil Rights Division, U.S. Department of Justice, September 2, 1977, Washington, D.C.

27. Hunter interview.

28. Jones interview.

29. Robert O'Connor and Thomas Ingersoll, "The Impact of Judicial Decisions on the Implementation of the 1965 Voting Rights Act," paper presented at the 1980 meeting of the Midwest Political Science Association.

30. Hunter interview.

31. Ibid.

32. Ibid.

33. Jones interview.

34. Ibid.

35. Hunter interview.

36. Jones interview.

37. U.S. Comptroller General, *Voting Rights Act*, pp. 10-20.

38. As one Civil Rights Division lawyer put it, "[Section 5 compliance] is probably easier than a lot of areas. We are not asking them to do anything special, spend money that they wouldn't have otherwise, or have new programs. We're just asking them to do their normal business, but not discriminate." Hunter interview.

39. Randall B. Ripley and Grace A. Franklin, *Congress, The Bureaucracy and Public Policy* (Homewood, Ill.: The Dorsey Press, 1976), pp. 121-53.

40. Hunter interview.

41. 383 U.S. 301 (1966) at 328.

PART FOUR

THE POLICY EVALUATED

6 Appraisals of Voting Rights Enforcement

Even after extensive effort and expenditures, the implementation of a public program does not guarantee its success. Quite to the contrary, the current citizen displeasure with the cost, delay, and underachievement of many government activities can be traced directly to the complexities of "moving from a decision to operations in such a way that what is put in place bears a reasonable resemblance to the decision and is functioning well in its institutional environment."[1] Evaluation is necessary to judge the degree to which policy choice resembles policy performance and to support recommendations for modification (or even termination) of a given program. Positive or negative assessments depend on the authorship and motivation of the evaluation exercise. As advocates, opponents, and nonpartisan watchdogs make competing and frequently conflicting pronouncements about a program's efficacy, it becomes obvious that, within such a crowded arena, performance appraisal "is seldom a value-free endeavor."[2]

PROCESS VERSUS IMPACT EVALUATIONS: SOME DISTINCTIONS

Performance appraisals of administrative agencies frequently mix policy research with the political controversy surrounding the program under consideration.[3] Evaluating merit becomes intertwined with justifications for the value positions of either the policy's supporters or detractors. This tangling of analysis with advocacy leads to James Wilson's Laws of Policy Evaluation: (1) a program's proponents will evaluate it favorably, and (2) a program's opponents will evaluate it unfavorably.[4] A second source of confusion in performance appraisal stems from the distinction between process evaluation and impact evaluation. "Process evaluation," according to David Nachmias, "is concerned with the extent to which a particular policy or program is implemented according to its stated guidelines."[5] By contrast, "impact evaluation is concerned with examining the extent to which a policy causes change in the intended direction."[6] The importance of this difference turns on the enormous obstacles to effective program implementation in a federal system.[7] That is, the result of an impact evaluation can be misleading in cases where the policy suffers from poor program implementation. Consequently, impact evaluations should be preceded or accompanied by process evaluations.[8] Third, evaluations of federal policies tend to suffer from what Martha Derthick calls "the danger of taking a 'top-down' view of the world of implementation." This perceptual bias, Martha Derthick explains, leads to two serious fallacies: (1) the tendency to see the American federal system as hierarchical, and (2) the tendency to overlook the capacity of local officials to modify or even subvert national policy guidelines.[9]

Since the implementation of any new policy involves "the process of interaction between the setting of goals and the actions geared to achieving them,"[10] performance appraisals should examine the mechanisms of goal definition and redefinition within the administrative agency and the agency's strategic adjustments to its larger political context. To gauge the consequences resulting from the interactive adaptation of a program and its multiple organizational environments, evaluations should explore a policy's genesis and evolution. Walter Williams, in his effort to develop a methodology of implementation assessment, suggests that process evaluations should investigate "(1) the technical capacity to implement, (2) political feasibility, and (3) the technical and political strategies for implementation."[11] He goes on to say

The critical feature of these studies is their capacity to provide rich detail about both an organization's history and procedures, and the four kinds of dynamic staff behavior listed earlier [that is, (1) what organizational staff members do with nonhuman resources (inputs), such as programmatic elements and internal organizational arrangements; (2) how staff members behave with each other; (3) how they behave with staff members of other organizations with which their organization must interact in its external environment; and (4) what they do in treating those who are expected to benefit from their services]. Through careful observation and questioning one can assess how much confusion, lack of clarity, or outright contradiction exist in terms of desired organizational behavior; how administrative duties are executed; how staff delivers services; and what happens in the decision-making process, including the extent to which clients and other citizens have a real say.[12]

THE CONFLICTING EVALUATIONS OF VOTING RIGHTS ENFORCEMENT

As with other areas of public policy, the performance of the administrative agency responsible for voting rights enforcement comes under the scrutiny of a number of different overseers. Some performance reviewers, having been established by statute or executive order, are an institutionalized component of the substantive policy area, such as the U.S. Commission on Civil Rights. Other governmental performance appraisers function as part of the more general policy process and evaluate performance in all policy areas, such as the U.S. General Accounting Office. Nongovernmental, but very active and vocal, policy critics in the form of pressure groups like the Voter Education Project also operate solely in the substantive policy area. Similarly, many nongovernmental policy critics who range more widely in the national policy process, such as the NAACP and Common Cause, also evaluate the work of this agency. Appraisals of the implementing agency's effectiveness by both the governmental and nongovernmental overseers vary from sympathetic support to even-handed evaluations to demonstrative denunciations. These critiques not only affect the agency's annual budgetary gains or losses, but also influence the broader public perception of the agency's "success" or "failure."

Since passage of the 1965 Act, the CRD has enforced voting rights policy under the spotlight of constant critical review. Because of the pivotal importance of the Act to black political progress, close oversight of voting enforcement is a routine feature of the CRD's political environment; what is unusual, however, is the diversity of critical opinion and especially its polar conclusions. One set of evaluation lauds the DOJ's actions as a signal accomplishment in civil rights policy.[13] Favorable judgments about the Voting Rights Act (and its enforcement) base the measurement of "success" on the immediate and monumental increase in black voter registration after August, 1965. Supporting evidence includes higher rates of increase in voter turnout for southern blacks compared to any other major demographic group,[14] the decline of racial rhetoric in state and local election campaigns,[15] some evidence of pro-civil rights roll-call votes by "Black Belt" congressmen,[16] and a noticeable reduction in police abuse and sentence severity for minority citizens.[17] This growing body of evidence documents what Numan Bartley and Hugh Graham have labeled as "the new political realities" of southern politics.[18]

A second set of evaluations takes sharp exception to proclamations of "success" in the area of voting rights policy. The principal indictment of the CRD's enforcement activities emphasizes the frustration of equal political rights for black southerners.[19] Negative assessments of voting policy ground their measure of "failure" in the persistent underrepresentation of blacks in elected as well as in appointed offices throughout the covered jurisdictions. Supporting evidence points to the ceaseless and ingenious patterns of racial gerrymanders,[20] the minimal number and even the absence of black officials in jurisdictions with black, voting-age majority populations,[21] the negligible or at best uneven shift of public goods and services toward the black community in covered jurisdictions,[22] and the limitations of translating votes into influence over public policy decisions.[23]

These conflicting evaluations of voting rights enforcement can be attributed to a definitional muddle over the meaning and measurement of "success." For example, many of the evaluations that label the VRA a successful piece of legislation only focus on Section 4 actions; that is, these appraisals measure "success" by using gross registration totals, which are appropriate for gauging vote denial, but not vote dilution. Another problem afflicting some "positive" evaluations is the confusion that "success" (defined as voting by black citizens) in federal elections indicates "success" in subnational elections. Very simply, while the collective black population of each Deep South state now constitutes a formidable voting bloc for presidential and often congressional elections, the same cannot be said for many state and local offices. Various forms of gerrymandering and other dilution schemes continue to fragment the full electoral potential of black citizens in their home states and communities.

To some extent, definitional issues also bedevil "negative" evaluations. A serious issue is the determination of the "final outcome" of the Act. The absence of a clear consensus on the intended effects of the Voting Rights Act prohibits cumulative comparisons among the various "negative" evaluations. Studies that examine the number and types of black public officials lead to conclusions that are often different from studies that measure the equality of public service provision.

Faced with such mixed reviews, an effective examination of voting rights enforcement must cut through a single point of view and minimize the errors typically associated with a narrow analysis of a complex policy problem. Since any one data source or perspective has particular strengths and weaknesses, utilization of multiple perspectives, or "triangulation," yields a firmer evidentiary base and permits the corroboration of the individual pieces of information against each other.[24] Second, because most previous appraisals have been "final-outcome" evaluations, some polar conclusions can be eliminated by first developing sufficient information for a "process" evaluation. Triangulation on the voting rights enforcement process is perhaps best achieved by a contrastive analysis of the Department of Justice's position with the viewpoints of the institutionalized oversight agencies that have evaluated the CRD's actions over the past 16 years. The following sections provide an assessment of voting rights implementation from the perspective of the U.S. Commission on Civil Rights (CCR), the U.S. General Accounting Office (GAO), and local county attorneys in two southern states. By adopting a *Rasho-mon-* like retelling of the same story from different angles,[25] the approach taken here more accurately assesses the linkage of legislative mandate with policy performance as it is embodied in the current voting rights enforcement process.

THE VIEW FROM THE U.S. COMMISSION ON CIVIL RIGHTS

Created by Congress in 1957 to act as a central clearinghouse for information and research in respect to discrimination or denial of equal protection of the laws, the U.S. Commission on Civil Rights serves as an in-house conscience for the federal government and the nation. Its collection of horror stories concerning violations of personal freedoms was an important element in building public support for the civil rights legislation of the 1960s. Having had an almost midwife-like role in the passage of this set of legislation, the CCR's research and reports on voting rights enforcement typify the agency's "maternal" regard for the growth and development of civil rights throughout the country.

In its first report on the 1965 Voting Rights Act to the President and the Congress (pursuant to PL 85-315), the CCR in November, 1965 triumphantly announced "in many areas of the South there is full compliance with the Voting Rights Act of 1965. In most areas, tests and devices which have been used in the past to deny Negroes the right to vote have been effectively suspended."[26] The report, which essentially offered a chronology of enforcement actions from August to November, 1965, contained only a few remarks suggestive of the prevailing massive resistance and noncompliance with the provisions of the Act. Instead, with justification, the CCR preferred to highlight the real progress of these first up-beat months.

Once the euphoria produced by the success of the voter registration drives subsided, complaints about VRA enforcement voiced by minority citizens and civil rights organizations soon received powerful reinforcement from the Commission. In 1968, the CCR issued its first comprehensive review of voting rights enforcement. Entitled *Political Participation*, the document presented a more balanced picture of minority gains in the South.[27] The Commission opened this in-depth report with a history of Negro political participation and a detailed statement of increased minority registration and turnout. Facts, figures, and photographs supported the CCR's conclusion that "in a relatively short period since the passage of the Voting Rights Act, there has been significant progress in voter registration and political activity by Negro Citizens."[28] Counterbalancing the evidence depicting progress contained in the report's first two chapters, the report's next nine chapters illuminate in explicit terms the multiplicity of obstacles to Negro participation in electoral and political processes erected by the southern states in reaction to the 1965 Act (see Table 6.1). The Commission went to great lengths to demonstrate the powerful negative effects of these barriers on black political participation.

In contrast to the November, 1965, report, the CCR closed *Political Participation* with a somber and realistic assessment.

Despite this progress, however, it is clear that we are still a long way from the goal of full enfranchisement for Negro citizens. As this report discloses, many problems remain in securing to the Negroes of the South the opportunity to participate equally with white citizens in voting and political activity. There remain areas where the number of Negroes registered to vote is disproportionately low. Some Negroes, still discouraged by past discrimination, in effect are penalized for residing in counties and parishes which have not been designated for Federal examiners and where there has been no local voter registration drive. *In areas where registration has increased, we have moved into a new phase of the problem* [our emphasis]. Political boundaries have been changed in an effort to dilute the newly gained voting strength of Negroes. Various devices have been used to prevent Negroes from becoming candidates or obtaining office. Discrimination has occurred against Negro registrants at the polls and discriminatory practices—ranging from the exclusion of Negro poll watchers to discrimination in the selection of election officials to vote fraud—have been pursued which violate the integrity of the electoral process. Moreover, in some areas there has been little or no progress in the entry and participation by Negroes in political party affairs—the key to meaningful participation in the electoral process. Some of the practices found are reminiscent of those which existed at an earlier time during Reconstruction when fear of "Negro government" gave rise to intimidation and a number of election contrivances which finally led to disenfranchisement of the Negro citizen.[29]

Although the CCR's conclusion identified "a new phase" in the struggle for equal voting rights, the 1968 report did not probe at

Table 6.1
Obstacles to Negro Participation in the Electoral and Political Process

A. Diluting the Negro vote
1. Switching to at-large elections
2. Consolidating counties
3. Reapportionment and redistricting measures
4. Full-slate voting required

B. Preventing Negroes from becoming candidates or obtaining office
1. Abolishing the office
2. Extending the term of incumbent white officials
3. Substituting appointment for election
4. Increase filing fees
5. Adding requirements for getting on the ballot
6. Withholding information or providing false information
7. Withholding or delaying certification of nominating petition
8. Improving barriers to the assumption of office

C. Discrimination against Negro registrants
1. Exclusion from precinct meeting
2. Omission of registered Negroes from voter lists
3. Failure to provide sufficient voting facilities
4. Harassment of Negro voters by election officals
5. Refusal to assist or permit assistance to illiterate voters
6. Giving inadequate or erroneous information to Negro voters
7. Disqualification of Negro ballots on technical grounds
8. Denial of equal opportunity to vote absentee
9. Discriminatory location of polling places
10. Racially segregated voting facilities and voter lists

D. Exclusion of and interference with Negro poll watchers

E. Vote Fraud

F. Discriminatory selection of election officials

G. Intimidation and economic dependence
1. Intimidation and harassment of polically active Negroes
2. General intimidation affecting the exercise of political rights
3. Economic dependence as a deterrent to free political activity by Negroes

Source: U.S. Commission on Civil Rights, *Political Participation* (Washington, D.C., 1968).

length the DOJ's failure to activate Section 5. The Commission's most telling statement on Section 5 came in its recommendation for prompt and full enforcement.

Failure to enforce the flat prohibition of Section 5 in the face of repeated violations—most notably in Mississippi—is bound to encourage the enforcement and enactment of additional measures having the purpose or effect of diluting or inhibiting the Negro vote.[30]

The events of the 1970s have confirmed, in the Commission's perspective, the validity of the 1968 report. For the CCR, what is absolutely necessary is "effective enforcement" of the law. Because the first half decade after *South Carolina v. Katzenbach* saw no movement on Section 5 enforcement, the CCR staff became convinced that the CRD's policy and enforcement strategy also constituted a major obstacle to equal political opportunity. With the publication of the 1971 preclearance guidelines, Commission and civil rights activists in the field quickly identified some of the basic deficiencies in the CRD's procedures. Given CRD's reliance on negotiated settlements, it is understandable that Commission staffers were uneasy about voting rights enforcement. Dissatisfaction with the DOJ's slow progress increasingly came to the Commission's attention in the form of letters, newspaper stories, and telephone calls. An attorney active in civil rights work commented about the CRD's strategy in a way that probably captured the attitude of most civil rights advocates. Armand Derfner, of the Lawyer's Committee for Civil Rights Under the Law, said that "the quickest way to get compliance with Section 5 would be for the Justice Department to file *one* criminal information. I daresay this would bring instant compliance throughout the South within about 45 seconds!"[31]

In January, 1975, ten years after the passage of the Voting Rights Act and four years after the development of DOJ regulations for implementing Section 5 of that Act, the CCR responded to the litany of complaints with a massive volume entitled *The Voting Rights Act: Ten Years After*.[32] The Commission's second major evaluation of voting enforcement reiterated with up-to-date evidence the themes of the 1968 report. Extensive statistical documentation again bolstered the conclusion:

Clearly, substantial progress has been made toward full enjoyment of political rights. Because the headlines and front-page pictures of blacks marching to registrars' offices have faded, it is fitting to review the status of voting rights 10 years after passage of the Voting Rights Act. The very real gains that have been made, however, must not be allowed to obscure the persistence of racial discrimination in the electoral process.[33]

Similarly, several chapters of the 1975 publication replicated the finding of the 1968 report of serious barriers to minority registration, voting, candidacy, and representation throughout the South. The following excerpts convey the Commission's dismay over the continuing existence of voting rights obstacles.

Although blacks are beginning to catch up, the U.S. Assistant Attorney General for Civil Rights noted recently, "Some of the gains of the past ten years are more apparent than real!" Analysis of current statistics shows that, though the gaps between white and black participation rates have diminished, there remain significant disparities. Furthermore, though the number of black elected officials has increased rapidly, blacks have gained only a meager hold on the most significant offices....[34]

There is only one black representative in Congress from the seven Southern States which are wholly or partially covered by the Voting Rights Act. No black holds statewide office in the South and no black candidate for statewide office has even come close to election. Under the impact of the Voting Rights Act and court-ordered, single-member districting, blacks have begun to appear in State legislatures, county commissions, school boards, and city councils. But this occurs almost always in places where blacks are sufficiently numerous and concentrated residentially to dominate a district by a substantial population margin and a comfortable registration margin....[35]

What these changes have in common is that they were made by whites in political control. Minority political strength, despite progress under the Voting Rights Act, is not yet able to prevent structural changes that limit the effectiveness of that strength. For example, when the Richmond annexation was agreed to in 1969, three of the nine city council members were black. They were excluded from the negotiations that led to the annexation and had no way to prevent its taking place. The only safeguard of minority voting rights in this situation was Section 5 of the Voting Rights Act, enforced by the Attorney General, and the judicial system. In other cities and counties where changes similar in their effect have been made, minorities have had even less political strength than had been gained in Richmond by 1969. For example, when Leflore County, Mississippi, adopted at-large election for its board of supervisors and when it later adopted (as required by court order) a single-member district plan that a Federal court found to be racially gerrymandered, there was not even token black representation on the county board of supervisors.[36]

The blame for this state of affairs, in the Commission's view, could be attributed to white public officials still defending supremacist positions and, for the first time, to the failure of the Department of Justice to enforce the law vigorously. "The central problem is that of dilution of the vote—arrangements by which the vote of a minority elector is made to count less than the vote of a white."[37]

To the Commission, "Section 5 has become the focus of the Voting Rights Act in recent years," and "the history of Section 5 provides an index of the types of discriminatory practices that covered jurisdictions have attempted to put into effect since 1965 and 1970. . . ."[38] On review of the evidence, the CCR concluded that there was uneven compliance with the Section 5 mandate to have all voting changes in the covered jurisdictions precleared by the U.S. government. "Compliance with the submission requirement has been uneven, *and the DOJ does not have an effective monitoring system* to bring to its attention unsubmitted changes."[39] Without such a monitoring system effectively in place, which would identify those jurisdictions that did not comply, how could sanctions be employed to punish those white southern officials who refused to submit voting changes for preclearance and, therefore, were depriving minorities of their right to vote?

In the 1975 document, the CCR recommended strengthening the enforcement powers of the DOJ. Specifically with regard to Section 5, the CCR called upon Congress to amend the Voting Rights Act "to provide for *civil penalties* or damages against state and local officials who violate Section 5 of the Act by enforcing or implementing changes in their electoral laws and procedures without having first obtained preclearance from the Attorney General of the United States or the U.S. District Court for the

District of Columbia."[40] The effectiveness of the preclearance procedure, concluded the CCR, "has been limited by the failure of covered jurisdictions to submit all changes in their electoral laws and procedures for review and *by the absence of direct procedures to enforce compliance* with the preclearance requirement." If southern officials who did not preclear before implementing a new voting change were assessed personal damages, "without reimbursement from public funds, . . . timely submissions of changes" would be the reality.[41] The 1975 CCR recommendation would have given leverage to the very persons who were adversely affected by these discriminatory voting changes—the black voters themselves. The plan would have awarded damages to those who instituted the proceedings against the local officials—the minorities in the local jurisdictions.

If implemented by the Congress, the recommendations would have significantly broadened the scope of the battle for equal protection in voting. The CRD attorneys would have had an enormous support mechanism—the white official's fear of civil damage suits brought by black residents of a town that adopted a voting change without preclearance. This would have meant an increase in the number of submissions to the Justice Department. However, there would have to be additional appropriations for this full enforcement of the Act. The CCR recommendations in 1975 called for such expanded resources: "the President should request and Congress should appropriate additional funds for the DOJ and the Department should increase its allocation of resources to the Voting Section."[42] The recommendations were not well received, and there was no additional funding for the DOJ, nor was there an amendment to the Act that would have enabled citizens to institute civil proceedings against local officials who ignored the command of Section 5.

In January, 1980, the CCR would write that it "is evident that minorities still need the protection of the Voting Rights Act."[43] In a recent report on *The State of Civil Rights: 1979*, the CCR concluded:

We are at the threshold of the 1980's. The 1960's brought us good laws, and they were enhanced in the 1970's by strong judicial decisions. Yet the *lack of enforcement* by the Executive Branch of Government, the weakening of good legislation by the Congress, and the diminishing will and vision on the part of many Americans are discouraging.[44]

In sum, the position of the U.S. Commission on Civil Rights is that a good law has been emasculated for a number of reasons: (1) no effective penalties existed in the 1965 Act (and subsequent regulations of the DOJ) to compel white leaders in the South to preclear; (2) not enough CRD manpower was assigned to enforce effectively the regulations as they were developed in 1971; and (3) DOJ bureaucrat-attorneys developed a "professional" relationship with local officials, many of whom have long sought to exclude minorities from the political process. While the CCR and civil rights leaders are not totally discouraged, they remain fearful of the time when there will no longer be a Voting Rights Act.

THE VIEW FROM THE GENERAL ACCOUNTING OFFICE

The CCR's accusations about the CRD's enforcement practices found receptive listeners on Capitol Hill. Efforts to dilute the growth of black electoral strength were investigated by the U.S. Senate's Committee on the Judiciary in 1975, and in the same year, dilution schemes provoked considerable concern during the renewal hearings for the VRA. After extension of the Act (with the addition of the bilingual provisions), Representative Don Edwards (Chairman, Subcommittee on Civil and Constitutional Rights, House Committee on the Judiciary) requested a full-scale investigation of voting rights policy from the Comptroller General. Representative Edward's letter stressed the subcommittee's desire to evaluate the Department of Justice's enforcement of the Voting Rights Act, so that the subcommittee could "carefully monitor the progress of the Act in removing barriers to full electoral participation by minority citizens."[45]

The subsequent GAO report, issued on February 6, 1978, assessed the implementation and impact of the Voting Rights Act. In addition to a standard review of the Justice Department's policies, regulations, practices, and procedures, the GAO systematically surveyed and interviewed a number of important clients and administrators including state and local election officials, minority organization leaders, private citizens who expressed an interest in minority voting rights, and selected officials in the Department of Justice. Entitled *Voting Rights Act—Enforcement Needs Strengthening*, the report enumerated major implementation failures in agency management policies, program monitoring of local compliance, preparation of evidence, and intergovernmental communications.

It is no surprise, given its oversight function, that the General Accounting Office identified several managerial shortcomings limiting VRA enforcement. What is surprising, however, is the relatively simple character of the administrative practices GAO proposed as changes in the Voting Section's operating procedures. For example, Civil Rights Division managers (i.e., the Assistant Attorney General, the Deputy Assistant Attorney General, and the Chief of the Voting Section) did not know which cases were pending and which cases were in fact closed.[46] Prior to the GAO request, the litigative staff did not maintain a list of cases and their status.[47] Similarly, recordkeeping by the Submission Unit was deemed cumbersome and often the cause of confusion.[48] The absence of a computerized retrieval system delayed the processing of submissions because the paralegal staff had to cope with an overflowing filing system that has expanded exponentially as submissions have increased.[49]

Had the program evaluation been restricted to managerial snafus, it could be treated as a minor affair between an executive branch bureau and Congress' watchdog. However, in a provocative statement, GAO leveled a serious charge at DOJ's enforcement practices.

The Voting Rights Act has been in effect for over 12 years, yet there is little assurance that covered States and localities are complying with the Act's preclearance provision. We found that the Department of Justice had limited formal procedures for determining that voting changes were submitted for review as required by the Act or for determining whether jurisdictions implemented changes over the Department's objections.[50]

To document this charge, the report described breakdowns in the Voting Section's efforts to monitor local government compliance.

Problems cited include the absence of any systematic method of uncovering voting changes, the lack of follow-up procedures after objections had been interposed, and the sporadic use of the FBI to obtain necessary information from reluctant jurisdictions. Incomplete monitoring means covered jurisdictions might implement voting changes without preclearance or despite objections interposed by the U.S. Attorney General. GAO found numerous instances of both situations, including requests by the Voting Section for information from covered jurisdictions that have remained unanswered for at least two years.[51] One damning piece of evidence in the GAO indictment listed the number of unsubmitted changes that resulted from the passage of session laws in covered states. Session laws are statutes passed during an assembly of a state legislature. Based on its investigation, the GAO discovered 318 unreported session law changes during the period between 1970 and 1974.[52] Given the Voting Section's staffing deficiencies, the failure to uncover an unreported change in some small, isolated town or village in the deep South is quite understandable, but for the Voting Section to miss several hundred unreported changes that were the product of state legislative activity borders on the unimaginable. The session law problem apparently stems from the CRD's sporadic, rather than regular, monitoring of legislative action. For example, the Voting Section reviewed session laws in Virginia in 1971, in Alabama and Louisiana in 1972, and Alabama again in 1974. The Chief Attorney for the Voting Section succinctly describes their work: "We've done reviews of session laws at various times trying to pick out things that look like they might need changing and then write letters listing them to the jurisdictions."[53]

The GAO report also observed that, even with FBI assistance, the CRD still experienced difficulty in tracking down unreported changes in jurisdictions throughout the covered states. The complexity of the monitoring problem is clear in this description of the Voting Section's operation.

We've done several things. One project that we launched, in early 1975, made a study of all of the places from which we had received submissions. Then we listed all of those [from] which we had received none.

Then we sent the FBI to those cities. In order to make it a manageable number, we looked at census data and picked them, we were limited to some extent because census data is only reported from cities over a certain size, 10,000 or something like that. We looked at those cities and found the ones in which there were a substantial number of minority population and sent them to all of those cities to talk to officials to find out if there had been any voting changes since the applicable date, and to provide them with the requirements of Section 5 and the need for the submission. That netted us quite a large number. Then we sent them to all counties of respectable size and composition in selected states, so that in conjunction with the session law project, which would not pick up local changes—it only pertained to state-enacted laws—we really got a substantial response from that project. What we have done since on a continuing basis is not initiate a new project in terms of locating unsubmitted changes necessarily. When we send out requests for additional information to complete a submission, many times those things just fall through the cracks; we just never hear from them, the submitting authority again. What we have done is to do a review of those outstanding requests periodically. Now we are trying to get it down to thirty days. If they are out thirty days or more, we will send out the FBI to meet with the official and find out what the problem is.[54]

However, sending out the FBI, even many times to one jurisdiction, does not necessarily yield the required information, as the GAO report pointedly observes. The Voting Section's own description of its methods also confirms the inadequacy of limiting compliance monitoring to cities of a population over 10,000. The South, in spite of all its economic growth and urbanization, still retains a large rural population located in small communities, many of which are unincorporated.

Inadequate preparation of evidence is another enforcement weakness mentioned in the GAO report. On the basis of a random sample of submissions, GAO investigators discovered "that 59 percent of 271 changes decided did not have all the data required by Federal regulations."[55] Another data handicap confronting the Voting Section is the obsolescence of census information on covered jurisdictions. Without up-to-date census records, the significant population shifts that have occurred in many covered jurisdictions have left the Voting Section at the mercy of locally commissioned and executed surveys. The Voting

Section, as noted in the previous chapter, does not employ a trained demographer who understands census data and its statistical manipulation, even though much of the information required by the submission regulations is demographic in nature. In regard to the GAO dissatisfaction with Voting Section data deficiencies, the Bureau of Census has responsibility under the Voting Rights Act for conducting biennial surveys (concurrent with congressional election years) of jurisdictions covered under the preclearance requirements of the Act to assist DOJ in identifying those jurisdictions with voting problems and to provide the Congress with data to measure the impact of the Act. Unfortunately, these surveys are flawed by their incompleteness as well as by the variability in turnout by different types of elections.[56] These flawed supplementary census surveys mean that the 1970 Census and estimates based on it have been the principal data base for Section 5 determinations.[57]

One other complaint raised by the GAO highlights the Voting Section's system of communications with local election officials and local minority leaders. To make sure that local communities comply with 28 CFR 51, the Voting Section beginning in 1973 distributed information packets to all covered jurisdictions. However, respondents to the GAO survey of election officials indicate that the local attorneys who must initiate the preclearance process do not have copies of the relevant regulations and that they also have difficulty interpreting the regulations, once they obtain copies of the requirements. Similarly, the Voting Section's communications with minority groups does not reach all interested parties. The Voting Section mails a weekly listing of submissions to anyone upon request, but the weekly listing only contains the date, type of change, and name of jurisdiction. A serious defect of the mailing lists is the appearance of new civil rights organizations; unless they contact CRD, the new group will not be visible to the Washington staff and, therefore, not become part of the Voting Section's "network" of local informants. On another aspect of communication, the GAO observes that minority persons commented on 55 percent of the submissions, but local minority groups were informed of the Voting Section's review decision in less than one percent of the cases sampled.[58] Finally, DOJ does not make announcements of public hearings as required by law.[59]

These communication failures deserve further elaboration. To supplement its study of CRD management practices, GAO conducted interviews with a sample of minority interest group representatives and election officials in the covered jurisdictions.[60] The survey's results delineate the present battlelines over Section 5 procedures, as perceived by the opposing sides. Turning first to state and local officials, their responses can be examined in three areas: (1) knowledge of the Act and Section 5 requirements, (2) compliance with the Act, and (3) assessment of the Act. Subnational officials' knowledge was decidedly uneven. Most state and local officials (83 percent) had received copies of the Act, while 73 percent of the state officials and 42 percent of local officials stated they received copies of Section 5 guidelines after their publication in *The Federal Register*. Fully one-third of these officials expressed a desire for further assistance under the Act and over 25 percent of the local officials displayed only a marginal understanding of why their jurisdiction was covered. On the critical issue of submissions, 16 percent said they have implemented election changes without having first reported them to the U.S. Attorney General. Among the reasons given for this failure to report were difficulty in identifying an electoral change, supposed insignificance of changes, and length of time required for DOJ approval. No official cited administrative costs or staffing requirements as an obstacle to reporting. In assessing CRD's assistance with Section 5, less than 30 percent considered Justice as their prime source of assistance, yet, most (85 percent) agreed that the CRD staff service was fair to very good. As expected, 50 percent of the state and local election officials felt the protection afforded by Section 5 and the Voting Rights Act was excessive, and only 3 percent saw a need to expand the level of protection.[61]

Minority perceptions of Section 5 coverage and CRD compliance methods are the converse of the responses by local election officials. Answers given by interest group representatives can be categorized by: (1) knowledge of the Act and Section 5 procedures, (2) participation in the preclearance decision, and (3) assessment of the Act. Lack of knowledge about DOJ procedures was cited by 35 percent of the minority respondents, and over 90 percent said they were not on the Voting Section's mailing list—over half were unaware of its existence. Approximately 25 percent stated they know of unreported changes, and most felt the changes were significant enough to cause concern in the local community. In terms of participation in the preclearance process, about 80 percent of the minority interviewees noted that they were rarely or never consulted by the CRD or local election officials. This sense of removal from the decision process was reinforced by the minority respondents' belief that DOJ approval of changes opposed by minority leaders was a more important problem than a covered jurisdiction's failure to submit. Minority assessment of the Act reflected several views. Approximately 50 percent judged coverage of the Act to be about right, but over 40 percent judged present coverage to be too limited or much too limited. Disagreeing with the Commission on Civil Rights, minority respondents expressed little difficulty with local registration and polling place practices, as depicted in Table 6.2. Eighty percent credited the Voting Rights Act with improving minority participation, and 73 percent said less restrictive requirements would compromise minority political activity.[62]

On balance, the GAO survey verifies the disappearance of grosser techniques to prevent minority electoral participation and a shift by local officials to a vote dilution strategy that relies on the manipulation of less obvious and visible (to the average voter) legal parameters of elections, such as boundaries, candidate qualifications, governmental forms, and polling place, precinct, and reregistration rules. Decisions about these structural changes usually occur within the context of CRD's bargaining-compromise enforcement pattern. As the GAO survey indicates, the negotiated settlement does not usually include input from the affected minorities.

The GAO report, which concluded that the "limited federal efforts preclude assurance that all States and localities are complying with the Voting Rights Act," put forward several suggestions to improve DOJ's enforcement operations. The recommendations address both management practices and legislative refinements.

—Improve compliance activity by developing procedures for (1) informing jurisdictions periodically of their submission responsibilities, (2) identifying systematically jurisdictions not submitting voting changes, (3)

Table 6.2
Minority Interest Group Representatives' Assessment of Obstacles to Electoral Participation

Possible Problem	Little Or No Problem	Somewhat Of A Problem	Moderate Problem	Serious Problem	Very Serious Problem
Uncomfortable atmosphere at registration	73	7	3	12	5
Harassment	82	5	2	10	1
Misinformation of registration requirements	85	3	4	4	4
Difficulty in finding registration location	88	8	2	1	1
Registration materials Not in minority language	77	5	14	-	4
Inconvenient registration locations	51	19	8	13	9
Inconvenient registration hours	45	21	11	14	10

PERCENT OF INTERVIEWEES RESPONDING

Source: U.S. General Accounting Office, *Impact of Voting Rights Act as Seen by Minority Interest Groups and Selected Individuals* (unpublished document in GAO files; mimeographed), 1978.

monitoring whether States and localities are implementing election law changes over the Department's objection, and (4) soliciting the views of interest groups and individuals.[63]

—Improve the preclearance review process by (1) reassessing submission guidelines to determine data needs for the review of various types of change submissions and (2) implementing procedures for achieving more timely submission reviews.[64]

—Improve the Department's efforts to maintain submission information by (1) implementing procedures for locating submission files and (2) making necessary corrections to the computer data base and developing procedures for increased computer utilization in managing the election law review process. . . .[65]

—Expand the Voting Section paraprofessionals' responsibilities to allow attorneys more time to be involved in litigative matters.[66]

—Develop and initiate a systematic approach to more extensively identify litigative matters in the voting rights area.[67]

—Congress should reassess the adequacy and need for the biennial survey mandated by the Voting Rights Act in light of its limited usefulness and substantial costs.[68]

None of these recommendations entail sweeping adjustments inside the CRD and would have a salutary effect on Section 5 compliance.

THE DEPARTMENT OF JUSTICE RESPONDS

In accordance with Section 236 of the Legislative Reorganization Act of 1970, Kevin Rooney, Assistant Attorney General for Administration, submitted to the Committee on Governmental Affairs, U.S. Senate, the Department of Justice's reply to the GAO report. The rejoinder (dated June 7, 1978) opened with the admission that the Comptroller General's report "is a fairly thorough critique of the Department's voting rights enforcement program and contains several appropriate recommendations to the Attorney General towards improving the effectiveness of our compliance efforts."[69] After arguing that the GAO misperceived the CRD role under the Voting Rights Act, Rooney's report settles down to serious rebuttal, interspersed with occasional signs of willingness to modify current management practices.

The items that the CRD agreed to upgrade include its recordkeeping and filing systems, its computerized data systems, and its methods for utilizing the paralegal staff. To quote the DOJ memorandum, "the Division [CRD] has recently hired an administrator experienced in the use of computerized information retrieval systems and we intend to revise and modernize our system."[70] In regard to the efficient and effective use of the paralegals, the CRD agrees with the GAO suggestions to expand their responsibilities, but only to a certain point.

> ...the task of monitoring elections is one that often requires skill and experience in making and communicating legal judgments involving the application of State, local, and Federal law to discrete and sometimes sensitive fact situations....Thus, while paralegals may assist in such field work, we would hesitate to have paralegals supplant field attorneys.[71]

Besides this basic objection to nonlawyers replacing lawyers, the DOJ also reminds the GAO and the Senate committee that the paralegals' workload of submission reviews is extremely heavy and that the Voting Section really needs at least 11 more paralegals.

On June 16, 1978, Drew Days, III, Assistant Attorney General for Civil Rights, stated "the Justice Department has neither the personnel nor the resources to become the primary enforcer of the Voting Rights Act."[72] Responding to members of the House Judiciary subcommittee on civil and constitutional rights, Days defended the DOJ's record on voting enforcement by adding:

> It was never contemplated that an official of the federal government would be on hand in each jurisdiction to prevent violations of this act. While we do have a substantial role in monitoring compliance, it is impossible for a unit [the Voting Section] which consists of 17 attorneys and 15 paralegals to be looking over the shoulder of officials in some 1,115 jurisdictions.[73]

Days' testimony also included the observation that the DOJ shares responsibility for enforcement with private citizens who can challenge in court the denial of voting rights and with the covered jurisdictions subject to the law. This "shared responsibility," Day argued, is in accord with original congressional intent. The Assistant Attorney General, in answering the oversight committee's charges of less-than-thorough enforcement, placed some of the blame on Congress itself, as he pointed out the legislature's refusal to approve the CRD's request for an extra 11 positions to be assigned to voting enforcement.

The DOJ's hostility to the GAO investigation appears in a number of firm and uncompromising stands. First, the rejoinders refuse to give ground on the issue of faulty monitoring, as illustrated by the following statement.

We do not believe our procedures for monitoring future compliance with our objections require revision. We have a registry of 408 organizations and individuals who are notified of submissions. Those who comment on a submission are then notified if we interpose an objection. These groups and persons are in the best position to become aware of implementation of such changes and bring them to our attention.[74]

Second, DOJ challenges the GAO's contention that preclearance review decisions are performed without complete and pertinent data. The DOJ insists:

rather our experience and research show that, when significant information is lacking, an objection to the implementation of the change is interposed, which is a procedure specifically provided for in our Section 5 guidelines.[75]

Third, the DOJ forcefully rejects the GAO's indictment of delayed preclearance decisions.

We are not aware of a single instance in recent years where an objection was interposed after the 60-day period expired, nor are we aware of any prevalence of other late responses even remotely approaching the volume claimed by the report. Perhaps G.A.O.'s perception of what constitutes the 60-day period is different from ours because of some confusion in calculating the statutory period. This is somewhat evident from a subsequent statement on page 18 of the report concerning a finding that "in about 6.8 percent of the submissions reviewed, a Departmental decision was not rendered until at least 100 days from the *initial* receipt of the submission" [emphasis added]. However, our "more information" procedure (adopted by our guidelines and approved by the Supreme Court in *Georgia v. United States*, 411 U.S. 526 (1973), specifically allows for a tolling of the 60-day period when additional information is necessary to a proper analysis of the change.[76]

Clearly these three issues are at the heart of the compliance controversy. The Comptroller General's investigation by reinforcing many of the Civil Rights Commission's claims has further polarized the CRD from its critics. While the Voting Section has introduced some of the GAO recommended changes of in-house administrative procedures (see Appendix G), its fundamental strategy to obtain compliance has not been altered.

THE VIEW FROM THE COUNTY COURTHOUSE

Curiously, an essential element missing from the institutional evaluations of voting rights enforcement is the appraisal of those officials in the covered jurisdictions who actually must abide by the law. To fill this gap, this section reports the perspective of county attorneys in Georgia and Mississippi who have direct responsibility for complying with the Voting Rights Act.[77] The responses to our inquiries provide interesting glimpses into the behaviorial interaction of local-level officials with the CRD staff in Washington, D.C. This information also illustrates the diversity of voting rights compliance by local attorneys. Finally, these responses capture the local attorney's attitudes about their federal counterparts in the Section 5 negotiations. While these images constitute only another piece of the complete enforcement process, nevertheless, the responses of the local attorneys reveal much about their compliance behavior and thus permit some assessment of existing appraisals of voting rights policy.

The compliance behavior of county attorneys can be examined in four areas: (1) their sources of information, (2) their perceptions of CRD actions, (3) their perceptions of their own compliance, and (4) their responses to the interposition of an objection. Since voting rights enforcement depends upon the local officials' understanding of the federal law, the sources of information about the Act utilized by county attorneys in the covered jurisdictions directly condition compliance. Half of the county attorneys rely primarily on the DOJ for voting rights information, while the other half rely on their own skills or on their state attorney general. While 70 percent of the attorneys stated that the DOJ had sent them information about the Act, only 15 percent said they received a copy of the interpretation guidelines. This meager informational support from Washington prompted 58 percent of the county attorneys to communicate with the Voting Section prior to a submission. The most typical forms of communication are, of course, telephone (57 percent) and letter (31 percent); by contrast, county attorneys seldom make personal visits to the Justice Department or ask their Congressman to intervene on their behalf. Once a county attorney contacts the Voting Section, most attorneys (62 percent) rate the assistance received as adequate. The principal complaints with the Voting Section's assistance include lack of timely response, ambiguous answers to questions, and difficulty in identifying the appropriate official within DOJ. These responses match the GAO finding of weaknesses in the Justice Department's communication with covered jurisdictions and support the CCR call for a campaign by the CRD to educate local attorneys. With 81 percent of the county attorneys stating that they were either "unsure" (45.4 percent) or "unaware" (36.3 percent) of the CRD standards for Section 5 determinations, the need for a training program throughout the covered states is obvious.

The county attorneys' perceptions of CRD actions add fuel to the controversy surrounding the Voting Section's adherence to the 60-day time limit. Fifty-three percent of the county attorneys said they received notification of the Attorney General's decision by the sixtieth day, but fully 46 percent claimed that the notification arrived after the legal time limit. This issue may seem significant from the perspective of legislative intent and procedural correctness, but the controversy diminishes in importance upon the discovery that the vast majority of revisions (58.5 percent) made in voting change submissions are deemed by the local attorneys to be "one or two minor points." That is, even though some confusion exists in the federal-local understanding about the operation of the 60-day clock, the actual decision, even if it arrives "late" by local perceptions, most typically is either approval or approval contingent upon one or two minor revisions. Put the other way, only 5 percent of the county attorneys state that the CRD required a wholesale revision of an original submission. This confusion over the 60-day time limit could be remedied quite simply. The CRD, according to 75 percent of the local attorneys, requests more information about a voting change after the initial submission of the documents. It would seem most appropriate (and efficient) to reiterate the rules about re-starting the 60-day clock at this point. Apparently, the Voting Section's form letters have not been sufficient to eliminate misunderstandings.

On the critical point of compliance, about 41 percent of the county attorneys we contacted have never submitted a voting change. Attorneys in Mississippi (66 percent) were more likely to have filed a preclearance request than attorneys in Georgia (47 percent). As might be expected, a number of the county attorneys who have never submitted a voting change represent counties with small nonwhite populations (i.e., less than 25 percent).[78] Yet, in each state, one finds counties not only with significant proportions of black citizens (i.e., 25-49 percent), but also counties with majority black populations in which the county attorney has never submitted a voting change. Several of the county attorneys (29 percent) who themselves had not filed a preclearance request recalled that their county had, in fact, made a submission since August, 1965. Combining these two pieces of information, approximately 24 percent of the county attorneys (Georgia: 36 percent; Mississippi: 16 percent) have not made a Section 5 submission or remember if their county had ever made a submission. This estimate exceeds the GAO figure derived from their survey of state and local officials and more closely matches the GAO findings based on responses from minority group representatives. All of these estimates far exceed the DOJ's claim of 94 percent compliance.

Our contacts and the GAO survey results indicate that local attorneys do not find administrative costs, staffing requirements, or preparation time to be an obstacle to reporting voting changes. The principal reason offered for failure to submit a voting change was the absence of voting changes in a covered jurisdiction.

When asked about the manner of elections in the county and the length of time this form of election has been used, the county attorneys who have never filed a preclearance request typically answered with responses such as "50 years" or "forever." In effect, many counties have simply ignored the 1965 Voting Rights Act by not modifying their election laws or procedures. This situation might be tolerable from a pragmatic viewpoint in counties with a very small percent of black citizens, but even a number of counties with a majority black voting-age population have deliberately not changed their electoral procedures. Simply put, in this type of county, local white political groups have adopted a strategy of "no change" in the hope of outlasting either lawsuits or the lifespan of the 1965 Voting Rights Act. Another important dimension of compliance concerns the conduct of elections prior to approval of a preclearance request. Despite the claims of the Voting Section that such elections are insignificant and small in number, almost 40 percent of the county attorneys assert that elections have proceeded in their jurisdiction while submissions were still pending in the Voting Section. Such action reduces the effectiveness of the CRD's reliance on minority group monitoring of local elections.

Finally, county attorneys (14 percent) in Georgia and Mississippi claim that the U.S. Attorney General interposed objections more frequently than documented by DOJ records (approximately 2 percent). This discrepancy derives most likely from the form letters used by the CRD. Some confusion apparently exists in the minds of local officials between requests for additional information and an actual objection. Besides this matter of occasional confusion, local attorneys (90 percent) express a strong dislike for the CRD's failure to provide information or justification in support of an interposed objection. While most objections are eventually resolved, 60 percent of the attorneys for counties incurring objections declared that their jurisdiction proceeded with elections prior to removal of the objection. Again, this statement hardly squares with the compliance claim of the Justice Department.

County attorneys in Georgia and Mississippi display a range of compliance behavior in regard to Section 5 requirements. The attorneys (60 percent) that responded they were aware of the law and had filed all voting changes with the U.S. Attorney General can be considered to be in full compliance. Another 16 percent of the county attorneys admit to not reporting "insignificant" voting changes, but they do claim to report most voting changes. This group can be considered to be in substantial compliance. The remaining county attorneys (24 percent) who have not filed preclearance reports nor have their jurisdictions ever filed a voting change are clearly at odds with the legislative intent of Section 5. The two most frequently offered reasons for noncompliance are ignorance of the law and deliberate avoidance of the law. A small portion of county attorneys (approximately 9-10 percent) do not realize that their county is covered by the 1965 Act or do not understand the law sufficiently to comply with it in a meaningful fashion. The last group of county attorneys (15-16 percent) have not submitted a preclearance request because their county election commission has chosen not to initiate any electoral changes. A very common situation is the existence of at-large elections often coupled with commission-form governments (see the Mobile, Alabama cases[79]) which pre-date the 1965 Act. By carefully refraining from modification of long-standing electoral procedures, these jurisdictions remain outside the domain of Section 5 coverage. In addition to these general categories of compliance, almost 40 percent of the counties go ahead with elections even though a preclearance request is still pending with the Department of Justice.

This courthouse view of Section 5 enforcement helps cut through some of the polar positions taken by the Voting Section and its institutional overseers. By applying the responses of the local attorneys to each of the DOJ's fundamental differences with the GAO investigation, it becomes possible to assess the merits of the contradictory points between the two agencies. First, despite the last-minute filing game attempted by some jurisdictions, the processing routines of the Submission Unit appear to work remarkably well. Although some local attorneys remain confused by the tolling of the 60-day clock, on balance, the Voting Section's track record for timely Section 5 determinations must be conceded. The strongest pressure keeping the Submission Unit "on time" is the legislative rule that allows a preclearance submission to become effective if a determination is not rendered by the Attorney General within the 60-day time limit.

Ironically, it is this haste to meet the 60-day deadline which gives some credence to the GAO charge that Section 5 decisions are made without complete data. As the paralegal research assistants readily admit, the "biggest hang-up" they face is the time limit coupled with staff size.[80] The necessity for the Submission Unit staff to beat the 60-day clock becomes especially severe in the two-to-three month period before elections in the various states.[81] With preclearance materials piling up, the paralegal staff relies heavily on its bureaucratic routine of "spotting red flags." Such hurried action easily explains minority group leaders' perception that they are often left out of the Section 5 process. Unless a paralegal "spots a red flag" in a given preclearance submission, the chances are good that few, if any, local minority leaders will be contacted and that the proposed change(s) will be approved with at most "one or two minor revisions."[82]

While the problem of incomplete data is forced on the Submission Unit by virtue of the time limit-staff size dilemma, the GAO indictment of faulty monitoring falls squarely at the feet of the Voting Section and its CRD managers. Of the three sticking-points between DOJ and the GAO (and the principal one from the CCR's perspective), the CRD's inability to detect the numerous and recurring instances of noncompliance discredits the DOJ's claim of almost 94 percent compliance. The similarity between the percentage of county attorneys who state that their jurisdiction has never filed a Section 5 request (24 percent) and the percentage of minority group leaders who claim to know of unreported changes (25 percent) is too close to be passed off as coincidence. By adopting a reactive, almost court-like pattern of implementation, the Voting Section, in effect, depends on the volition of local attorneys employed by the covered jurisdictions to initiate the process of minimizing nondiscrimination. Given the previous and enduring history of voting rights discrimination, this strategic choice by the CRD managers is naive at best and at worst perpetuates vote dilution. In summary, this courthouse view of Section 5 enforcement supports many of the issues raised in the reports of the U.S. Commission on Civil Rights and the General Accounting Office.

TRIANGULATING COMPLIANCE AND ACCOUNTABILITY

The critiques produced by the U.S. Commission on Civil Rights and the General Accounting Office identify the CRD's administrative shortcomings and the political consequences of its strategy of negotiated settlements. Although both of these performance appraisals contain significant information and make accurate judgments, by Williams' standards of implementation assessment, each agency's review of voting rights enforcement is incomplete. The CCR, in its extensive catalogues of the difficulties encountered by black citizens in the deep South, calls attention to the CRD's failure to implement voting rights policy in consonance with legislative intent. In effect, the Commission concentrates on "what they [the staff] do in treating those who are expected to benefit from their [the agency] services." Similarly, the GAO's well-documented investigation comes down hard on the CRD's managerial mistakes and correctly stresses organizational changes feasible within the CRD's current administrative means. The GAO report zeroes in on "what organizational staff members do with nonhuman resources (inputs), such as programmatic elements and internal organizational arrangements." Both the CCR and the GAO evaluations presume a reasonably detailed knowledge of "how staff members behave with each other," such as was presented earlier in Chapter 3. Finally, the survey of county attorneys working for the covered jurisdictions helps complete the picture of "how they [the agency staff] behave with staff members of other organizations with which their organization must interact in its external environment."

The contrastive analysis of the different evaluations of voting rights enforcement removes much of the confusion and contradictions contained in the debate over Section 5 compliance. From this comparison of conflicting performance appraisals, a corollary to Wilson's Two Laws of Policy Evaluation appears to be operating: statutory authority predestines evaluatory conclusions. That is, oversight agencies produce evaluations which reflect their policy mission as it is embodied in the oversight agency's enabling legislation. Certainly, this is an obvious point; but, nevertheless, it must be made because this evalutory behavior explains the uni-dimensional thrust of a given oversight agency's work. The lesson here is simple and straightforward: process evaluations in order to serve as adequate foundations for impact studies need to investigate the complete range of an administrative agency's implementation actions. Only by marshalling a multidimensional appraisal of voting rights enforcement and comparatively examining the strengths and weaknesses of each evaluation does it become possible to triangulate on compliance.

No one oversight agency can easily do a complete performance appraisal of a program. In response to the basic constraints of unique legislative mandates and limited budgetary resources, oversight agencies choose assessment tasks in line with the different connotations of evaluation. Guy Benveniste elaborates on this natural organizational tendency to specialize on a particular function in his typology of bureaucratic accountability.[82] From his perspective, accountability has three distinct usages, and therefore, different types of evaluations and appraisal agents develop and cluster around each meaning. For example, Benveniste identifies the verification of an agency's use of organizational resources as one form of accountability. Evaluations of this type emphasize "efficiency" and "management." In the case of voting rights appraisals, the GAO report would fit this category. The next type of accountability investigates an administrative agency's planning, programming, decision making, and implementation of desired outputs. This kind of evaluation stresses "effectiveness" of organizational processes and routines that permit the agency to hit its policy target (that is, what types of goods and/or services does the agency deliver to which types of clients?). Such a process evaluation is a main theme of the first part of this book. Benveniste lists the determination of an agency's goal achievement as the third type of accountability. The issue here is the consonance between the agency's service targets and the legislatively mandated targets, or in a word, the policy "validity" of an agency's actions. In the area of voting rights, the CCR has been the agency primarily concerned with validity questions.

To Benveniste's three types of accountability, one additional and ultimate form of accountability—democratic control—must be incorporated in implementation assessments. Performance

appraisals which recognize that an administrative agency's behavior is conditioned by the organization's structure and available resources as well as by demands from the external environment
of other organizations lay the groundwork for addressing the
question of democratic accountability. While a policy's effect on
individual citizens gives impact evaluations their analytic significance, the assignment of responsibility depends on a process
evaluation sufficiently detailed to allow assessment of the nature
of popular control over the policy's execution. The viewpoints on
voting enforcement make it clear that responsibility for compliance is shared by a series of public officials (federal, state, and
local), interest group representatives (black and white), and private citizens who have acted to shape the policy formulation and
implementation phases. This interplay between the formulation
and implementation of Section 5 and the determination of accountability will be considered in the next chapter.

NOTES

1. Walter Williams, "Special Issue on Implementation: Editor's
Comments,"*Policy Analysis* 1, 3 (Summer 1975): 451.
2. Charles O. Jones,*An Introduction to the Study of Public Policy*, 2nd
edition (North Scituate, Mass.: Duxbury Press, 1977), p. 175.
3. Carol Weiss, "The Politization of Evaluation Research,"*Journal of
Social Issues* 26, 4 (Autumn 1970): 57-68.
4. James Q. Wilson, "On Pettigrew and Armor,"*The Public Interest* 31
(Spring 1973): 132-34.
5. David Nachmias,*Public Policy Evaluation: Approaches and Methods*
(New York: St. Martin's Press, 1979), p. 5.
6. Ibid.
7. Eugene Bardach, *The Implementation Game: What Happens After a Bill
Becomes a Law* (Cambridge, Mass.: The MIT Press, 1977).
8. Howard Freeman, "Evaluation Research and Public Policies," in
Gene M. Lyons, ed., *Social Research and Public Policies*. The Public Affairs
Center. Dartmouth College (Hanover, N.H.: University Press of New
England, 1975), p. 146; Dennis Palumbo and Elaine Sharp, "Process
Versus Impact Evaluation of Community Corrections," in David Nachmias,
ed., *The Practice of Policy Evaluation* (New York: St. Martin's Press, 1980),
pp. 288-90.

9. Martha Derthick, *New Towns In-Town* (Washington, D.C.: The Urban Institute, 1972).

10. Jeffrey L. Pressman and Aaron B. Wildavsky, *Implementation* (Berkeley: University of California Press, 1973), p. xv.

11. Walter Williams, "Implementation Analysis and Assessment," *Policy Analysis* 1, 3 (Summer 1975): 558.

12. Walter Williams, *The Implementation Perspective: A Guide for Managing Social Service Delivery Programs* (Berkeley: University of California Press, 1980), p. 90.

13. Harrell R. Rodgers, Jr. and Charles S. Bullock, III, *Law and Social Change: Civil Rights Laws and Their Consequences* (New York: McGraw-Hill, 1972), pp. 23-37.

14. Thomas E. Cavanaugh, "Changes in American Electoral Turnout, 1964-1976," paper presented at the annual meeting of the Midwest Political Science Association, Chicago, Ill., April 1979.

15. Earl Black, *Southern Governors and Civil Rights: Racial Segregation as a Campaign Issue in the Second Reconstruction* (Cambridge, Mass.: Harvard University Press, 1976).

16. Merle Black, "Racial Composition of Congressional Districts and Support for Federal Voting Rights in the American South," *Social Science Quarterly* 59 (December 1978): 435-50; Mark Stern, "Southern Congressional Civil Rights Voting and the New Southern Democracy," paper presented at the annual meeting of the American Political Science Association, Washington, D.C., August 31-September 3, 1979.

17. Gerald M. Pomper and Susan S. Lederman, *Elections in America: Control and Influence in Democratic Politics* (New York: Longman, 1980), pp. 194-205.

18. Numan V. Bartley and Hugh D. Graham, *Southern Politics and the Second Reconstruction* (Baltimore, Md.: Johns Hopkins University Press, 1975).

19. David Hunter, *The Shameful Blight: The Survival of Racial Discrimination in Voting in the South* (Washington, D.C.: Washington Research Project, 1972).

20. Armand Derfner, "Racial Discrimination and the Right to Vote," *Vanderbilt Law Review* 26 (April 1973). Stanley Halpin, Jr. and Richard L. Engstrom, "Racial Gerrymandering and Southern State Legislative Redistricting: Attorney General Determinations Under the Voting Rights Act," *Journal of Public Law* 22 (1973): 37-66; Frank R. Parker, "County Redistricting in Mississippi: Case Studies in Racial Gerrymandering," *Mississippi Law Journal* 44 (June 1973): 391-424; Richard L. Engstrom, "Racial Discrimination in the Electoral Process: The Voting Rights Act

and the Vote Dilution Issue," in Robert P. Steed, Laurence W. Moreland, and Tod A. Baker, eds., *Party Politics in the South* (New York: Praeger Publishers, 1980), pp. 197-213.

21. Mack H. Jones, "The Voting Rights Act and Political Symbolism," paper presented at the annual meeting of the Southern Political Science Association, Gatlinburg, Tenn., November 1-3, 1979.

22. Hanes Walton, Jr., *Black Politics: A Theoretical and Structural Analysis* (New York: J.B. Lippincott, 1972), pp. 196-224; Milton D. Morris, *The Politics of Black America* (New York: Harper and Row, 1975), pp. 291-302; Hanes Walton, Jr., "Black Politics in the South: Projections for the Coming Decade," in Marguerite Ross Barnett and James A. Hefner, eds., *Public Policy for the Black Community* (New York: Alfred, 1976), pp. 79-100; James Button, Richard Scher, and Larry Berkson, "The Quest for Equality: The Impact of the Civil Rights Movement on Black Public Services in the South," paper presented at the annual meeting of the Midwest Political Science Association, Chicago, Ill., April 20-22, 1978.

23. Matthew Holden, Jr., *The Politics of the Black "Nation"* (New York: Chandler, 1973), pp. 193-211; Lucius J. Barker and Jesse J. McCorry, Jr., *Black Americans and the Political System* (Cambridge, Mass.: Winthrop, 1976), pp. 92-96; Joel A. Thompson, "The Voting Rights Act in North Carolina: A Quasi-Experimental Analysis of Policy Effectiveness," paper presented at The Citadel Symposium on Southern Politics, Charleston, S.C., March 27-29, 1980.

24. David C. Leege and Wayne L. Francis, *Political Research: Design, Measurement, and Analysis* (New York: Basic Books, 1974), pp. 140-41; Earl R. Babbie, *The Practice of Social Research*, 2nd edition (Belmont, Calif.: Wadsworth, 1979), p. 110.

25. *Rasho-Mon* is Akira Kurosawa's movie which describes the events leading to a murder and a rape. Kurosawa uses a series of flashbacks to narrate the story from the viewpoint of each participant. However, Kurosawa never gives the audience a definitive version, so they must decide guilt or innocence and motivations after the movie concludes.

26. U.S. Commission on Civil Rights, *The Voting Rights Act . . . The First Months*, November, 1965, p. 3.

27. U.S. Commission on Civil Rights *Political Participation: A Study of the Participation by Negroes in the Electoral and Political Processes in 10 Southern States Since Passage of the Voting Rights Act of 1965*, May, 1968.

28. Ibid., p. 177.

29. Ibid., pp. 177-78.

30. Ibid., p. 184.

31. Armand Derfner, "Racial Discrimination and the Right to Vote," *Vanderbilt Law Review* 26 (1973): 523.

32. U.S. Commission on Civil Rights, *The Voting Rights Act: Ten Years After*, January 1975.

33. Ibid., p. 1.

34. Ibid., p. 52.

35. Ibid., pp. 61-62.

36. Ibid., p. 326.

37. Ibid., p. 204.

38. Ibid., pp. 25-26.

39. Ibid., p. 337.

40. Ibid., p. 331.

41. Ibid., pp. 346-47.

42. Ibid., p. 350.

43. U.S. Commission on Civil Rights, *The State of Civil Rights: 1979*, January, 1980, p. 33.

44. Ibid., p. 37.

45. U.S. Comptroller General, U.S. General Accounting Office, *Voting Rights Act—Enforcement Needs Strengthening*, February 6, 1978, pp. 47-49.

46. Ibid., p. 30.

47. Ibid., pp. 61-74. Appendix XII of the GAO report contains the first complete list of VRA cases and the disposition.

48. Ibid., pp. 18-19.

49. While the Voting Section does have access to a computer for information retrieval purposes, the bulk of the agency's records are stored in traditional filing cabinets scattered throughout a number of anterooms and hallways. During a tour of the office area, the Submission Unit Staff Attorney showed the authors the "Texas Room"—a substantial office stuffed with submissions from only the state of Texas.

50. U.S. Comptroller General, *Voting Rights Act*, p. 10.

51. Ibid., pp. 13-14.

52. Ibid., p. 13. GAO's figure for unreported session law changes does include other types of unreported changes.

53. Interview with Gerald Jones, Chief, Voting Section, Civil Rights Division, U.S. Department of Justice, September 2, 1977, Washington, D.C.

54. Ibid.

55. U.S. Comptroller General, *Voting Rights Act*, p. 17.

56. Ibid., pp. 30-31.

57. One of the most important and least discussed methodological issues relevant to Section 5 enforcement is the quality of the demographic data available to the Voting Section.

58. U.S. Comptroller General, *Voting Rights Act*, pp. 10-19.

59. Ibid., pp. 45-46.

60. All percentages cited in this paragraph are contained in an internal GAO memorandum, entitled "Election Official Reaction to Implementation of the Voting Rights Act," made available to the authors by the GAO's General Government Division.

61. Ibid.

62. All percentages cited in this paragraph are contained in an internal GAO memorandum, entitled "Impact of Voting Rights Act as Seen by Minority Interest Groups and Selected Individuals," made available to the authors by the GAO's General Government Division.

63. U.S. Comptroller General, *Voting Rights Act*, p. 20.

64. Ibid.

65. Ibid.

66. Ibid., p 32.

67. Ibid.

68. Ibid.

69. Letter from Kervin D. Rooney, Assistant Attorney General for Administration, Voting Service Department of Justice, submitted to the Honorable Abraham Ribicoff, Chairman, Committee on Governmental Affairs, U.S. Senate, Washington, D.C., June 7, 1978, p. 1.

70. Ibid., p. 5.

71. Ibid., p. 12.

72. *Jackson Clarion-Ledger* (Jackson, Miss.), June 16, 1978.

73. Ibid.

74. Rooney, letter to Ribicoff, p. 5.

75. Ibid., p. 6.

76. Ibid., pp. 7-8.

77. Other than the small sampling of state and local election officials (who usually do not file Section 5 submissions) cited in the 1978 GAO report, attorneys working for counties throughout the original Section 5 states have not had their attitudes and behavior considered in other evaluations. To obtain their views on Section 5 requirements, we mailed questionnaires to counties in Georgia and Mississippi and in some cases had telephone follow-ups about their responses. While the responses (33 percent) do not constitute a random sample, the responses come from the complete range of counties by population size, racial mix, and degree of urbanization and give some insights into Section 5 compliance.

78. In Georgia, 37.5 percent of the county attorneys stating that they had never submitted a voting change represent counties with small nonwhite populations. In Mississippi, 43.8 percent of the county attor-

neys stating that they had never submitted a voting change represent counties with small nonwhite populations.

79. Bolden v. Mobile, Alabama, 64 LEd 2d47 (1980).

80. Interview with Janet Blizzard, Supervisor of the Research Assistants, Voting Section, Civil Rights Division, U.S. Department of Justice, September 2, 1977, Washington, D.C.

81. Ibid.

82. Interview with Elizabeth A. Dunagin, Research Assistant, Voting Section, Civil Rights Division, U.S. Department of Justice, September 2, 1977, Washington, D.C.

83. Guy Benveniste, *Bureaucracy* (San Francisco: Boyd and Fraser Publishing Co., 1977), pp. 141-42.

PART FIVE

CONCLUSION

7 Compromised Compliance

THE POLICY MADE AND THE ENSUING DILEMMA

This book has attempted to examine the development and implementation of a legislative policy directed toward the enforcement of the Fifteenth Amendment, a policy that would protect voting rights of blacks in the South. The 1965 Voting Rights Act was the radical culmination of an effort by the national government that began with the 1954 *Brown* decision of the U.S. Supreme Court and, politically, with passage of the 1957 Civil Rights Act. With a nation shocked at the outbreaks of violence in Mississippi in 1964 and in Alabama in 1965, both the Executive branch and the Congress moved from a decade-long litigation-oriented policy to a direct-action policy (validated by the Judicial Branch) in order to protect blacks in their efforts to register and to vote.

The 1965 Voting Rights Act delegated power to the U.S. Department of Justice to ensure the protection of the black citizen's right to vote in the South. The Voting Section in the Civil Rights Division of the DOJ, a small band of attorney-administrators, was given the immense task of implementing this dramatic piece of legislation. It was legislation that suspended tests and devices, that enabled examiners and observers to enter many towns and counties in the South to assist in the registration of blacks, and that, in Section 5, called for administrative (or judicial) examination of all voting changes *before* they were implemented to determine whether their purpose or effect was to deny or dilute the voting rights of the newly enfranchised blacks.

Examining the shift from policymaking to policy implementation, one cannot ignore the dynamics of politics in a federal system. Administrators charged with implementing policy are part of a larger whole. It is a system that includes national leaders such as the President, the Attorney General (the highest legal officer in the government but a political appointee of the President), congressional leaders such as the key chairmen of the DOJ's authorization and appropriations committees and subcommittees in the House and Senate, bar association leaders, clientele groups such as the NAACP and county and statewide legal associations, and the persons who are or should be directly affected by the legislation: black Americans who had been denied the right to vote and white powerholders who were denying them that fundamental right.

Given these various forces impacting on the administrators of the VRA, the lawyers and paralegals in the Voting Section, their decisions were based on political assessments and made with great deliberation. From 1965 to 1971, the CRD concentrated its authority on the enforcement of Section 4 of the Act, registration of black voters in the covered jurisdictions. Decisions were made by the President and his political advisors, including the Attorney General, and for three years, Civil Rights Division attorneys, working with other federal bureaucrats (who functioned as observers and examiners), implemented Section 4. By 1968, however, active DOJ implementation of Section 4 ended. With the advent of the Nixon Administration in 1969, a moratorium on VRA implementation occurred. During the three years of Section 4 implementation, under the occasionally watchful eyes of President Lyndon Johnson and his Attorney Generals Nicholas Katzenbach, succeeded by Ramsey Clark, there was informal discretionary action by the DOJ. For obvious political reasons, certain counties in the southern states were not targeted for Section 4 enforcement by the DOJ—for example Sunflower County, Mississippi, the home of U.S. Senator James Eastland.

During this time, Section 5 was not dealt with positively by the administrators in the DOJ. Probably the greatest informal discretionary power of administrators is just this power not to act, in this case, the decision not to implement Section 5 of the Voting

Rights Act. Nothing short of continual political pressures can get administrators to act in a manner contrary to their desires. Lyndon Johnson had been interested in the visible manifestation of the Voting Rights Act, moving swiftly to register the masses of black citizens in the deep South. He was not very interested in the implementation of Section 5, and so it was not enforced by the DOJ bureaucrats. Certainly, Richard Nixon's "southern strategy" precluded any commitment to enforcement of Section 5,[1] and so it was not enforced by the bureaucrats in the DOJ. It was not until 1971 that the various demands—by legislative oversight committees, by the U.S. Commission on Civil Rights, by civil rights groups, and by some white government attorneys and politicians in the South—led the Civil Rights Division administrators to formulate basic regulations that spelled out the manner by which Section 5 of the Voting Rights Act would now be administered by the Voting Section.

The regulations, published in the Federal Register in September, 1971, became a critical element in the administrative response to the imperatives of the 1965 legislative policy. Congress had passed legislation that, hopefully, would enable blacks to register, vote, and develop a sense of political power that ordinarily goes along with the right to vote. Section 5 was included to guarantee the fruits of the registration process: the development of "political consciousness" on the part of the newly enfranchised black voters. Full compliance with the intent of the 1965 Voting Rights Act would mean, ultimately, that blacks would, through voting and the formation of a viable political voting bloc, improve the quality of their life. Professor Leslie D. McLemore, Chairman of the Political Science Department at Jackson State University, said recently that "the primary overriding significance of participating in the political process is that it gives people access to the entire spectrum of society—political, social, economic. That is really what the American dream is all about, access and the ability to improve oneself."[2] For a black person living in the covered states, full compliance would lead to paved roads, new parks, improved police protection, street lights, regular garbage collection, and a good education for his or her children.[3]

This full compliance could take place only if certain antecedent conditions were present: the right to vote, the development of cohesive, viable black political organizations at the local level in the South, and Section 5 review of all voting changes that would be introduced in these jurisdictions (to determine whether a particular voting change would adversely affect the voting right and the development of a sense of political power on the part of blacks). Section 5, in short, was and is seen as the linchpin of the Voting Rights Act. The right to vote would prove to be meaningless (and the many struggles to win that right prove to be Pyrrhic victories) if the white power structure could simply change the rules of the game so as to continue to deny or dilute the power of the black voter.

The obvious dilemma for the administrators in the Voting Section of the DOJ, then, was this: how to implement a portion of the Voting Rights Act, Section 5, that so vitally affected both parties to the dispute. If the DOJ vigorously enforced both the spirit and the letter of Section 5, there would surely be evasion, avoidance, and delay by the white powerholders who were being asked, in the words of dissenting U.S. Supreme Court Justice Black, to go begging to Washington, D.C., on their hands and knees for permission to act in matters affecting voting. Yet there had to be some kind of enforcement because administrative inaction was no longer a politically viable strategy for the DOJ bureaucrats. Thus there developed, as we have described in earlier chapters, a compliance process that reflected the reality of policymaking and policy implementation in a federal system. It is a process we have labeled "compromised compliance."

POLICY REFINEMENT OR REDEFINEMENT

Jay Sigler captures the essence of voting rights implementation in his insightful comment that the reality of voting rights policy "rests in its actual enforcement...the enforcement of voting rights policy is more important than the existence of printed rights."[4] Certainly, the passage of the 1965 Voting Rights Act was critically important; but without effective enforcement and compliance, it and every other civil rights law remain a symbolic victory and not a meaningful actuality for persons deprived of the basic rights of citizenship. To solve the dilemma of voting rights enforcement, DOJ had to invent an implementation strategy that could function within the limits imposed by our constitutional order and by the political pressures from the competing social groups.

Writing in *Federalist 48*, James Madison explains how our constitutional system places "executive magistrates" under the authority and direction of Congress. This close consonance of executive action with legislative intent defined the norm of accountability in our system of legislative supremacy. However, changes in our society and government have invalidated the premises of 1787. With the growth of the public sector and the expansion of federal action, Congress has devolved more and more authority to "executive magistrates." To the extent that administrative execution of a policy diverges from its articulation by Congress, then serious questions of accountability arise.

Policymaking is no longer a solely legislative exercise. Following the passage of legislation hammered out in traditional fashion between the President and the Congress, the flow of policy moves to a phase of policy refinement in which "an executive agency or bureau interprets congressional (or presidential) intent and provides the context in which the policy will be carried out."[5] It is in the policy-refinement phase that administrative discretion first appears and initiates the choices that condition the implementation process.

Administrative discretion is, at once, a virtue and a vice. Through the possession of discretion, a government agency can "fine tune" its implementation activities to specific situations and circumstances.[6] On the other side of the discretionary coin, freedom to translate legislative mandates into administrative action can lead to a wide range of interpretations from minor modifications to goal distortion and displacement.[7] Bureaucratic responsibility for policy implementation can easily produce simple irritants such as the "red-tape" necessary to law enforcement as well as *policy redefinement* in which agency decision rules and standard operating procedures create outcomes that diverge sharply from the original legislative intent. Policy interpretation, defined as the promulgation of rules and procedures, is the first critical juncture in the implementation process where administrative action can become uncoupled from legislative intent. Besides the valid translation of a policy into operational terms, rule-making also entails the development of bureaucratic routines capable of inducing compliance from the targeted individuals and groups. Rule enforcers must somehow match or modify existing administrative resources and routines to the behavioral problem requiring social control.[8] This "matching" of bureaucratic capacities with the diversity of responses is the second juncture at which administrative action and legislative logic can become separated. Finally, the ability of targeted individuals and groups to discover new means by which to avoid imposed rules is a third point at which legislative intent can be frustrated.[9] Such "learning" over time can quickly subvert the effectiveness of the most diligent administrators and, if left unchecked, can yield substantial divergence between the actual and the desired forms of compliance behavior.

The political resistance and the social turbulence prevailing in the covered jurisdictions left the DOJ with little choice in the application of the Section 5 remedy. To create a viable enforcement strategy, CRD policymakers had to knit together the three strands of policy implementation. "Moving from decision to operations" includes more than simply putting the organizational gears in motion. Besides this first requirement of policy implementation—establish a satisfactorily functioning administrative unit—the CRD also had to elicit cooperation from subnational officials.

The second dimension of implementation—gain compliance— is distinct from organizational administration because compliance involves the relationship between the governmental agency and its external constituencies (in contrast to administration, which is the relationship between managers and employees). Finally, while the DOJ enforcement strategy had to obtain compliance, the process also had to build a political base for the program. In a sense, this third dimension of implementation— institutionalize the policy and its derivative programs—is the litmus test of policy survival. Unless a program generates favorable political support from its clientele, the program will face a shaky and uncertain political future.

Implementation, as Eugene Bardach so forcefully demonstrates, entails more than routine administrative actions. The extent to which operational policy reflects the legislative mandate will depend on the tradeoffs made by the administrative decision makers as they try to balance their choices along the three dimensions of implementation. In the case of voting rights enforcement, the degree of compliance has become a function of the accommodations made by the CRD in its efforts to adapt available resources to the hostile environment in which it has to operate.

As we noted at the outset of this consideration of voting rights enforcement, it is not particularly useful to think about policy compliance as a simple matter of obedience or disobedience with the law, administrative regulation, or court decision. Because those of whom compliance is sought are usually policymakers in their own right with the ability to respond in a variety of ways to legislative, executive, or judicial directives, it is more appropriate to think of compliance as consisting of a range of possible responses by officials in covered jurisdictions which fall within some zone of acceptability for the administrators charged with the implementation of federal voting rights policy.

Having discretion as its primary instrument, a compliance strategy of bargaining and negotiation became the only viable route combining some sense of effectiveness and political survival for the CRD's Section 5 enforcement program. To gain control over the massive hostility encountered in the covered jurisdictions, the CRD concentrated its Section 5 actions on a limited repertoire of behavior by local elections officials. In operationalizing discrimination as "non-retrogression," the CRD sought to define the range of minority electoral participation the agency would guarantee. Since any organization lacks the capacity to control all aspects of its internal components, let alone its external environment, a common managerial approach is the deliberate narrowing of actions and behaviors the organization will try to influence. This strategy of "partial inclusion" allows an organization to align its limited resources to a reasonable set of tasks.[10] A Voting Section attorney describing the goals of Section 5 enforcement aptly captures this "partial inclusion" of those aspects of voting rights that were believed amenable to CRD control.

The primary goal of the administration of Section 5 is to prevent the implementation of discretionary voting changes by objecting to such changes under Section 5. A necessary part of this, of course, is making sure that possibly discriminatory changes are submitted for review. A secondary goal is to facilitate the implementation of nondiscriminatory voting changes.[11]

By making the efficient operation of the submission process the primary goal and the implementation of nondiscriminatory changes the secondary goal, the Voting Section ratifies changes in electoral procedures that do not violate retrogression, but also do not foster full or effective minority participation.

Compliance, then, emerges out of the balance between the agency's powers of enforcement and the "sting" of the techniques of control. Giandomenico Majone and Aaron Wildavsky emphasize that "one cannot discount the possibility that successful implementation may be made possible only by a lowering of standards, a reformulation of evaluative criteria, or a shift in viewpoints...."[12] James Anderson explains that this compliance-control trade-off inherent in policy implementation also takes into account the acceptability of the enforcement procedures.

There appears to be general agreement that policies should be implemented in such a manner as to cause the least necessary material and psychological disturbance to the affected persons. This being so, the most technically or economically efficient method of enforcement may not be the most acceptable politically.... Another consideration in the choice of control techniques stems from the fact that the general objective of public policy is to control behavior [or secure compliance] and not to punish violators except as a last resort. Consequently, there will usually be a preference for less harsh or coercive techniques.... Government tends to follow a rule of parsimony in the employment of legal restraint and compulsion in policy implementation.[13]

When an administrative agency must enforce the law in a political atmosphere of pressure from contending parties, Leon

Mayhew reminds us that "the protection of stability and legitimacy through compromise is an inescapable condition of successful enforcement."[14] Only in the unlikely event that Congress would write a clealy unambiguous voting rights statute with teeth in it and then insist on its execution to the letter of the law would an administrative agency such as the Voting Section be able to avoid the tradeoffs between political survival and other standards of performance. However, without clear-cut, meaningful legislative standards, agency discretion is the norm.

Although the level of compliance with voting rights policy is generally believed to be somewhat higher than compliance in other civil rights policy areas,[15] the manner in which the Department of Justice administrators have chosen to implement the Section 5 preclearance requirement has resulted in a level of compliance that has engendered criticism from two influential sources. Local government officials, preferring not to be required to preclear changes in voting procedures in the first place, tend to perceive Section 5 enforcement as an unnecessary intrusion by the federal government into matters that are strictly local in nature. In contrast, spokespersons for a more stringent standard of Section 5 enforcement (for example, the Commission on Civil Rights) tend to view Department of Justice implementation of that section of the 1965 Act as generally suboptimal and, therefore, a series of missed opportunities to foster equality in political participation for minority citizens. Department of Justice spokespersons, however, hold that the level of compliance currently achieved is very close to the best that can be attained under the prevailing circumstances.

In their significant studies of civil rights policy enforcement, Harrell Rodgers, Jr. and Charles Bullock, III delineate a range of enforcement techniques beginning with voluntary compliance, moving through litigation, to such coercive sanctions as termination of federal and/or state funds or the use of physical force (such as federal marshals or the National Guard) to achieve adherence to policy directives.[16] The story of administrative implementation of Section 5 of the 1965 Voting Rights Act is one in which a relatively small staff of lawyer and paralegal Civil Rights Division bureaucrats, who are (1) accustomed to case-by-case resolution of legal disputes, (2) mindful of the fact that covered jurisdictions are unwilling partners in their administrative interactions, (3) sensitive to political realities of congressional and presidential predilections in voting rights enforcement, and (4) operating without benefit of a fiscal coercive instrument, seek to maintain an acceptable balance between the letter and spirit of the law and the realities of intergovernmental politics. Clearly, the Voting Section's approach to obtaining compliance with the requirements of Section 5 is one of attempting voluntary compliance (through negotiation and compromise) rather than coercive sanctions.

The picture that emerges from this review of voting rights policy is one of substantial dissonance between the legislative statement and its enforcement by the Department of Justice. In effect, two distinct policies live side by side. Through the 1965 Act, Congress affirmed the democratic importance of extending the franchise to minorities in the covered jurisdictions. The Civil Rights Division, by contrast, has translated legislative intent into a series of regularized procedures—the preclearance process—which reduce the CRD's enforcement costs and increase the local official's convenience. As cooperation between the intergovernmental actors has evolved, the original congressional intentions with respect to voting equality for all citizens have receded into the background. This is the cost incurred in maintaining *positive* relationships between federal and local officials. This excessive commitment to negotiated settlements has diminished the substance of the voting rights policy created in 1965. Because intergovernmental bargaining persists as the principal mode of enforcement, the Department of Justice remains trapped in a dilemma of compromised compliance and the possibility of continued dilution of the black vote in southern states still exists 16 years after the passage of the legislation.

THE DEMOCRATIC DILEMMAS

Voting rights enforcement presents us with somewhat of a paradox. In a society that alleges to be democratic, the right of each individual to participate in the processes of leadership selection and to have his or her vote freely cast, fairly counted, and equally weighed must be guaranteed. This is what the voting rights struggle in the United States during this century has been all about.

Without question, popular participation in voting—the central civic act in a democracy—must be protected. There is, however, another facet of democratic theory which is also important to our understanding of Section 5 implementation. The pluralist interpretation of American politics holds that conflicts among groups of individuals over the distribution of social and economic benefits and burdens tend to be carried on through a process of continual bargaining in which policy agreements get worked out that contending parties are willing to accept at least in the short run. The policy decisions that emerge through the mutual adjustment of partisan interests are thought to be preferable to any other possible policy outcomes because partisan pursuit of self-interest ensures that all important alternatives and positions will be considered during policy deliberations.[17] From this perspective, Department of Justice lawyer-bureaucrats and officials from covered jurisdictions can be viewed as participants in a process of partisan mutual adjustment of interests. It is not at all surprising, therefore, that the Section 5 enforcement decisions that emerge from such a process are forged in compromise.

Given the primacy of Congress in our domestic policy process, should the Voting Section be held totally accountable for the character of voting rights enforcement across the deep South (and with the 1975 minority language provisions, across all or portions of 22 states)? Without new appropriations, can an agency that is administratively hamstrung by a deprivation of compliance-inducing instruments (that is, grant money, field personnel, civil penalties) be effective considering the logistical scope of its enforcement task? If Congress creates a policy and sees it transmogrified by bureaucrats, but fails to redirect the agency, where does accountability lie? If Congress ignores the administrative conduct of policy, then the Madisonian linkage between citizens and executive magistrates disintegrates.

Even if external checks on administrative action break down, can citizens not depend on internal agency control mechanisms to guarantee bureaucratic fidelity to legislative standards? Once the legislative branch has defined the problem and devised the remedy, is it too much to expect that executive branch managers develop appropriate organizational arrangements and method-ologies that produce results not significantly different from legis-lative mandates?[18] For example, since the compliance-monitoring system used by the Voting Section is faulty, one solution within the means of DOJ's pocketbook would be the use of mail surveys of local election officials to construct an up-to-date catalogue of election practices and an official record of responsible parties. Akin to EEOC surveys, this simple technique would put local officials under oath to provide accurate information. A corollary step could be the increased use of the FBI to probe local contro-versies. Because the FBI is a "free" resource to units within Justice, the Voting Section can readily expand its "field person-nel." Without totally abandoning its present passive mode of reacting to preclearance submissions (that is, waiting for reports of voting changes to be sent to the Attorney General), the Voting Section could systematically map the covered jurisdictions and establish a solid benchmark against which to measure its performance.[19]

Improvements in legislative oversight and agency performance are a function of a policy's political context. Eugene Bardach explains that "implementation is the continuation of politics by other means" and exhibits "a great deal of energy [which] goes into maneuvering to avoid responsibility, scrutiny, and blame."[20] His remarks reaffirm E. E. Schattschneider's thesis that losers at one point in the policy process will continue the fight at some other point.[21] Southern white leaders did not cease and desist their resistance after 1965. Quite the contrary, their rearguard battles moved from the legislature to the bureaucracy and the courts. This "defensive politics" characteristic of policy imple-mentation leads in several possible directions including "trim-ming goals back, distorting or preventing goals, and even adding to them in a manner that eventually leads to an unsupportable political burden."[22] Trapped in the crossfire from segregationists and civil rights advocates, the Voting Section opted for the role of "peacemaker." With little new congressional support following on the heels of added responsibilities, and confronted by Supreme Court decisions that narrow the meaning of Section 5 (for example, *Richmond v. United States* and *Beer v. United States*), it was probably rational for Voting Section leadership to have made "concessions to Realpolitik necessary for survival..."[23] and to redefine voting rights policy by choosing to guarantee only a partial range of minority electoral participation instead of the fullest extent possible.

One conclusion that may be drawn from this interpretation of events is that compromised compliance has been functional because, by encouraging covered jurisdictions to continue to participate in the preclearance process, it has made improvements possible (albeit incremental ones) in the voting status of minority citizens. By not insisting on a more radical departure from the status quo in voting practices, the strategy of negotiated settlements has minimized resistance and reduced the need for coercion. An alternative conclusion, as discussed in this book, is that by accepting anything less than the fullest measure of voting rights each and every time a change is submitted for preclearance, the Justice Department becomes an accomplice in the continuing resistance to voting parity for minority citizens.

Although both conclusions are partially compelling, they are not equally appealing. If voting rights for minority citizens are to be a meaningful reality in the decade of the 1980s and beyond, then the process of compromised compliance—whatever its virtues—is, on balance, just not good enough. However, having said that compromised compliance is not good enough, a profound questions remains: where does society go from this type of enforcement? Can the ultimate goal, that is, equal political participation by black citizens in the democratic process, be achieved by the ending of enforcement, albeit "compromised," of Section 5 by the Department of Justice?

RENEWAL OF THE VOTING RIGHTS ACT—AND BEYOND

The Voting Rights Act of 1965 is scheduled to expire in 1982. White city and county attorneys we have surveyed are fairly unanimous in calling for either the outright repeal or the demise of the Voting Rights Act at that time. "All other suggestions," said one attorney, "are unprintable!" For these men who have filed the Section 5 preclearance papers, only "civil rights lawyers, the NAACP organization, black racist groups, and known black agitators" have benefited from Section 5 enforcement. In the eyes of some local white attorneys, Section 5 means "black incompetent so-called civil rights specialists who can't read, . . . holding degrees in sociology, Greek history, English literature, or the philosophy of black thought in America," positively responding to "attempts by political agitators or organizers to vote [sic] for large numbers of illiterate blacks."

By contrast, black political leaders are genuinely fearful about the consequences should the Voting Rights Act not be renewed. While less than happy with the DOJ's Section 5 policy of "compromised compliance," blacks are fully aware of its value to their communities. For them, the repeal of Section 5 or its death before there is full compliance would lead to a return to a system of white repression and coercion of blacks in the South.[24]

Even though it has not been vigorously enforced, the Act has helped open voting booths and some positions of local political power to black citizens (and other minorities) in America. If the VRA is not continued in 1982 by Congress, even in its present form, there will be pervasive gloom in the civil rights community. With growing calls for retrenchment of affirmative action and other civil rights programs now moving to the center stage of public opinion, the expiration of the Act in 1982 could well be the signal to return black voting rights to the pre-1965 reliance on costly and time-consuming litigation. The "years of catching up" could be halted and possibly rolled back in the reshuffling of electoral disticts following the 1980 census. The shortcomings of the CRD's procedures combined with the attractiveness of the district court route (viz., *Connor*) make the Civil Rights Commission's "worst-case" scenario a distinct possibility. To repeal or to let the 1965 Voting Rights Act die in 1982 would be to quash the hope of achieving the ultimate outcome of compliance with the policy—the betterment of life for blacks and for other minorities in the covered jurisdictions.

Still another suggestion has been developed by opponents of the

1965 Voting Rights Act and that is the "nationalization" of the Voting Rights Act. First presented (unsuccessfully) by Attorney General John Mitchell, during the debates in Congress prior to the passage of the 1970 amendments to the Voting Rights Act, the position of the advocates of nationalization of Section 5 is: (1) that the 1965 Voting Rights Act unfairly treats a segment of the national community (the covered jurisdictions), and (2) that, if the 1965 legislation is to be continued, in the name of fairness and constitutional propriety, the coverage of the 1965 Voting Rights Act should be broadened to cover *all* voting changes in *all* political subdivisions of *all* the states, including those voting changes that *all* the states propose to enact.

The basic call, then, of the proponents of nationalizing the Voting Rights Act is the monitoring (discovery) and the systematic review by the U.S. Department of Justice of all election laws and other voting changes. Given the marred character of the implementation process as it exists now (the focus of this book), any attempt to introduce a nationwide application of the Voting Rights Act will force the Civil Rights Division attorneys handling Section 5 implementation to break down under the impossible burden of implementing that section nationally. The cry for nationalization, uttered by opponents of the Act such as John Mitchell, Richard M. Nixon, and most recently by the Chairman of the Senate Judiciary Committee, U.S. Senator Strom Thurmond (R-S.C.), and President Ronald Reagan, will have the effect of thoroughly immobilizing the staff in CRD, thereby effectively destroying the impact of Section 5 as a device to prevent prospective discriminatory vote dilution.

Which is the way to go? How does one answer the question of renewal of the Voting Rights Act? Examining the impact of the Voting Rights Act on the South since 1965, we believe that "compromised compliance," while not good enough, has moved the affected groups—blacks, other minorities, and whites—along the road to an open society. American society, however, has not yet reached the final objective at the heart of the Voting Rights Act. Continuation of the Voting Rights Act, especially Section 5, might very well move portions of our society closer to the ideal of representative government.

We cannot say that this would be the case if the 1965 Act and its Section 5 were no longer in existence. We have attempted to understand and to explain the nature and the complexities of administrative implementation of national policy in the area of voting rights enforcement. We believe it is imperative that the 1965 Voting Rights Act be extended for as long as it takes to educate the affected publics, black and white, to the meaning and the responsibility of representative government in a free society. To do less would be to lose sight of the goal of the Fifteenth Amendment. We believe that this ought not to happen. Retention of Section 5, or some other mechanism that will enable voters to expeditiously challenge voting changes that they believe unfairly deprive them of their voting rights or that dilutes the value of their vote, is one viable road that can be taken to maintain democratic, representative government in our society.[25]

NOTES

1. Indeed, as the text indicates, p. 69, his Attorney General, John Mitchell, vigorously argued before the Congress in 1970 that Section 5 should be abolished. Minimally, he argued, the burden of proof in Section 5 preclearances should be on the Department of Justice attorneys (to show discriminatory purpose or effect) rather than on the local jurisdictions to show that there was no dilution of the black vote.

2. Reginald Stuart quote "Where the Right to Vote Was like Reaching the Moon." *New York Times*, April 14, 1981, pp. 1, 8.

3. In a report entitled *A Decade of Frustration*, published in April, 1981, by the Southern Regional Council, Atlanta, Georgia, it was pointed out that public schools in the Black Belt of the deep South (southern Alabama and Georgia) were clearly inferior to most schools in the South and nationally "despite a decade of school desegregation aimed at relieving such conditions." The Report focused on 34 rural counties in the two states where blacks constitute a majority of the population; "nearly all of these school districts have school boards with white majorities. . . . the report asserted that public education remained inferior...'often as a result of local government decision-making.' " The news story indicated that "where improvements have been made in education in the counties of the Black Belt, two factors have been responsible: *mandatory state and Federal standards and school boards with a black elected majority*." [our empha-

sis] " 'Black controlled school districts [have made progress],' " Steve
Suitts, Executive Director of the Southern Regional Council noted in his
remarks to the press. All those counties covered in the Southern Regional Council report are covered by Section 5 of the Voting Rights Act.
Evidently, in those counties that elect the local school board, there were
no voting changes filed with the Department of Justice since 1965, since
most of the counties in the report still have white majorities on the School
Board, yet the counties are heavily black in population. As such, white
minorities still control the educational policy making in these heavily
black populated counties. The Report concluded that "local resistance to
desegregation has been transformed into 'total neglect.' " Until majority
black voting power is capable of making changes in the methods of
selecting members of the local school board, there is not full voting
participation in that jurisdiction. Reginald Stuart, "Local Governments
Hurt Rural Black Belt Schools Despite Integration, Report Claims," Jackson,
Mississippi *Clarion-Ledger*, April 8, 1981, p. 1.

4. Jay A. Sigler, *American Rights Policies* (Homewood, Ill: Dorsey
Press, 1975), p. 258.

5. Lawrence C. Dodd and Richard L. Schott, *Congress and the Administrative State* (New York: Wiley, 1979), pp. 291-92.

6. Andrew Dunsire, *Control in a Bureaucracy* (New York: St. Martin's
Press, 1978), pp. 102-9.

7. Francis E. Rourke, *Bureaucracy, Politics, and Public Policy*, 2nd edition (Boston: Little, Brown and Co., 1976), p. 54.

8. Dunsire, *Control in a Bureaucracy*, p. 228.

9. Christopher C. Hood, *The Limits of Administration* (London: John
Wiley, 1976), pp. 79-82.

10. Arnold S. Tannenbaum, *Control in Organizations* (New York: McGraw-
Hill, 1968), p. 10.

11. David H. Hunter, "The Administrators' Dilemmas for the Enforcement of Section 5 of the Voting Rights Act of 1965," p. 2. Paper
presented at the national conference of the American Society for Public
Administration, Phoenix, AZ., April 9-12, 1978.

12. Giandomenico Majone and Aaron Wildavsky, *Implementation*, 2nd
edition (Berkeley: University of California Press, 1979), p. 193.

13. James E. Anderson, *Public Policy-Making*, 2nd edition (New York:
Holt, Rinehart and Winston, 1979), p. 142.

14. Leon Mayhew, *Law and Equal Opportunity* (Cambridge, Mass.:
Harvard University Press, 1968), p. 271, quoted in Eugene Bardach, *The
Implementation Game: What Happens After a Bill Becomes a Law* (Cambridge,
Mass.: The MIT Press, 1977), p. 95.

15. Harrell R. Rodgers, Jr. and Charles S. Bullock, III, *Law and Social Change: Civil Rights Laws and Their Consequences* (New York: McGraw-Hill, 1972), pp. 15-54.

16. Harrell R. Rodgers, Jr. and Charles S. Bullock, III, *Coercion to Compliance* (Lexington, Mass.: Lexington Books, 1976), pp. 47-52.

17. Robert A. Dahl, *A Preface to Democratic Theory*, (Chicago: The University of Chicago Press, 1956); David Braybrooke and Charles E. Lindblom, *A Strategy of Decision: Policy Evaluation as a Social Process* (New York: The Free Press, 1963).

18. Kenneth J. Meier, *Politics and the Bureaucracy* (North Scituate, Mass.: Duxbury Press, 1979), pp. 162-85.

19. Interview with John Ols, Assistant Director, General Government Division, U.S. General Accounting Office, September 4, 1979, Washington, D.C.

20. Eugene Bardach, *The Implementation Game: What Happens After a Bill Becomes a Law* (Cambridge, Mass.: The MIT Press, 1977), pp. 37-82.

21. E. E. Schattschneider, *The Semi-Sovereign People: A Realist's View of Democracy in America* (New York: Holt, Rinehart, and Winston, 1960).

22. Bardach, *Implementation Game*, p. 85.

23. Robert C. Fried, *Performance in American Bureaucracy* (Boston, Mass.: Little, Brown, 1976), p. 77.

24. At the National League of Cities' 57th Annual Congress of Cities meeting in Atlanta, December, 1980, black delegates urged the incoming Reagan administration not to support efforts to kill the renewal of the 1965 Voting Rights Act. If the Act is not renewed, said NAACP Mississippi Field Director Robert Walker, "we'll [blacks] find ourselves in a different position." Quoted in Jackson, Mississippi *Clarion-Ledger*, December 4, 1980, p. 3. Other black leaders raised similar concerns should the Voting Rights Act expire in 1982. Tyrone Ellis, a 34-year-old black state representative from Oktibbeha County, Mississippi, was the first black elected to state office from his district in over 100 years. "If the VRA were allowed to expire it would set us back 100 years." Another black Mississippi legislator, state Senator Henry Kirksey, added: "We have only begun to scratch the surface, there are still black people who don't know the law exists." Quoted in Reginald Stuart, "Where the Right to Vote Was Like Reaching the Moon," *New York Times*, April 14, 1981, pp. 1, 8.

25. In an article in the *Kentucky Law Journal*, U.S. District Court (Northern District-Miss.) Judge William Keady and University of Mississippi Law School Professor George C. Cochran, urge a revision of Section 5 due to reasons we have developed in the body of our book: lack of monitoring by the DOJ and compromised compliance with respect to those

preclearances that have been filed by the covered jurisdictions. In their article, entitled "Section 5 of the Voting Rights Act: A Time for Revision," the two lawyer-scholars propose that any state or political subdivision of a state desiring to implement a voting change having a "potential for discrimination" (based on the *Allen* definition of 1969), be required to file a complaint in federal district court naming the U.S. as a defendant. Filed in the federal court in which the submitting jurisdiction is located, the relief sought would be identical to that currently found in the Section 5 procedures that now exist. The local city or county or state would seek a declaratory judgement from the federal court that the voting change would not have the effect of denying the right to vote on the basis of race or color. Burden of proof would be on the jurisdiction bringing the complaint. Notice would be published in the press, the DOJ would be involved, and expeditious consideration would be given to the complaint. A judgment adverse to the U.S. or citizen intervenors will be subject to an automatic stay with an expedited appeal granted as a matter of right. See Keady and Cochran, "Section 5 of the Voting Rights Act: A Time for Revision," *Kentucky Law Journal* 69, 4 (1981): 32-37.

APPENDICES

Appendix A

The Voting Rights Act of 1965, with Amendments

VOTING RIGHTS ACT OF 1965

Public Law 91-285

PUBLIC LAW 89-110, 89TH CONGRESS, S. 1564,
AUGUST 6, 1965

AN ACT To enforce the fifteenth amendment to the Constitution
of the United States, and for other purposes

Be it enacted by the Senate and House of Representatives of the United States of America in Congress assembled, That this Act shall be known as the "Voting Rights Act of 1965".

TITLE I—VOTING RIGHTS

SEC. 2. No voting qualification or prerequisite to voting, or standard, practice, or procedure shall be imposed or applied by any State or political subdivision to deny or abridge the right of any citizen of the United States to vote on account of race or color, or in contravention of the guarantees set forth in section 4(f)(2).

Public Law 94-73

SEC. 3. (a) Whenever the Attorney General or an aggrieved person institutes a proceeding under any statute to enforce the voting guarantees of the fourteenth or fifteenth amendment in any State or political subdivision the court shall authorize the appointment of Federal examiners by the United States Civil Service Commission in accordance with section 6 to serve for such period of time and for such political subdivisions as the court shall determine is appropriate to enforce the voting guarantees of the fourteenth or fifteenth amendment (1) as part of any interlocutory order if the court determines that

Public Law 94-73

the appointment of such examiners is necessary to enforce such voting guarantees or (2) as part of any final judgment if the court finds that violations of the fourteenth or fifteenth amendment justifying equitable relief have occurred in such State or subdivision: *Provided*, That the court need not authorize the appointment of examiners if any incidents of denial or abridgement of the right to vote on account of race or color, or in contravention of the guarantees set forth in section 4(f)(2). (1) have been few in number and have been promptly and effectively corrected by State or local action, (2) the continuing effect of such incidents has been eliminated, and (3) there is no reasonable probability of their recurrence in the future.

Public Law
94-73

(b) If in a proceeding instituted by the Attorney General or an aggrieved person under any statute to enforce the voting guarantees of the fourteenth or fifteenth amendment in any State or political subdivision the court finds that a test or device has been used for the purpose or with the effect of denying or abridging the right of any citizen of the United States to vote on account of race or color, or in contravention of the guarantees set forth in section 4(f)(2), it shall suspend the use of tests and devices in such State or political subdivisions as the court shall determine is appropriate and for such period as it deems necessary.

Public Law
93-373

(c) If any proceeding instituted by the Attorney General or an aggrieved person under any statute to enforce the voting guarantees of the fourteenth or fifteenth amendment in any State or political subdivision the court finds that violations of the fourteenth or fifteenth amendment justifying equitable relief have occurred within the territory of such State or political subdivision, the court, in addition to such relief as it may grant, shall retain jurisdiction for such period as it may deem appropriate and during such period no voting qualification or prerequisite to voting, or standard, practice, or procedure with respect to voting different from that in force or effect at the time the proceeding was commenced shall be enforced unless and until the court finds that such qualification, prerequisite, standard, practice, or procedure does not have the purpose and will not have the effect of denying or abridging the right to vote on account of race or color, or in contravention of the guarantees set forth in section 4(f)(2): *Provided*, That such qualification, prerequisite, standard, practice, or procedure may be enforced if the qualification, prerequisite, standard, practice, or procedure has been submitted by the chief legal officer or other appropriate official of such State or subdivision to the Attorney General and the Attorney General has not interposed an objection within sixty days after such submission, except that neither the court's finding nor the Attorney General's failure to object shall bar a subsequent action to enjoin enforcement of such qualification, prerequisite, standard, practice, or procedure.

SEC. 4. (a) To assure that the right of citizens of the United States to vote is not denied or abridged on account of race or color, no citizen shall be denied the right to vote in any Federal, State, or local election because of his failure to comply with any test or device in any State with respect to which the determinations have been made under the first two sentences of subsection (b) or in any political subdivision with respect to which such determinations have been made as a separate unit, unless the United States District Court for the District of Columbia in an action for a declaratory judgment brought by such State or subdivision against the United States has determined that no such test or device has been used during the seventeen years preceding the filing of the action for the purpose or with the effect of denying or abridging the right to vote on account of race or color: *Provided*, That no such declaratory judgment shall issue with respect to any plaintiff for a period of seventeen years after the entry of a final judgment of any court of the United States, other than the denial of a declaratory judgment under this section, whether entered prior to or after the enactment of this Act, determining that denials or abridgments of the right to vote on account of race or color through the use of such tests or devices have occurred anywhere in the territory of such plaintiff. No citizen shall be denied the right to vote in any Federal, State, or local election because of his failure to comply with any test or device in any State with respect to which the determinations have been made under the third sentence of subsection (b) of this section or in any political subdivision with respect to which such determinations have been made as a separate unit, unless the United States District Court for the District of Columbia in an action for a declaratory judgment brought by such State or subdivision against the United States has determined that no such test or device has been used during the ten years preceding the filing of the action for the purpose or with the effect of denying or abridging the right to vote on account of race or color, or in contravention of the guarantees set forth in section 4(f)(2): *Provided*, That no such declaratory judgment shall issue with respect to any plaintiff for a period of ten years after the entry of a final judgment of any court of the United States, other than the denial of a declaratory judgment under this section, whether entered prior to or after the enactment of this paragraph, determining that denials or abridgments of

Public Law
94-73
Public Law
91-285

the right to vote on account of race or color, or in contravention of the guarantees set forth in section 4(f)(2) through the use of tests or devices have occurred anywhere in the territory of such plaintiff.

An action pursuant to this subsection shall be heard and determined by a court of three judges in accordance with the provisions of section 2284 of title 28 of the United States Code and any appeal shall lie to the Supreme Court. The court shall retain jurisdiction of any action pursuant to this subsection for five years after judgment and shall reopen the action upon motion of the Attorney General alleging that a test or device has been used for the purpose or with the effect of denying or abridging the right to vote on account of race or color, or in contravention of the guarantees set forth in section 4(f)(2).

Public Law 94-73
If the Attorney General determines that he has no reason to believe that any such test or device has been used during the seventeen years preceding the filing of an action under the first sentence of this subsection for the purpose or with the effect of denying or abridging the right to vote on account of race or color, he shall consent to the entry of such judgment.

Public Law 91-285
If the Attorney General determines that he has no reason to believe that any such test or device has been used during the ten years preceding the filing of an action under the second sentence of this subsection for the purpose or with the effect of denying or abridging the right to vote on account of race or color, or in contravention of the guarantees set forth in section 4(f)(2) he shall consent to the entry of such judgment.

(b) The provisions of subsection (a) shall apply in any State or in any political subdivision of a State which (1) the Attorney General determines maintained on November 1, 1964, any test or device, and with respect to which (2) the Director of the Census determines that less than 50 per centum of the persons of voting age residing therein were registered on November 1, 1964, or that less than 50 per centum of such persons voted in the presidential election of November 1964. On and after August 6, 1970, in addition to any State or political subdivision of a State determined to be subject to subsection (a) pursuant to the previous sentence, the provisions of subsection (a) shall apply in any State or any political subdivision of a State which (i) the Attorney General determines maintained on November 1, 1968, any test or device, and with respect to which (ii) the Director of the Census determines that less than 50 per centum of the persons of voting age residing therein were registered on November 1, 1968, or that less than 50 per centum of such persons voted in the presidential election of November 1968.

On and after August 6, 1975, in addition to any State or political subdivision of a State determined to be subject to subsection (a) pursuant to the previous two sentences, the provisions of subsection (a) shall apply in any State or any political subdivision of a State which (i) the Attorney General determines maintained on November 1, 1972, any test or device, and with respect to which (ii) the Director of the Census determines that less than 50 per centum of the citizens of voting age were registered on November 1, 1972, or that less than 50 per centum of such persons voted in the Presidential election of November 1972.

Public Law 94-73

A determination or certification of the Attorney General or of the Director of the Census under this section or under section 6 or section 13 shall not be reviewable in any court and shall be effective upon publication in the Federal Register.

(c) The phrase "test or device" shall mean any requirement that a person as a prerequisite for voting or registration for voting (1) demonstrate the ability to read, write, understand, or interpret any matter, (2) demonstrate any educational achievement or his knowledge of any particular subject, (3) possess good moral character, or (4) prove his qualifications by the voucher of registered voters or members of any other class.

(d) For purposes of this section no State or political subdivision shall be determined to have engaged in the use of tests or devices for the purpose or with the effect of denying or abridging the right to vote on account of race or color, or in contravention of the guarantees set forth in section 4(f)(2) if (1) incidents of such use have been few in number and have been promptly and effectively corrected by State or local action, (2) the continuing effect of such incidents has been eliminated, and (3) there is no reasonable probability of their recurrence in the future.

Public Law 94-73

(e)(1) Congress hereby declares that to secure the rights under the fourteenth amendment of persons educated in American-flag schools in which the predominant classroom language was other than English, it is necessary to prohibit the States from conditioning the right to vote of such persons on ability to read, write, understand, or interpret any matter in the English language.

(2) No person who demonstrates that he has successfully completed the sixth primary grade in a public school in, or a private school accredited by, any State or territory, the District of Columbia, or the Commonwealth of Puerto Rico in which the predominant classroom language was other than English, shall be denied the right to vote in any Federal, State, or local election because of his inability to read, write, understand, or

interpret any matter in the English language, except that in States in which State law provides that a different level of education is presumptive of literacy, he shall demonstrate that he has successfully completed an equivalent level of education in a public school in, or a private school accredited by, any State or territory, the District of Columbia, or the Commonwealth of Puerto Rico in which the predominant classroom language was other than English.

Public Law
94-73
Public Law
91-285

(f) (1) The Congress finds that voting discrimination against citizens of language minorities is pervasive and national in scope. Such minority citizens are from environments in which the dominant language is other than English. In addition they have been denied equal educational opportunities by State and local governments, resulting in severe disabilities and continuing illiteracy in the English language. The Congress further finds that, where State and local officials conduct elections only in English, language minority citizens are excluded from participating in the electoral process. In many areas of the country, this exclusion is aggravated by acts of physical, economic, and political intimidation. The Congress declares that, in order to enforce the guarantees of the fourteenth and fifteenth amendments to the United States Constitution, it is necessary to eliminate such dis-. crimination by prohibiting English-only elections, and by prescribing other remedial devices.

(2) No voting qualification or prerequisite to voting, or standard, practice, or procedure shall be imposed or applied by any State or political subdivision to deny or abridge the right of any citizen of the United States to vote because he is a member of a language minority group.

(3) In addition to the meaning given the term under section 4(c), the term "test or device" shall also mean any practice or requirement by which any State or political subdivision provided any registration or voting notices, forms, instructions, assistance, or other materials or information relating to the electoral process, including ballots, only in the English language, where the Director of the Census determines that more than five per centum of the citizens of voting age residing in such State or political subdivision are members of a single language minority. With respect to section 4(b), the term "test or device", as defined in this subsection, shall be employed only in making the determinations under the third sentence of that subsection.

(4) Whenever any State or political subdivision subject to the prohibitions of the second sentence of section 4(a) provides any registration or voting notices, forms, instructions, assistance, or other materials or information relating to the electoral process, including ballots, it shall

provide them in the language of the applicable language
minority group as well as in the English language: *Provided*, That where the language of the applicable minority group is oral or unwritten, the State or political subdivision is only required to furnish oral instructions, assistance, or other information relating to registration and
voting.

SEC. 5. Whenever a State or political subdivision with
respect to which the prohibitions set forth in section
4(a) based upon determinations made under the first
sentence of section 4(b) are in effect shall enact or seek to
administer any voting qualification or prerequisite to
voting, or standard, practice, or procedure with respect to
voting different from that in force or effect on November
1, 1964, or whenever a State or political subdivision with
respect to which the prohibitions set forth in section 4(a)
based upon determinations made under the second sentence of section 4(b) are in effect shall enact or seek to administer any voting qualification or prerequisite to voting, or standard, practice, or procedure with respect to
voting different from that in force or effect on November
1, 1968, or whenever a State or political subdivision with
respect to which the prohibitions set forth in section 4(a)   Public Law
based upon determinations made under the third sen-   94-73
tence of section 4(b) are in effect shall enact or seek to
administer any voting qualifications or prerequisite to
voting, or standard, practice, or procedure with respect
to voting different from that in force or effect on November 1, 1972, such State or subdivision may institute an
action in the United States District Court for the District of Columbia for a declaratory judgment that such
qualification, prerequisite, standard, practice, or procedure does not have the purpose and will not have the
effect of denying or abridging the right to vote on account
of race or color, or in contravention of the guarantees set
forth in section 4(f)(2), and unless and until the court
enters such judgment no person shall be denied the right
to vote for failure to comply with such qualification, prerequisite, standard, practice, or procedure: *Provided*,
That such qualification, prerequisite, standard, practice,
or procedure may be enforced without such proceeding if
the qualification, prerequisite, standard, practice, or procedure has been submitted by the chief legal officer or
other appropriate official of such State or subdivision to
the Attorney General and the Attorney General has not
interposed an objection within sixty days after such submission, or upon good cause shown, to facilitate an expedited approval within sixty days after such submission, the Attorney General has affirmatively indicated
that such objection will not be made. Neither an affirmative indication by the Attorney General that no objection
will be made, nor the Attorney General's failure to ob-

ject, nor a declaratory judgment entered under this section shall bar a subsequent action to enjoin enforcement of such qualification, prerequisite, standard, practice, or procedure. In the event the Attorney General affirmatively indicates that no objection will be made within the sixty-day period following receipt of a submission, the Attorney General may reserve the right to reexamine the submission if additional information comes to his attention during the remainder of the sixty-day period which would otherwise require objection in accordance with this section. Any action under this section shall be heard and determined by a court of three judges in accordance with the provisions of section 2284 of title 28 of the United States Code and any appeal shall lie to the Supreme Court.

SEC. 6. Whenever (a) a court has authorized the appointment of examiners pursuant to the provisions of section 3(a), or (b) unless a declaratory judgment has been rendered under section 4(a), the Attorney General certifies with respect to any political subdivision named in, or included within the scope of, determinations made under section 4(b) that (1) he has received complaints in writing from twenty or more residents of such political subdivision alleging that they have been denied the right to vote under color of law on account of race or color, or in contravention of the guarantees set forth in section 4 (f) (2), and that he believes such complaints to be meritorious, or (2) that in his judgment (considering, among other factors, whether the ratio of nonwhite persons to white persons registered to vote within such subdivision appears to him to be reasonably attributable to violations of the fourteenth or fifteenth amendment or whether substantial evidence exists that bona fide efforts are being made within such subdivision to comply with the fourteenth or fifteenth amendment), the appointment of examiners is otherwise necessary to enforce the guarantees of the fourteenth or fifteenth amendment, the Civil Service Commission shall appoint as many examiners for such subdivision as it may deem appropriate to prepare and maintain lists of persons eligible to vote in Federal, State, and local elections. Such examiners, hearing officers provided for in section 9(a), and other persons deemed necessary by the Commission to carry out the provisions and purposes of this Act shall be appointed, compensated, and separated without regard to the provisions of any statute administered by the Civil Service Commission, and service under this Act shall not be considered employment for the purposes of any statute administered by the Civil Service Commission, except the provisions of section 9 of the Act of August 2, 1939, as amended (5 U.S.C. 118i), prohibiting partisan political activity: *Provided,* That the Commission is authorized, after con-

Public Law
94–73

sulting the head of the appropriate department or agency, to designate suitable persons in the official service of the United States, with their consent, to serve in these positions. Examiners and hearing officers shall have the power to administer oaths.

SEC. 7. (a) The examiners for each political subdivision shall, at such places as the Civil Service Commission shall by regulation designate, examine applicants concerning their qualifications for voting. An application to an examiner shall be in such form as the Commission may require and shall contain allegations that the applicant is not otherwise registered to vote.

(b) Any person whom the examiner finds, in accordance with instructions received under section 9(b), to have the qualifications prescribed by State law not inconsistent with the Constitution and laws of the United States shall promptly be placed on a list of eligible voters. A challenge to such listing may be made in accordance with section 9(a) and shall not be the basis for a prosecution under section 12 of this Act. The examiner shall certify and transmit such list, and any supplements as appropriate, at least once a month, to the offices of the appropriate election officials, with copies to the Attorney General and the attorney general of the State, and any such lists and supplements thereto transmitted during the month shall be available for public inspection on the last business day of the month and in any event not later than the forty-fifth day prior to any election. The appropriate State or local election official shall place such names on the official voting list. Any person whose name appears on the examiner's list shall be entitled and allowed to vote in the election district of his residence unless and until the appropriate election officials shall have been notified that such person has been removed from such list in accordance with subsection (d): *Provided*, That no person shall be entitled to vote in any election by virtue of this Act unless his name shall have been certified and transmitted on such a list to the offices of the appropriate election officials at least forty-five days prior to such election.

(c) The examiner shall issue to each person whose name appears on such a list a certificate evidencing his eligibility to vote.

(d) A person whose name appears on such a list shall be removed therefrom by an examiner if (1) such person has been successfully challenged in accordance with the procedure prescribed in section 9, or (2) he has been determined by an examiner to have lost his eligibility to vote under State law not inconsistent with the Constitution and the laws of the United States.

SEC. 8. Whenever an examiner is serving under this Act in any political subdivision, the Civil Service Commission may assign, at the request of the Attorney General, one or more persons, who may be officers of the United States, (1) to enter and attend at any place for holding an election in such subdivision for the purpose of observing whether persons who are entitled to vote are being permitted to vote, and (2) to enter and attend at any place for tabulating the votes cast at any election held in such subdivision for the purpose of observing whether votes cast by persons entitled to vote are being properly tabulated. Such persons so assigned shall report to an examiner appointed for such political subdivision, to the Attorney General, and if the appointment of examiners has been authorized pursuant to section 3(a), to the court.

SEC. 9. (a) Any challenge to a listing on an eligibility list prepared by an examiner shall be heard and determined by a hearing officer appointed by and responsible to the Civil Service Commission and under such rules as the Commission shall by regulation prescribe. Such challenge shall be entertained only if filed at such office within the State as the Civil Service Commission shall by regulation designate, and within ten days after the listing of the challenged person is made available for public inspection, and if supported by (1) the affidavits of at least two persons having personal knowledge of the facts constituting grounds for the challenge, and (2) a certification that a copy of the challenge and affidavits have been served by mail or in person upon the person challenged at his place of residence set out in the application. Such challenge shall be determined within fifteen days after it has been filed. A petition for review of the decision of the hearing officer may be filed in the United States court of appeals for the circuit in which the person challenged resides within fifteen days after service of such decision by mail on the person petitioning for review but no decision or a hearing officer shall be reversed unless clearly erroneous. Any person listed shall be entitled and allowed to vote pending final determination by the hearing officer and by the court.

(b) The times, places, procedures, and form for application and listing pursuant to this Act and removals from the eligibility lists shall be prescribed by regulations promulgated by the Civil Service Commission and the Commission shall, after consultation with the Attorney General, instruct examiners concerning applicable State law not inconsistent with the Constitution and laws of the United States with respect to (1) the qualifications required for listing, and (2) loss of eligibility to vote.

(c) Upon the request of the applicant or the challenger or on its own motion the Civil Service Commission shall have the power to require by subpoena the attendance and testimony of witnesses and the production of documentary evidence relating to any matter pending before it under the authority of this section. In case of contumacy or refusal to obey a subpoena, any district court of the United States or the United States court of any territory or possession, or the District Court of the United States for the District of Columbia, within the jurisdiction of which said person guilty of contumacy or refusal to obey is found or resides or is domiciled or transacts business, or has appointed an agent for receipt of service or process, upon application by the Attorney General of the United States shall have jurisdiction to issue to such person an order requiring such person to appear before the Commission or a hearing officer, there to produce pertinent, relevant, and nonprivileged documentary evidence if so ordered, or there to give testimony touching the matter under investigation; and any failure to obey such order of the court may be punished by said court as a contempt thereof.

SEC. 10. (a) The Congress finds that the requirement of the payment of a poll tax as a precondition to voting (i) precludes persons of limited means from voting or imposes unreasonable financial hardship upon such persons as a precondition to their exercise of the franchise, (ii) does not bear a reasonable relationship to any legitimate State interest in the conduct of elections, and (iii) in some areas has the purpose or effect of denying persons the right to vote because of race or color. Upon the basis of these findings, Congress declares that the constitutional right of citizens to vote is denied or abridged in some areas by the requirement of the payment of a poll tax as a precondition to voting. Public Law 94–73

(b) In the exercise of the powers of Congress under section 5 of the fourteenth amendment, section 2 of the fifteenth amendment and section 2 of the twenty-fourth amendment, the Attorney General is authorized and directed to institute forthwith in the name of the United States such actions, including actions against States or political subdivisions, for declaratory judgment or injunctive relief against the enforcement of any requirement of the payment of a poll tax as a precondition to voting, or substitute therefor enacted after November 1, 1964, as will be necessary to implement the declaration of subsection (a) and the purposes of this section.

(c) The district courts of the United States shall have jurisdiction of such actions which shall be heard and determined by a court of three judges in accordance with the provisions of section 2284 of title 28 of the United States Code and any appeal shall lie to the Supreme Court. It shall be the duty of the judges designated to hear the case to assign the case for hearing at the earliest practicable date, to participate in the hearing and determination thereof, and to cause the case to be in every way expedited.

SEC. 11. (a) No person acting under color of law shall fail or refuse to permit any person to vote who is entitled to vote under any provision of this Act or is otherwise qualified to vote, or willfully fail or refuse to tabulate, count, and report such person's vote.

(b) No person, whether acting under color of law or otherwise, shall intimidate, threaten, or coerce, or attempt to intimidate, threaten, or coerce any person for voting or attempting to vote, or intimidate, threaten, or coerce, or attempt to intimidate, threaten, or coerce any person for urging or aiding any person to vote or attempt to vote, or intimidate, threaten, or coerce any person for exercising any powers or duties under section 3(a), 6, 8, 9, 10, or 12(e).

Public Law
94-73

(c) Whoever knowingly or willfully gives false information as to his name, address, or period of residence in the voting district for the purpose of establishing his eligibility to register or vote, or conspires with another individual for the purpose of encouraging his false registration to vote or illegal voting, or pays or offers to pay or accepts payment either for registration to vote or for voting shall be fined not more than $10,000 or imprisoned not more than five years, or both: *Provided, however,* That this provision shall be applicable only to general, special, or primary elections held solely or in part for the purpose of selecting or electing any candidate for the office of President, Vice President, presidential elector, Member of the United States Senate, Member of the United States House of Representatives, Delegate from the District of Columbia, Guam, or the Virgin Islands, or Resident Commissioner of the Commonwealth of Puerto Rico.

(d) Whoever, in any matter within the jurisdiction of an examiner or hearing officer knowingly and willfully falsifies or conceals a material fact, or makes any false, fictitious, or fraudulent statements or representations, or makes or uses any false writing or document knowing the same to contain any false, fictitious, or fraudulent statement or entry, shall be fined not more than $10,000 or imprisoned not more than five years, or both.

Public Law
94-73

(e)(1) Whoever votes more than once in an election referred to in paragraph (2) shall be fined not more than $10,000 or imprisoned not more than five years, or both.

(2) The prohibition of this subsection applies with respect to any general, special, or primary election held solely or in part for the purpose of selecting or electing any candidate for the office of President, Vice President, presidential elector, Member of the United States Senate, Member of the United States House of Representatives, Delegate from the District of Columbia, Guam, or the Virgin Islands, or Resident Commissioner of the Commonwealth of Puerto Rico.

(3) As used in this subsection, the term "votes more than once" does not include the casting of an additional ballot if all prior ballots of that voter were invalidated, nor does it include the voting in two jurisdictions under section 202 of this Act, to the extent two ballots are not cast for an election to the same candidacy or office.

Sec. 12. (a) Whoever shall deprive or attempt to deprive any person of any right secured by section 2, 3, 4, 5, 7, or 10 or shall violate section 11(a), shall be fined not more than $5,000, or imprisoned not more than five years, or both.

Public Law 90-284

(b) Whoever, within a year following an election in a political subdivision in which an examiner has been appointed (1) destroys, defaces, mutilates, or otherwise alters the marking of a paper ballot which has been cast in such election, or (2) alters any official record of voting in such election tabulated from a voting machine or otherwise, shall be fined not more than $5,000, or imprisoned not more than five years, or both.

(c) Whoever conspires to violate the provisions of subsection (a) or (b) of this section, or interferes with any right secured by section 2, 3, 4, 5, 7, 10, or 11(a) shall be fined not more than $5,000, or imprisoned not more than five years, or both.

Public Law 90-284

(d) Whenever any person has engaged or there are reasonable grounds to believe that any person is about to engage in any act or practice prohibited by section 2, 3, 4, 5, 7, 10, 11, or subsection (b) of this section, the Attorney General may institute for the United States, or in the name of the United States, an action for preventive relief, including an application for a temporary or permanent injunction, restraining order, or other order, and including an order directed to the State and State or local election officials to require them (1) to permit persons listed under this Act to vote and (2) to count such votes.

(e) Whenever in any political subdivision in which there are examiners appointed pursuant to this Act any persons allege to such an examiner within forty-eight hours after the closing of the polls that notwithstanding (1) their listing under this Act or registration by an appropriate election official and (2) their eligiblity to vote, they have not been permitted to vote in such election, the examiner shall forthwith notify the Attorney General if such allegations in his opinion appear to be well founded. Upon receipt of such notification the Attorney General may forthwith file with the district court an application for an order providing for the marking, casting, and counting of the ballots of such persons and requiring the inclusion of their votes in the total vote before the results of such election shall be deemed final and any force or effect given thereto. The district court shall hear and determine such matters immediately after the filing of such application. The remedy provided in this subsection shall not preclude any remedy available under State or Federal law.

(f) The district courts of the United States shall have jurisdiction of proceedings instituted pursuant to this section and shall exercise the same without regard to whether a person asserting rights under the provisions of this Act shall have exhausted any administrative or other remedies that may be provided by law.

Sec. 13. Listing procedures shall be terminated in any political subdivision of any State (a) with respect to examiners appointed pursuant to clause (b) of section 6 whenever the Attorney General notifies the Civil Service Commission, or whenever the District Court for the District of Columbia determines in an action for declaratory judgment brought by any political subdivision with respect to which the Director of the Census has determined that more than 50 per centum of the nonwhite persons of voting age residing therein are registered to vote, (1) that all persons listed by an examiner for such subdivision have been placed on the appropriate voting registration roll, and (2) that there is no longer reasonable cause to believe that persons will be deprived of or denied the right to vote on account of race or color, or in contravention of the guarantees set forth in section 4(f)(2) in such subdivision, and (b), with respect to examiners appointed pursuant to section 3(a), upon

Public Law
94–73

order of the authorizing court. A political subdivision may petition the Attorney General for the termination of listing procedures under clause (a) of this section. and may petition the Attorney General to request the Director of the Census to take such survey or census as may be appropriate for the making of the determination provided for in this section. The District Court for the District of Columbia shall have jurisdiction to require such survey or census to be made by the Director of the Census and it shall require him to do so if it deems the Attorney General's refusal to request such survey or census to be arbitrary or unreasonable.

Sec. 14. (a) All cases of criminal contempt arising under the provisions of this Act shall be governed by section 151 of the Civil Rights Act of 1957 (42 U.S.C. 1995).

(b) No court other than the District Court for the District of Columbia or a court of appeals in any proceeding under section 9 shall have jurisdiction to issue any declaratory judgment pursuant to section 4 or section 5 or any restraining order or temporary or permanent injunction against the execution or enforcement of any provision of this Act or any action of any Federal officer or employee pursuant hereto.

(c)(1) The terms "vote" or "voting" shall include all action necessary to make a vote effective in any primary, special, or general election, including, but not limited to, registration, listing pursuant to this Act, or other action required by law prerequisite to voting, casting a ballot, and having such a ballot counted properly and included in the appropriate totals of votes cast with respect to candidates for public or party office and propositions for which votes are received in an election.

(2) The term "political subdivision" shall mean any county or parish, except that where registration for voting is not conducted under the supervision of a county or parish, the term shall include any other subdivision of a State which conducts registration for voting.

(3) The term "language minorities" or "language minority group" means persons who are American Indian, Asian American, Alaskan Natives or of Spanish heritage.

Public Law 94–73

(d) In any action for a declaratory judgment brought pursuant to section 4 or section 5 or this Act, subpenas for witnesses who are required to attend the District Court for the District of Columbia may be served in any judicial district of the United States: *Provided,* That no writ of subpena shall issue for witnesses without the District of Columbia at a greater distance than one hundred miles from the place of holding court without the permission of the District Court for the District of Columbia being first had upon proper application and cause shown.

(e) In any action or proceeding to enforce the voting guarantees of the fourteenth or fifteenth amendment, the court, in its discretion, may allow the prevailing party, other than the United States, a reasonable attorney's fee as part of the costs.

Public Law 94–73

SEC. 15. Section 2004 of the Revised Statutes (42 U.S.C. 1971), as amended by section 131 of the Civil Rights Act of 1957 (71 Stat. 637), and amended by section 601 of the Civil Rights Act of 1960 (74 Stat. 90), and as further amended by section 101 of the Civil Rights Act of 1964 (78 Stat. 241), is further amended as follows:

(a) Delete the word "Federal" wherever it appears in subsections (a) and (c);

(b) Repeal subsection (f) and designate the present subsections (g) and (h) as (f) and (g), respectively.

SEC. 16. The Attorney General and the Secretary of Defense, jointly, shall make a full and complete study to determine whether, under the laws or practices of any State or States, there are preconditions to voting, which might tend to result in discrimination against citizens serving in the Armed Forces of the United States seeking to vote. Such officials shall, jointly, make a report to the Congress not later than June 30, 1966, containing the results of such study, together with a list of any States in which such preconditions exist, and shall include in such report such recommendations for legislation as they deem advisable to prevent discrimination in voting against citizens serving in the Armed Forces of the United States.

Sec. 17. Nothing in this Act shall be construed to deny, impair, or otherwise adversely affect the right to vote of any person registered to vote under the law of any State or political subdivision.

Sec. 18. There are hereby authorized to be appropriated such sums as are necessary to carry out the provisions of this Act.

Sec. 19. If any provision of this Act or the application thereof to any person or circumstances is held invalid, the remainder of the Act and the application of the provision to other persons not similarly situated or to other circumstances shall not be affected thereby.

TITLE II—SUPPLEMENTAL PROVISIONS

APPLICATION OF PROHIBITION TO OTHER STATES

Public Law
94-73
Public Law
91-285

Sec. 201. (a) No citizen shall be denied, because of his failure to comply with any test or device, the right to vote in any Federal, State, or local election conducted in any State or political subdivision of a State.

(b) As used in this section, the term "test or device" means any requirement that a person as a prerequisite for voting or registration for voting (1) demonstrate the ability to read, write, understand, or interpret any matter, (2) demonstrate any educational achievement or his knowledge of any particular subject, (3) possess good moral character, or (4) prove his qualifications by the voucher of registered voters or members of any other class.

RESIDENCE REQUIREMENTS FOR VOTING

Public Law
91-285

Sec. 202. (a) The Congress hereby finds that the imposition and application of the durational residency requirement as a precondition to voting for the offices of President and Vice President, and the lack of sufficient opportunities for absentee registration and absentee balloting in presidential elections—

(1) denies or abridges the inherent constitutional right of citizens to vote for their President and Vice President;

(2) denies or abridges the inherent constitutional right of citizens to enjoy their free movement across State lines;

(3) denies or abridges the privileges and immunities guaranteed to the citizens of each State under article IV, section 2, clause 1, of the Constitution;

(4) in some instances has the impermissible purpose or effect of denying citizens the right to vote for such officers because of the way they may vote;

(5) has the effect of denying to citizens the equality of civil rights, and due process and equal pro-

tection of the laws that are guaranteed to them under the fourteenth amendment; and

(6) does not bear a reasonable relationship to any compelling State interest in the conduct of presidential elections.

(b) Upon the basis of these findings, Congress declares that in order to secure and protect the above-stated rights of citizens under the Constitution, to enable citizens to better obtain the enjoyment of such rights, and to enforce the guarantees of the fourteenth amendment, it is necessary (1) to completely abolish the durational residency requirement as a precondition to voting for President and Vice President, and (2) to establish nationwide, uniform standards relative to absentee registration and absentee balloting in presidential elections.

(c) No citizen of the United States who is otherwise qualified to vote in any election for President and Vice President shall be denied the right to vote for electors for President and Vice President, or for President and Vice President, in such election because of the failure of such citizen to comply with any durational residency requirement of such State or political subdivision; nor shall any citizen of the United States be denied the right to vote for electors for President and Vice President, or for President and Vice President, in such election because of the failure of such citizen to be physically present in such State or political subdivision at the time of such election, if such citizen shall have complied with the requirements prescribed by the law of such State or political subdivision providing for the casting of absentee ballots in such election.

(d) For the purposes of this section, each State shall provide by law for the registration or other means of qualification of all duly qualified residents of such State who apply, not later than thirty days immediately prior to any presidential election, for registration or qualification to vote for the choice of electors for President and Vice President or for President and Vice President in such election; and each State shall provide by law for the casting of absentee ballots for the choice of electors for President and Vice President, or for President and Vice President, by all duly qualified residents of such State who may be absent from their election district or unit in such State on the day such election is held and who have applied therefor not later than seven days immediately prior to such election and have returned such ballots to the appropriate election official of such State not later than the time of closing of the polls in such State on the day of such election.

(e) If any citizen of the United States who is otherwise qualified to vote in any State or political subdivision in any election for President and Vice President has begun residence in such State or political subdivision after the thirtieth day next preceding such election and, for that reason, does not satisfy the registration requirements of such State or political subdivision he shall be allowed to vote for the choice of electors for President and Vice President, or for President and Vice President, in such election, (1) in person in the State or political subdivision in which he resided immediately prior to his removal if he had satisfied, as of the date of his change of residence, the requirements to vote in that State or political subdivision, or (2) by absentee ballot in the State or political subdivision in which he resided immediately prior to his removal if he satisfies, but for his nonresident status and the reason for his absence, the requirements for absentee voting in that State or political subdivision.

(f) No citizen of the United States who is otherwise qualified to vote by absentee ballot in any State or political subdivision in any election for President and Vice President shall be denied the right to vote for the choice of electors for President and Vice President, or for President and Vice President, in such election because of any requirement of registration that does not include a provision for absentee registration.

(g) Nothing in this section shall prevent any State or political subdivision from adopting less restrictive voting practices than those that are prescribed herein.

(h) The term "State" as used in this section includes each of the several States and the District of Columbia.

(i) The provisions of section 11(c) shall apply to false registration, and other fraudulent acts and conspiracies, committed under this section.

BILINGUAL ELECTION REQUIREMENTS

Public Law 94-73

SEC. 203. (a) The Congress finds that, through the use of various practices and procedures, citizens of language minorities have been effectively excluded from participation in the electoral process. Among other factors, the denial of the right to vote of such minority group citizens is ordinarily directly related to the unequal educational opportunities afforded them, resulting in high illiteracy and low voting participation. The Congress declares that, in order to enforce the guarantees of the fourteenth and fifteenth amendments to the United States Constitution, it is necessary to eliminate such discrimination by prohibiting these practices, and by prescribing other remedial devices.

(b) Prior to August 6, 1985, no State or political subdivision shall provide registration or voting notices, forms, instructions, assistance, or other materials or information relating to the electoral process, including ballots, only in the English language if the Director of the Census determines (i) that more than 5 percent of the citizens of voting age of such State or political subdivision are members of a single language minority and (ii) that the illiteracy rate of such persons as a group is higher than the national illiteracy rate: *Provided*, That the prohibitions of this subsection shall not apply in any political subdivision which has less than five percent voting age citizens of each language minority which comprises over five percent of the statewide population of voting age citizens. For purposes of this subsection, illiteracy means the failure to complete the fifth primary grade. The determinations of the Director of the Census under this subsection shall be effective upon publication in the Federal Register and shall not be subject to review in any court.

(c) Whenever any State or political subdivision subject to the prohibition of subsection (b) of this section provides any registration or voting notices, forms, instructions, assistance, or other materials or information relating to the electoral process, including ballots, it shall provide them in the language of the applicable minority group as well as in the English language: *Provided*, That where the language of the applicable minority group is oral or unwritten or in the case of Alaskan natives, if the predominant language is historically unwritten, the State or political subdivision is only required to furnish oral instructions, assistance, or other information relating to registration and voting.

(d) Any State or political subdivision subject to the prohibition of subsection (b) of this section, which seeks to provide English-only registration or voting materials or information, including ballots, may file an action against the United States in the United States District Court for a declaratory judgment permitting such provision. The court shall grant the requested relief if it determines that the illiteracy rate of the applicable language minority group within the State or political subdivision is equal to or less than the national illiteracy rate.

(e) For purposes of this section, the term "language minorities" or "language minority group" means persons who are American Indian, Asian American, Alaskan Natives, or of Spanish heritage.

JUDICIAL RELIEF

SEC. 204. Whenever the Attorney General has reason to believe that a State or political subdivision (a) has enacted or is seeking to administer any test or device as a prerequisite to voting in violation of the prohibition contained in section 201, or (b) undertakes to deny the right to vote in any election in violation of section 202, or 203, he may institute for the United States, or in the name of the United States, an action in a district court of the United States, in accordance with sections 1391 through 1393 of title 28, United States Code, for a restraining

Public Law
94–73
Public Law
91–285

order. a preliminary or permanent injunction. or such other order as he deems appropriate. An action under this subsection shall be heard and determined by a court of three judges in accordance with the provisions of section 2284 of title 28 of the United States Code and any appeal shall be to the Supreme Court.

PENALTY

Public Law 91-285

SEC. 205. Whoever shall deprive or attempt to deprive any person of any right secured by section 201. 202, or 203 of this title shall be fined not more than $5.000, or imprisoned not more than five years. or both.

SEPARABILITY

Public Law 91-285

SEC. 206. If any provision of this Act or the application of any provision thereof to any person or circumstance is judicially determined to be invalid. the remainder of this Act or the application of such provision to other persons or circumstances shall not be affected by such determination.

Public Law 94-73

SEC. 207. (a) Congress hereby directs the Director of the Census forthwith to conduct a survey to compile registration and voting statistics: (i) in every State or political subdivision with respect to which the prohibitions of section 4(a) of the Voting Rights Act of 1965 are in effect. for every statewide general election for Members of the United States House of Representatives after January 1, 1974: and (ii) in every State or political subdivision for any election designated by the United States Commission on Civil Rights. Such surveys shall only include a count of citizens of voting age. race or color. and national origin. and a determination of the extent to which such persons are registered to vote and have voted in the elections surveyed.

(b) In any survey under subsection (a) of this section no person shall be compelled to disclose his race. color. national origin. political party affiliation. or how he voted (or the reasons therefor). nor shall any penalty be imposed for his failure or refusal to make such disclosures. Every person interrogated orally. by written survey or questionnaire. or by any other means with respect to such information shall be fully advised of his right to fail or refuse to furnish such information.

(c) The Director of the Census shall. at the earliest practicable time. report to the Congress the results of every survey conducted pursuant to the provisions of subsection (a) of this section.

(d) The provisions of section 9 and chapter 7 of title 13 of the United States Code shall apply to any survey. collection. or compilation of registration and voting statistics carried out under subsection (a) of this section.

TITLE III—EIGHTEEN-YEAR-OLD VOTING AGE

Public Law
94-73

ENFORCEMENT OF TWENTY-SIXTH AMENDMENT

Sec. 301. (a)(1) The Attorney General is directed to institute, in the name of the United States, such actions against States or political subdivisions, including actions for injunctive relief, as he may determine to be necessary to implement the twenty-sixth article of amendment to the Constitution of the United States.

Public Law
94-73

(2) The district courts of the United States shall have jurisdiction of proceedings instituted under this title, which shall be heard and determined by a court of three judges in accordance with section 2284 of title 28 of the United States Code, and any appeal shall lie to the Supreme Court. It shall be the duty of the judges designated to hear the case to assign the case for hearing and determination thereof, and to cause the case to be in every way expedited.

(b) Whoever shall deny or attempt to deny any person of any right secured by the twenty-sixth article of amendment to the Constitution of the United States shall be fined not more than $5,000 or imprisoned not more than five years, or both.

DEFINITION

Sec. 302. As used in this title, the term "State" includes the District of Columbia.

Public Law
94-73

○

Appendix B
Alabama Literacy Test

Alabama Literacy Test*

1. Which of the following is a right guaranteed by the Bill of Rights?

   _____Public Education   _____Voting

   _____Employment   _____Trial by Jury

2. The federal census of population is taken each five years. (True or false)

3. If a person is indicted for a crime, name two rights which he has.

4. A United States senator elected at the general election in November takes office the following year on what date?_____

5. A President elected at the general election in November takes office the following year on what date?

6. Which definition applies to the word "amendment?"

   _____Proposed change, as in a Constitution

   _____Making of peace between nations at war

   _____A part of the government

7. A person appointed to the United States Supreme Court is appointed for a term of _____.

8. When the Constitution was approved by the original colonies, how many states had to ratify it in order for it to be in effect?

9. Does enumeration affect the income tax levied on citizens in various states?

10. Persons opposed to swearing in an oath may say, instead: "I solemnly_____."

11. To serve as President of the United States a person must have attained ____25, _____35, _____40, _____45 years.

12. What words are required by law to be on all coins and paper currency of the United States?

13. The Supreme Court is the chief lawmaking body of the state. (True or false)

14. If a law passed by a state is contrary to provisions of the United States Constitution, which law prevails?

*Voided by 1965 Voting Rights Act, U. S. Congress. Affirmed by U. S. Supreme Court, 1966.

15. If a vacancy occurs in the United States Senate, the state must hold an election but, meanwhile, the place may be filled by a temporary appointment made by _____.

16. A United States senator is elected for a term of _____ years.

17. Appropriation of money for the armed services can be only for a period limited to _____ years.

18. The chief executive and the administrative officers make up the _____ branch of government.

19. Who passes laws dealing with piracy?

20. The number of representatives which a state is entitled to have in the House of Representatives is based on _____.

21. The Constitution protects an individual against punishments which are _____ and _____.

22. When a jury has heard and rendered a verdict in a case, and the judgment on the verdict has become final, the defendant cannot again be brought to trial for the same cause. (true or false)

23. Communism is the type of government in: _____United States _____Russia _____England.

24. Name two levels of government which can levy taxes.

25. Cases tried before a court of law are of two types, civil and _____.

26. By a majority vote of the members of the Congress, the Congress can change provisions of the Constitution of the United States. (True of false)

27. For security, each state has a right to form a _____.

28. The electoral vote for President is counted in the presence of two bodies. Name them.

29. If no candidate for President receives a majority of the electoral vote, who decides who will become President?

30. Of the original 13 states, the one with the largest representation in the first Congress was _____.

31. Of which branch of state government is the Speaker of the House a part?

    _____Executive _____Legislative_____Judicial.

32. Capital punishment is the giving of a death sentence. (True or false)

33. In case the President is unable to perform the duties of his office, who assumes them?

34. "Involuntary servitude" is permitted in the United States upon conviction of a crime. (True or false)

35. If a state is a party to a case, the Constitution provides that original jurisdiction shall be in _____.

36. Congress passes laws regulating cases which are included in those over which the United States Supreme Court has _____jurisdiction.

37. Which of the following is a right guaranteed by the Bill of Rights of the United States Constitution?

    _____Public Housing   _____Education

    _____Voting   _____Trial by Jury

38. The Legislatures of the states decide how presidential electors may be chosen. (True or false)

39. If it were proposed to join Alabama and Mississippi to form one state, what groups would have to vote approval in order for this to be done?

40. The Vice President presides over _____.

41. The Constitution limits the size of the District of Columbia to _____.

42. The only laws which can be passed to apply to an area in a federal arsenal are those passed by _____provided consent for the purchase of the land is given by the _____.

43. In which document or writing is the Bill of Rights found?

44. Of which branch of government is a Supreme Court justice a part?

    _____Executive _____Legislative _____Judicial.

45. If no person receives a majority of the electoral votes, the Vice President is chosen by the Senate. (True or false)

46. Name two things which the states are forbidden to do by the United States Constitution.

47. If election of the President becomes the duty of the United States House of Representatives and it fails to act, who becomes President and when?

48. How many votes must a person receive in order to become President if the election is decided by the United States House of Representatives?

49. How many states were required to approve the original Constitution in order for it to be in effect?

50. Check the offenses below which, if you are convicted of them, disqualify you for voting. _____Murder _____Petty Larceny
    _____Issuing worthless checks _____Manufacturing Whiskey

51. The Congress decides in what manner states elect presidential electors. (True or false)

52. Name two of the purposes of the United States Constitution.

53. Congress is composed of _____.

54. All legislative powers granted in the United States Constitution may legally be used only by _____.

55. The population census is required to be made every _____years.

56. Impeachments of United States officials are tried by _____.

57. If an effort to impeach the President of the United States is made, who presides at the trial?

58. On the impeachment of the chief justice of the Supreme Court of the United States, who tries the case?

59. Money is coined by order of:

    _____U.S. Congress

    _____The President's Cabinet

    _____State Legislatures

60. Persons elected to cast a state's vote for United States President and Vice President are called presidential _____.

61. Name one power which is exclusively legislative and is mentioned in one of the parts of the United States Constitution above.

62. If a person flees from justice into another state, who has authority to ask for his return?

63. Whose duty is it to keep Congress informed of the state of the union?

64. If the two houses of Congress cannot agree on adjournment, who sets the time?

65. When the presidential electors meet to cast ballots for President, must all electors in a state vote for the same person for President or can they vote for different persons if they so choose?

66. After the presidential electors have voted, to whom do they send the count of their votes?

67. The power to declare war is vested in _____.

68. Any power and rights not given to the United States or prohibited to the states by the United States Constitution are specified as belonging to whom?

Appendix C
Number of Changes Submitted under Section Five and Reviewed by the Department of Justice, by State and Year, 1965-1980

STATE	1965	1966	1967	1968	1969	1970	1971	1972	1973	1974	1975	1976	1977	1978	1979	1980	TOTAL
ALABAMA	1	0	0	0	13	2	86	111	60	58	299	349	153	146	142	228	1,648
ALASKA***	0	0	0	0	—	0	0	0	—	—	0	3	0	25	1	1	30
ARIZONA****	0	0	0	0	0	0	19	69	33	28	52	228	180	311	163	444	1,527
CALIFORNIA*	—	—	—	—	—	0	0	6	1	5	0	382	99	105	8	57	663
COLORADO*	—	—	—	—	—	—	—	—	—	—	0	12	4	34	147	29	226
CONNECTICUT**	—	—	—	—	—	—	—	—	—	0	0	0	0	0	0	0	0
FLORIDA*	0	1	0	0	—	—	—	—	—	—	0	57	8	46	28	22	162
GEORGIA	0	1	0	62	35	60	138	226	114	173	284	252	242	444	371	495	2,897
HAWAII*	0	0	0	0	0	0	0	0	0	0	0	6	0	0	0	3	9
IDAHO*	0	0	—	—	—	—	—	—	—	—	0	0	0	0	0	1	1
LOUISIANA	0	—	—	—	2	3	71	136	283	137	255	303	460	254	336	214	2,454
MAINE**	—	—	—	—	—	—	—	—	—	—	—	3	—	—	—	—	3
MASSACHUSETTS**	—	—	—	—	—	—	—	—	—	0	0	11	0	3	0	0	14
MICHIGAN**	—	—	—	—	—	—	—	—	—	—	0	1	0	0	0	0	1
MISSISSIPPI	0	—	—	—	4	28	221	68	66	41	107	152	114	126	112	78	1,117
NEW HAMPSHIRE**	—	—	—	—	—	—	—	—	—	0	0	0	0	0	0	0	0
NEW MEXICO*	—	—	—	—	—	—	—	—	—	—	0	65	—	—	—	—	65
NEW YORK*	—	—	—	—	—	0	4	—	—	84	78	106	96	72	27	19	486
OKLAHOMA*	—	0	0	0	0	—	—	—	—	—	0	1	0	0	—	—	1
NORTH CAROLINA*	0	0	0	0	0	2	75	28	35	54	293	125	183	156	89	121	1,161
SOUTH CAROLINA	0	25	52	37	80	114	160	117	135	221	201	419	299	212	138	126	2,336
SOUTH DAKOTA	—	—	—	—	—	—	—	—	—	—	0	0	0	2	4	0	6
TEXAS	—	—	—	—	—	—	—	—	—	—	249	4,694	1,735	2,425	2,917	2,740	14,760

VIRGINIA	0	0	0	11	0	46	344	181	123	186	259	301	434	314	267	377	2,843
WYOMING*	--	--	--	--	--	--	0	0	0	1	0	0	0	0	0	0	0
TOTALS	1	26	52	110	134	255	1,118	942	850	988	2,078	7,470	4,007	4,675	4,750	4,955	32,411

*Selected county (counties) covered rather than entire state.

**Selected town (towns) covered rather than entire state.

***Entire state covered 1965-1968; selected election districts covered 1970-1972; since 1975 entire state covered.

****Selected county (counties) until 1975; entire state now covered.

----Not covered for years indicated.

Source: U.S. Department of Justice Voting Rights Section, September 1980.

245

Number of Changes Submitted under Section Five and Reviewed by the Department of Justice, by Type and Year, 1965-1980

TYPE OF CHANGE	1965	1966	1967	1968	1969	1970	1971	1972	1973	1974	1975	1976	1977	1978	1979	1980	TOTAL
REDISTRICTING		2	4		12	25	201	97	47	55	53	335	79	48	53	54	1,065
ANNEXATION		1	2		2	6	256	272	242	244	571	1,499	939	880	1,130	772	6,816
POLLING PLACE		2	4	4	7	28	174	127	131	154	408	1,983	844	1,402	1,122	2,142	8,532
PRECINCT		2	9	7	11	22	144	69	55	81	82	608	266	299	542	590	2,787
REREGISTRATION**			1			2	52	15	6	4	46	146	366	162	271	3	1,074
INCORPORATION			1				4	1	3	1	5	15	12	5	11	39	97
ELECTION LAW [1]***	1	18	24	96	67	105	226	332	258	422	620	1,831	1,094	1,450	1,230	---	7,774
BILINGUAL											22	780	171	280	294	123	1,670
MISCELLANEOUS [2]***				3	14	8	15	26	99	12	65	168	150	65	68	160	853
NOT WITHIN THE SCOPE OF SECTION 5***		1	7		21	59	46	3	9	15	206	105	86	84	29	---	671
METHOD OF ELECTION*													---	---	---	124	124
FORM OF GOVERNMENT*													---	---	---	32	32
CONSOLIDATIONS OR DIVISION OF POLITICAL UNITS*													---	---	---	10	10
SPECIAL ELECTION*													---	---	---	212	212
VOTING METHODS*													---	---	---	61	61
CANDIDATE QUALIFICATION*													---	---	---	9	9
VOTER REGISTRATION PROCEDURE*													---	---	---	624	624

| TOTALS | 1 | 26 | 52 | 110 | 134 | 255 | 1,118 | 942 | 850 | 988 | 2,078 | 7,470 | 4,007 | 4,675 | 4,750 | 4,955 | 32,411 |

[1]Ordinance or other legislation affecting election laws; this category was replaced in 1980 by several others. See page 2.
[2]Miscellaneous change not included in the above classifications.

*New computer classifications beginning in 1980.
**Modified in 1980; does not include other registration procedures listed above.
***Not used in 1980.

Source: U.S. Department of Justice Voting Rights Section, September 1980.

Appendix E
DOJ Memo:
Request for FBI Assistance

OPTIONAL FORM NO. 10
JULY 1973 EDITION
GSA FPMR (41 CFR) 101-11.6

UNITED STATES GOVERNMENT

Memorandum

TO : Director
Federal Bureau of Investigation

DATE:

FROM : Drew S. Days III
Assistant Attorney General
Civil Rights Division

SUBJECT: _____, _____
_____, _____
Section 5
VOTING RIGHTS ACT OF 1965 _____

A review of this Division's Section 5 files has
revealed that on _____, the Department
received a submission under Section 5 from _____, of
_____. Three copies of the
submitting authority's letter are attached as Attachment B.
On _____, a letter was sent to the
submitting authority requesting additional information
regarding the change, three copies of which are also
attached as Attachment C. To date that information has
not been received.

Please conduct the investigation set out in
Attachement A. The information requested should be
obtained from appropriate officials in _____.

Since the Department's responsibility in enforcing the Voting Rights Act of 1965 includes an obligation to insure that known changes covered by Section 5 are not implemented with a racially discriminatory effect, the information requested below is desired to enable this Division to determine an appropriate course of action with regard to the subject voting change. We note that one of the alternative actions available to the Department regarding a voting change which is implemented without the required federal preclearance is to bring suit to enjoin the implementation of the voting change until Section 5 clearance of the change has been obtained by the covered jurisdiction.

Accordingly, please conduct an investigation to determine:

1. Whether the subject voting change has been implemented (used or enforced).

a. If so, determine when the voting change was first implemented, how and for how long or how often it has been implemented, and the name, and title of office, of the persons responsible for the implementation or at whose direction the implementation occurred (if an official body is involved determine the names and titles of its members).

b. If not, determine whether implementation of the voting change is planned, and if so, when, and the name, and title of office of the persons who will direct the implementation of the change (if an official body is involved determine the names and titles of its members).

2. When the requested additional information regarding the change will be submitted.

We note that information regarding voting changes under Section 5 will be considered to have been properly submitted only if proper submission procedures are followed. These procedures, as set out in the procedural guidelines for the administration of Section 5, 28 C.F.R. Section 51.9, require that the submitting authority deliver or mail such information to Assistant Attorney General, Civil Rights Division, Department of Justice, Washington, D.C. 20530, and that the envelope and first page of any submission shall be clearly marked "Submission under Section 5, Voting Rights Act." Accordingly, an investigating agent's acceptance of information we have requested does not constitute submission of the information under Section 5, and any official who desire to provide such information to an investigating agent should be so advised.

ATTACHMENT A

By the operation of Section 5 of the Voting Rights
Act of 1965, as amended, 42 U.S.C. 1973c, changes in any
standard, practice or procedure affecting voting in
particular states or political subdivisions are not legally
enforceable until a decision has been made at the federal
level that the changes do not have the purpose and will
not have the effect of denying or abridging the right to
vote on account of race, color, or membership in a language
minority group. This decision may be obtained in an
action for a declaratory judgment before the United States
District Court for the District of Columbia, or from the
Attorney General, in which case the voting change and
information regarding it are submitted to the Attorney
General who then has 60 days to render his decision.

The Department has promulgated guidelines, published
at 28 C.F.R. Part 51, regarding submission, analysis of,
and response to, voting changes under Section 5. If a
submission to the Attorney General of a change affecting
voting is not accompanied by sufficient information to
enable us to properly evaluate the purpose and effect of
the change, Section 51.18 of the guidelines requires
us to request from the submitting authority such additional
information as is found necessary for an evaluation, and
advise the submitting authority that the 60-day period we
have to review the change will not commence until the
requested additional information is received by the
Department. Because a voting change covered by Section 5
is not legally enforceable until an appropriate federal
decision is made, i.e., that the change has no objectionable
racial purpose or effect, submitted voting changes for which
necessary additional information has been requested but not
received may not legally be implemented.

Appendix F

Sample Letter Paragraphs from the Voting Section's Communication with Covered Jurisdictions

SAMPLE LETTER PARAGRAPHS FROM THE VOTING SECTION'S
COMMUNICATION WITH COVERED JURISDICTIONS

1. (a) This is in reference to the _____
_____, submitted to the Attorney
General pursuant to Section 5 of the Voting Rights Act of 1965,
as amended. Your submission was received on _____.

   (b) This is in reference to the _____
_____, submitted to the Attorney
General purusant to Section 5 of the Voting Rights Act of 1965,
as amended. Your submission was completed on _____.

   (c) This is in reference to the _____
_____, submitted to the Attorney
General pursuant to Section 5 of the Voting Rights Act of 1965,
as amended. Your submission was received on _____.
In accordance with your equest expedited consideration has been
given this submission pursuant to the procedural guidelines for
the administration of Section 5 (28 C.F.R. Section 51.22).

   (d) This is in reference to the _____
_____, submitted pursuant to
Section 5 of the Voting Rights Act of 1965, as amended. Your
submission was completed on _____. In accordance
with your request expedited consideration has been given this

submission pursuant to the procedural guidelines for the administration of Section 5 (28 C.F.R. Section 51.22).

2. (a) The Attorney General does not interpose any objection to the change in question. However, we feel a responsibility to point out that Section 5 of the Voting Rights Act expressly provides that the failure of the Attorney General to object does not bar any subsequent judicial action to enjoin the enforcement of such change.

   (b) The Attorney General does not interpose any objections to the changes in question. However, we feel a responsibility to point out that Section 5 of the Voting Rights Act expressly provides that the failure of the Attorney General to object does not bar any subsequent judicial action to enjoin the enforcement of such changes.

3. (a) The Attorney General does not interpose any objection to the change in question. However, we feel a responsibility to point out that Section 5 of the Voting Rights Act expressly provides that the failure of the Attorney General to object does not bar any subsequent judicial action to enjoin the enforcement of such change. We should further point out that the Attorney General has no authority to waive the 60-day period for consiering a submission and, as our guidelines indicate (see 28 C.F.R. Section 51.22), we may re-examine our position on your submission should we receive additional information concerning the change in voting procedure prior to the expiration of the 60-day period. Should such information warrant a change in the Attorney General's determination, you will be so advised.

(b) The Attorney General does not interpose any objections to the changes in question. However, we feel a responsibility to point out that Section 5 of the Voting Rights Act expressly provides that the failure of the Attorney General to object does not bar any subsequent judicial action to enjoin the enforcement of such changes. We should further point out that the Attorney General has no authority to waive the 60-day period for considering a submission and, as our guidelines indicate (see 28 C.F.R. Section 51.22), we may re-examine our position on your submission should we receive additional information concerning the changes in voting procedure prior to the expiration of the 60-day period. Should such information warrant a change in the Attorney General's determination, you will be so advised.

4. (a) After a preliminary examination of the initial submission, this Department has determined that the information sent is insufficient to enable the Attorney General to determine that the proposed change does not have the purpose and will not have the effect of abridging the right to vote on account of race.

   (b) After a preliminary examination of the initial submission, this Department has determined that the information sent is insufficient to enable the Attorney General to determine that the proposed changes do not have the purpose and will not have the effect of abridging the right to vote on account of race.

5. In order to aid us in evaluating the submission we would appreciate your providing us with the following information:

6. (a) As you know the Attorney General has 60 days in which to

    consider a submission pursuant to Section 5. This 60 day

    period will commence when this Department receives the infor-

    mation necessary to evaluate properly the change proposed

    in your submission.

  (b) As you know the Attorney General has 60 days in which to

    consider a submission pursuant to Section 5. This 60 day

    period will commence when this Department receives the infor-

    mation necessary to evaluate properly the changes proposed

    in your submission.

7. If you have any questions concerning the matters discussed in this

    letter or if we can aid you in any way to obtain the additional

    information we have requested, please do not hesitate to call

    _____

    of my staff, who has been assigned to handle this submission.

    Please refer to File _____ in any

    written response to this letter so that your correspondence will

    be properly channeled.

8. For your information, I am enclosing copies of the guidelines cited

    above. Please refer to File _____ in any

    future correspondence on this matter so that your correspondence

    will be properly channeled.

9. As set forth in the procedural guidelines for the administration of

    Section 5, 28 C.F.R. 51.7, changes which are not finally enacted or

    capable of administration are not ripe for review by the Attorney

    General.

10. We wish to further point out that the only changes formally sub-

    mitted to the Attorney General are the _____

_____,

and our determination is limited to those changes. The state acts
which were included in your submission were only evaluated as
supporting materials since the proper submitting authority for
these acts would be the chief legal officer or other appropriate
official of the state (see 28 C.F.R. 51.8).

11. Although we noted your request for expedited consideration, we were
unable to comply.

Appendix G
Revision of Procedures for the Administration of Section Five, *Federal Register*, January 1981

DEPARTMENT OF JUSTICE

Office of the Attorney General

28 CFR Part 51

Procedures for the Administration of Section 5 of the Voting Rights Act of 1965; Revision of Procedures

AGENCY: Department of Justice.

ACTION: Final rule.

SUMMARY: Procedures with respect to the administration of Section 5 of the Voting Rights Act of 1965, as amended, the "preclearance" requirement of the Voting Rights Act, were established in 1971. 36 FR 18186 (Sept. 10, 1971), 28 CFR Part 51. As a result of experience under these Procedures, changes mandated by the 1975 Amendments to the Voting Rights Act, and interpretations of Section 5 contained in judicial decisions,

it was decided that revisions were required. Proposed revised Procedures were published for comments on March 21, 1980 (45 FR 18890).

EFFECTIVE DATE: January 5, 1981.

FOR FURTHER INFORMATION CONTACT: David H. Hunter, Attorney, Voting Section, Civil Rights Division, Department of Justice, Washington, D.C. 20530, (202) 724–7189.

SUPPLEMENTARY INFORMATION: In response to the March 21, 1980 request, 22 comments were received, including 1 from a Federal agency, 7 from representatives of State governments, 6 from representatives of local governments, 6 from private organizations, 1 from a political science professor, and 1 from a private citizen. (These comments are available for inspection at the Department of Justice.) All comments have been studied carefully, and a number of changes have been made in the Procedures as a result of the comments.

The discussion that follows focuses first on a number of general issues raised by the comments and second on a number of specific topics that were the subject of comments.

Scope. A number of commenters were concerned with issues outside the scope of the Procedures, for example, procedures and substantive standards required by statute, the legal consequences of the absence of preclearance, the Department's litigation policy, the Department's policy under the Freedom of Information Act (for which see 28 CFR 16.9), and the interests of particular jurisdictions.

Formality. To satisfy some commenters would require an increase in the formality of the preclearance process. They advocate, for example, requiring a limitation on telephone communication between Department personnel and submitting authorities, the inclusion of interested individuals and groups in any informal meetings held with submitting authorities, the preparation of transcripts of conferences held under § 51.46, adherence to the rules of evidence in the information gathering process, and increased notice requirements. Because submission of changes to the Attorney General was designed to be an expeditious alternative to declaratory judgement actions brought in the U.S. District Court for the District of Columbia, we believe the level of formality suggested is not appropriate.

Exercise of discretion. Some commenters sought assurance that the Attorney General would not abuse his discretion. Concern was expressed, for example, with respect to what would

Revision of Procedure for Section Five   265

Federal Register / Vol. 46. No. 2 / Monday. January 5. 1981 / Rules and Regulations   871

constitute "good cause" justifying expedited consideration by the Attorney General (§ 51.12) or with respect to the possibility of the Attorney General's issuance of an unjustified request for additional information (under § 51.35) to extend the 60-day period. Although written procedures can establish standards. they cannot by themselves guarantee reasonableness. To some exter. however. safeguards or alternatives do exist. For instance. submitting authorities always have the option of an action for a declaratory judgment (§ 51.1). On the other hand. interested individuals and groups are given the opportunity to participate in the preclearance process by the various notice requirements provided (see "Role of third parties" below) and, although a decision by the Attorney General not to object is not subject to judicial review (§ 51.46), independent actions otherwise available are preserved by the statute.

Misinterpretation. Misinterpretation of the intent of the proposed Procedures may be evidence of a lack of clarity. Where a commenter has failed to discern the intended meaning, we have given close scrutiny to whether that meaning could be more effectively communicated.

Some commenters misinterpreted the Procedures by reading one section in isolation from the remainder or by overlooking the section that addressed a particular issue. For example. one commenter believed that the Attorney General would not consider a change that must be adopted by referendum until after the referendum is held; this commenter failed to note that § 51.20 excepts from the finality requirement measures subject to a referendum requirement.

Role of third parties. Providing an opportunity for interested persons to express their views with respect to a submitted change is an important part of our preclearance procedures. A number of sections have been revised to indicate more clearly the practice of the Attorney General in this regard (see §§ 51.31. 51.35. 51.43. 51.44. 51.45 and 51.47). To summarize. the submitting authority is requested to provide names of minority contacts (§ 51.28(f)) and evidence of publicity and public participation (51.28(e)) and may be requested to publicize a reconsideration request (§ 51.44(c)). and the Attorney General may publicize a submission in some circumstances (§ 51.36(b)). Persons who have commented on a submission or who have requested notification with respect to action taken on a specific submission are sent copies of letters requesting further information

(§ 51.35(b)). letters of no objection (§ 51.40(c)). letters of objection (§ 51.43(f)). and letters following reconsiderations of objections (§ 51.47(d)). Such persons are also notified of reconsideration requests (§ 51.44(c)). reconsiderations at the instance of the Attorney General (§ 51.45(b)). and requests for conferences (§ 51.46(c)). Interested individuals and groups registered under § 51.30 are given notice of submissions (§ 51.31). requests for expedited consideration (§ 51.32(c)). additional information requests and receipts of additional information (§ 51.35(d)). objections (§ 51.43(e)). reconsiderations of objections (§§ 51.44(c) and 51.45(b)). and decisions after reconsideration (§ 51.47(e)). The 1971 Procedures had specified that "prompt" notice of submissions be given to registrants (§ 51.18); this was changed in the proposed Procedures (§ 51.31) to "regular" notice. In response to one comment, "weekly" notice. which has been the normal practice. is now specified.

One commenter objected to the maintenance of a registry of interested individuals and groups. Other commenters believe that the present notice system is inadequate. We believe the notice system as revised and described in the Procedures is both necessary and sufficient for the efficient and fair administration of the preclearance program.

Delegation of authority. §§ 51.2(b), 51.3. Two commenters, both representing States, expressed reservations with respect to the delegation of authority from the Attorney General to the Assistant Attorney General, Civil Rights Division. and opposed any delegation below the level of the Assistant Attorney General. As a practical matter, given the volume of Section 5 submissions. such delegation is unavoidable. It should be noted, however. that the Assistant Attorney General is the final decisionmaker when a determination adverse to a submitting authority is made.

Political parties, § 51.7. In response to one query, this section and § 51.21 have been revised to make it clear that a political party can make a submission on its own behalf.

Further clarification of what changes by political parties are subject to Section 5 has not been attempted. § 51.7 delineates in a general way which "political party" changes are covered; where there is uncertainty with respect to the applicability of Section 5. determinations should be made on a case-by-case basis.

Computation of time. § 51.8. Two commenters questioned the clarity and propriety of the method of determining when 60 days have elapsed. The method employed is identical to that of Rule 6(a) of the Federal Rules of Civil Procedure.

It was suggested that the 60-day period commence with the date of mailing of the submission rather than the date of receipt by the Attorney General. or that the date of the Attorney General's response be the date of receipt by the submitting authority rather than the date of mailing by the Attorney General. Section 5, however, provides for a 60-day period for review by the Attorney General, and it is proper for the Procedures to allow a full 60 days for review by the Attorney General. This would not be the case if delivery time for the submission and delivery time for the decision were counted in the 60-day period. In our view, the full period is necessary for proper administration. See also § 51.32.

Examples of changes. § 51.12. One commenter objected to including. as an example of a change cover by Section 5. a change with respect to vote-counting procedures. Such changes, however, are covered by Section 5. See *Allen v. State Board of Elections,* 393 U.S. 544, 563–68 (1969). Moreover, the submission requirement does not operate to prevent State and local governments from implementing voting changes which they decide are desirable.

A new subsection k has been added. based on experience since *Dougherty County, Board of Education v. White,* 439 U.S. 32 (1978). to clarify that governmental regulation of employee political activity is covered by Section 5. *Recurrent practices, enabling legislation, and procedural changes,* §§ 51.13, 51.14, 51.15. These sections constitute an attempt to clarify what constitutes a change. when a change has occurred. and what the consequences of preclearance of a change are. It is hoped that § 51.13 will result in the reduction of submissions made unnecessarily. For example, a county which always conducts voter registration at extra locations prior to elections does not have to make a submission prior to each election; a submission would be required only when the practice is first instituted or is changed. Sections 51.14 and 51.15 do not require that local implementation of a precleared State requirement of general. noncontingent application be precleared. For example, were a State to lower its voting age from 18 to 17, only one submission. by the State. would be required (See also § 51.21) On the other hand. if a State were to pass legislation making a 17-

year voting age a matter of local option, the preclearance of exercise of the option would be required (§ 51.14).

Court-ordered changes, § 51.16. Requested clarification of the exemption, from the preclearance requirement, of changes ordered by Federal courts has not ~~~ een attempted. This section is design, nly to alert affected jurisdictions and the p ıblic to the existence of this exemption. Its exact scope can only be determined through the application of the developing case law in this area to the particular situation in question. See *Sanchez* v. *McDaniel,* 615 F. 2d 1023 (5th Cir. 1980), application for stay pending consideration of petition for certiorari granted, ―― U.S. ―― (Aug. 14, 1980) (Powell, Circuit Justice).

The issue of the status of changes resulting from orders of State courts is not addressed in the Procedures. The reference in § 51.20 to approval by State courts is to the system in some States by which courts have an administrative role in the approval of some voting changes.

Premature Submissions, § 51.20. This section has been expanded to conform to present practice under which we consider unripe for review proposed changes which are based upon or are otherwise directly related to other voting changes which have not been precleared.

Contents of submissions, §§ 51.24, 51.25, 51.26. A number of commenters complained of the burden imposed on jurisdictions by these sections; some commenters sought additional clarity. The specific requests for information contained in §§ 51.25 and 51.26 should be read in conjunction with the general provisions of § 51.24(c). See especially § 51.24(c) and (e). Providing the information requested should usually not be burdensome for the submitting authority but will result in more prompt and efficient handling of submissions, fewer requests under § 51.35, and fewer objections. For example, in many instances, "the anticipated effect of the change on members of racial or language minority groups" (§ 51.25(m)) could be provided by a brief statement. Also, in our view, identifying minority group contacts (§ 51.26(f)) does not place an undue burden on the submitting authority. Moreover, we do not expect jurisdictions with insignificant minority populations routinely to provide the names of minority contacts.

Because legal descriptions are generally integral parts of acts or ordinances, excluding them from a submission will frequently be a greater inconvenience than including them; accordingly, the exception for legal descriptions has been dropped from § 51.25(a). Revisions to increase clarity and specificity have been made in § 51.26.

Obtaining information. § 51.35(c). One commenter noted that we did not specify the event that triggers the beginning of the 60-day period when information necessary to complete a submission is obtained from a source other than the submitting authority. § 51.35 has been revised to indicate that the 60-day period begins on the date on which the Attorney General sends notification to the submitting authority of the receipt of the information.

. Failure to complete submission, § 51.38. Two commenters were critical of the discretion allowed by § 51.38. That section provides that, if requested additional information is not received within 60 days, "the Attorney General, absent extenuating circumstances and consistent with the burden of proof under Section 5 * * * may object to the change * * *." One commenter advocated the substitution of "shall" for "may", explaining that in order to postpone an adverse determination, political subdivisions will deliberately fail to provide additional information requested by the Department of Justice. To the extent that such a problem may exist, we believe that the practice described in § 51.38 provides a sufficient remedy. Ordinarily, the schedule by which requested information is provided is of greater interest to the submitting authority than to the Attorney General.

Burden of proof. § 51.39(e). One commenter opposed placing the burden of proof on the submitting authority. In our view, the burden of proof described in § 51.39(e) is consistent with and required by the scheme of Section 5. See *Georgia* v. *United States,* 411 U.S. 526, 536–39 (1973); *South Carolina* v. *Katzenbach,* 383 U.S. 301, 335 (1966); see also *Evers* v. *State Board of Election Commissioners,* 327 F. Supp. 640 (S.D. Miss. 1971), appeal dismissed 405 U.S. 1001 (1972). *No objection, §§ 51.40, 51.42, 51.48.* Concern with respect to the finality of a decision not to interpose an objection was expressed by one commenter. However, Section 5 itself states: "Neither an affirmative indication by the Attorney General that no objection will be made, nor the Attorney General's failure to object, nor a declaratory judgment entered under this section shall bar a subsequent action to enjoin enforcement of such qualification, prerequisite, standard, practice, or procedure." It is the practice of the Attorney General, reflected in § 51.40, to notify submitting authorities of this provision. The "subsequent action" referred to could not be under Section 5 but would have to have some other legal basis and could not constitute judicial review of the action of the Attorney General (see § 51.48). Accordingly, the Attorney General's reservation of the right to reexamine within the 60-day period a decision not to object (§ 51.42) is necessary if the Attorney General is to continue the practice of accommodating jurisdictions by making decisions as early as possible within the 60-day period.

Failure to respond, § 51.41. One commenter asserted that there would be insufficient procedural safeguards if preclearance was accomplished by the failure of the Attorney General to respond within the 60-day period. As § 51.41 was intended to make clear, it is the practice of the Attorney General to respond within the 60-day period. This section was added to clarify the rare occasions when, through the failure of administrative mechanisms, no response is made. Another commenter considered the provisos contained in the section inappropriate. The first proviso, that the submission be properly addressed, is necessary to assure that the submission can be routed to the proper unit within the Department of Justice. The second proviso, that response on the merits be appropriate, only makes clear that, if Section 5 does not apply (for one of the reasons listed in § 51.33), no preclearance is possible. In response to concern expressed by a number of commenters, § 51.41 has been changed to indicate explicitly (what was implicit in § 51.6(c)) that actions of the Attorney General under Section 5 are in writing.

Objections and Reconsiderations, §§ 51.43, 51.44, 51.45, 51.46, 51.47. The sections relating to notification of the decision to interpose an objection and the procedures for the reconsideration of objections have been reorganized and renumbered, without substantive change, to improve the clarity of presentation.

Accordingly, 28 CFR Part 51 is revised to read as set forth below.

Dated: December 18, 1980.

Benjamin R. Civiletti,
Attorney General.

PART 51—PROCEDURES FOR THE ADMINISTRATION OF SECTION 5 OF THE VOTING RIGHTS ACT OF 1965, AS AMENDED

Subpart A—General Provisions

Sec.
51.1   Purpose.
51.2   Definitions.
51.3   Delegation of authority.

Revision of Procedure for Section Five   267

Federal Register / Vol. 46, No. 2 / Monday. January 5. 1981 / Rules and Regulations   873

Authority: The provisions of this Part 51
are issued under 5 U.S.C. 301; 28 U.S.C. 509,
510; and 42 U.S.C. 1973c.

Subpart A—General Provisions

§ 51.1 Purpose.

Section 5 of the Voting Rights Act of
1965. as amended, 42 U.S.C. 1973c,
prohibits the enforcement in any
jurisdiction covered by Section 4(b) of
the Act, 42 U.S.C. 1973(b), of any voting
qualification or prerequisite to voting, or
standard. practice, or procedure with
respect to voting different from that in
force or effect on the date used to
determine coverage, until either (1) a
declaratory judgment is obtained from
the U.S. District Court for the District of
Columbia that such qualification,
prerequisite, standard, practice, or
procedure does not have the purpose
and will not have the effect of denying
or abridging the right to vote on account
of race, color, or membership in a
language minority group, or (2) it has
been submitted to the Attorney General
and the Attorney General has
interposed no objection within a 60-day
period following submission. In order to
make clear the responsibilities of the
Attorney General under Section 5 and
the interpretation of the Attorney
General of the responsibility imposed on
others under this section, the procedures
in this part have been established to
govern the administration of Section 5.

§ 51.2 Definitions.

As used in this part—
(a) "Act" means the Voting Rights Act
of 1965, 79 Stat. 437, as amended by the
Civil Rights Act of 1968, 82 Stat. 73, the
Voting Rights Act Amendments of 1970,
84 Stat. 314, and the Voting Rights Act
Amendments of 1975, 89 Stat. 400. 42
U.S.C. 1973 *et seq.* Section numbers,
such as "Section 14(c)(3)," refer to
sections of the Act.
(b) "Attorney General" means the
Attorney General of the United States or
the delegate of the Attorney General.
(c) "Vote" and "voting" are used, as
defined in the Act, to include "all action
necessary to make a vote effective in
any primary, special, or general election,
including but not limited to, registration,
listing pursuant to this Act, or other
action required by law prerequisite to
voting, casting a ballot, and having such

ballot counted properly and included in
the appropriate totals of votes cast with
respect to candidates for public or party
office and propositions for which votes
are received in an election." Section
14(c)(1).
(d) "Change affecting voting" means
any voting qualification, prerequisite to
voting, or standard, practice, or
procedure with respect to voting
different from that in force or effect on
the date used to determine coverage
under Section 4(b) and includes, *inter.
alia,* the examples given in § 51.12.
(e) "Political subdivision" is used, as
defined in the Act, to refer to " * * *
any county or parish, except that where
registration for voting is not conducted
under the supervision of a county or
parish, the term shall include any other
subdivision of a State which conducts
registration for voting." Section 14(c)(2).
(f) "Covered jurisdiction" is used to
refer to a State, where the determination
referred to in § 51.4 has been made on a
statewide basis, and to a political
subdivision, where the determination
has not been made on a statewide basis.
(g) "Preclearance" is used to refer to
the obtaining of the declaratory
judgment described in Section 5 or to
the failure of the Attorney General to
interpose an objection pursuant to
Section 5.
(h) "Submission" is used to refer to
the written presentation to the Attorney
General by an appropriate official of
any change affecting voting.
(i) "Submitting authority" means the
jurisdiction on whose behalf a
submission is made.
(j) "Language minority" or "language
minority group" is used, as defined in
the Act, to refer to persons who are
American Indian, Asian American,
Alaskan Natives, or of Spanish heritage.
Section 14(c)(3). See 28 CFR Part 55,
Interpretative Guidelines:
Implementation of the Provisions of the
Voting Rights Act Regarding Language
Minority Groups.

§ 51.3 Delegation of authority.

The responsibility and authority for
determinations under Section 5 have
been delegated by the Attorney General
to the Assistant Attorney General, Civil
Rights Division. With the exception of
objections and decisions following the
reconsideration of objections, the Chief
of the Voting Section is authorized to act
on behalf of the Assistant Attorney
General.

§ 51.4 Date used to determine coverage;
list of covered jurisdictions.

(a) The requirement of Section 5 takes
effect upon publication in the Federal
Register of the requisite determinations

of the Director of the Census and the Attorney General under Section 4(b). These determinations are not reviewable in any court. Section 4(b).

(b) Section 5 requires the preclearance of changes affecting voting made since the date used for the determination of coverage. For each covered jurisdiction that date is one of the following: November 1, 1964; November 1, 1968; or November 1, 1972. A list of covered jurisdictions, together with the applicable date used to determine coverage, is contained in the appendix to this part. Any additional determinations of coverage will be published in the Federal Register.

§ 51.5   Termination of coverage.

A covered jurisdiction may terminate the application of Section 5 by obtaining the declaratory judgment described in Section 4(a) of the Act.

§ 51.6   Political subunits.

All political subunits within a covered jurisdiction (e.g., counties, cities, school districts) are subject to the requirement of Section 5.

§ 51.7   Political parties.

Certain activities of political parties are subject to the preclearance requirement of Section 5. A change affecting voting effected by a political party is subject to the preclearance requirement (1) if the change relates to a public electoral function of the party and (2) if the party is acting under authority explicitly or implicitly granted by a covered jurisdiction or political subunit subject to the preclearance requirement of Section 5. For example, changes with respect to the recruitment of party members, the conduct of political campaigns, and the drafting of party platforms are not subject to the preclearance requirement. Changes with respect to the conduct of primary elections at which party nominees, delegates to party conventions, or party officials are chosen are subject to the preclearance requirement of Section 5. Where appropriate the term "jurisdiction" (but not "covered jurisdiction") includes political parties.

§ 51.8   Computation of time.

(a) The Attorney General shall have 60 days in which to interpose an objection to a submitted change affecting voting.

(b) Except as specified in §§ 51.35, 51.37, and 51.41 the 60-day period shall commence upon receipt by the Department of Justice of a submission.

(c) The 60-day period shall mean 60 calendar days, with the day of receipt of the submission not counted. If the final

day of the period should fall on a Saturday, Sunday, any day designated as a holiday by the President or Congress of the United States, or any other day that is not a day of regular business for the Department of Justice, the Attorney General shall have until the close of the next full business day in which to interpose an objection. The date of the Attorney General's response shall be the date on which it is mailed to the submitting authority.

§ 51.9   Requirement of action for declaratory judgment or submission to the Attorney General.

Section 5 requires that, prior to enforcement of any change affecting voting, the jurisdiction that has enacted or seeks to administer the change must either (1) obtain a judicial determination from the U.S. District Court for the District of Columbia that denial or abridgment of the right to vote on account of race, color, or membership in a language minority group is not the purpose and will not be the effect of the change or (2) make to the Attorney General a proper submission of the change to which no objection is interposed. It is unlawful to enforce a change affecting voting without obtaining preclearance under Section 5. The obligation to obtain such preclearance is not relieved by unlawful enforcement.

§ 51.10   Right to bring suit.

Submission to the Attorney General does not affect the right of the submitting authority to bring an action in the U.S. District Court for the District of Columbia for a declaratory judgment that the change affecting voting does not have the prohibited discriminatory purpose or effect.

§ 51.11   Scope of requirement.

Any change affecting voting, even though it appears to be minor or indirect, even though it ostensibly expands voting rights, or even though it is designed to remove the elements that caused objection by the Attorney General to a prior submitted change, must meet the Section 5 preclearance requirement.

§ 51.12   Examples of changes.

Changes affecting voting include, but are not limited to, the following examples:

(a) Any change in qualifications or eligibility for voting.

(b) Any change concerning registration, balloting, and the counting of votes and any change concerning publicity for or assistance in registration or voting.

(c) Any change with respect to the use of a language other than English in any aspect of the electoral process.

(d) Any change in the boundaries of voting precincts or in the location of polling places.

(e) Any change in the constituency of an official or the boundaries of a voting unit (e.g., through redistricting, annexation, deannexation, incorporation, reapportionment, changing to at-large elections from district elections, or changing to district elections from at-large elections).

(f) Any change in the method of determining the outcome of an election (e.g., by requiring a majority vote for election or the use of a designated post or place system).

(g) Any change affecting the eligibility of persons to become or remain candidates, to obtain a position on the ballot in primary or general elections, or to become or remain holders of elective offices.

(h) Any change in the eligibility and qualification procedures for independent candidates.

(i) Any change in the term of an elective office or an elected official or in the offices that are elective (e.g., by shortening the term of an office, changing from election to appointment or staggering the terms of offices).

(j) Any change affecting the necessity of or methods for offering issues and propositions for approval by referendum.

(k) Any change affecting the right or ability of persons to participate in political campaigns which is effected by a jurisdiction subject to the requirement of Section 5.

§ 51.13   Recurrent practices.

Where a jurisdiction implements a practice or procedure periodically or upon certain established contingencies, a change occurs (1) the first time such a practice or procedure is implemented by the jurisdiction, (2) when the manner in which such a practice or procedure is implemented by the jurisdiction is changed, or (3) when the rules for determining when such a practice or procedure will be implemented are changed. The failure of the Attorney General to object to a recurrent practice or procedure constitutes preclearance of the future use of the practice or procedure if its recurrent nature is clearly stated or described in the submission or is expressly recognized in the final response of the Attorney General on the merits of the submission.

§ 51.14 Enabling legislation and contingent or nonuniform requirements.

(a) The failure of the Attorney General to interpose an objection to legislation (1) that enables or permits political subunits to institute a voting change or (2) that requires or enables political subunits to institute a voting change upon some future event or if they satisfy certain criteria does not exempt the political subunit itself from the requirement to obtain preclearance when it seeks or is required to institute the change in question, unless implementation by the subunit is explicitly included and described in the submission of such parent legislation.

(b) Such legislation includes for example, (1) legislation authorizing counties, cities, or school districts to institute any of the changes described in § 51.12, (2) legislation requiring a political subunit that chooses a certain form of government to follow specified election procedures, (3) legislation requiring or authorizing political subunits of a certain size or a certain location to institute specified changes, (4) legislation requiring a political subunit to follow certain practices or procedures unless the subunit's charter or ordinances specify to the contrary.

§ 51.15 Distinction between changes in procedure and changes in substance.

The failure of the Attorney General to interpose an objection to a procedure for instituting a change affecting voting does not exempt the substantive change from the preclearance requirement. For example, if the procedure for the approval of an annexation is changed from city council approval to approval in a referendum, the preclearance of the new procedure does not exempt an annexation accomplished under the new procedure from the preclearance requirement.

§ 51.16 Court-ordered changes.

Changes affecting voting that are specifically or   ed by a Federal court as a result of the court's equitable jurisdiction over an adversary proceeding are not subject to the preclearance requirement of Section 5. However, subsequent changes necessitated by the court order but decided upon by the jurisdiction are subject to the preclearance requirement. For example, although a court-ordered districting plan may not be subject to the preclearance requirement, changes in voting precincts and polling places made necessary by the new plan remain subject to Section 5.

§ 51.17 Request for notification concerning voting litigation.

A jurisdiction subject to the preclearance requirement of Section 5 that becomes involved in any litigation concerning voting is requested promptly to notify the Assistant Attorney General, Civil Rights Division, Department of Justice, Washington, D.C. 20530. Such notification will not be considered a submission under Section 5.

Subpart B—Procedures for Submission to the Attorney General

§ 51.18 Form of submissions.

Submissions may be made in letter or any other written form.

§ 51.19 Time of submissions.

Changes affecting voting should be submitted as soon as possible after they become final.

§ 51.20 Premature submissions.

The Attorney General will not consider on the merits (a) any proposal for a change affecting voting submitted prior to final enactment or administrative decision or (b) any proposed change which has a direct bearing on another change affecting voting which has not received Section 5 preclearance. However, with respect to a change for which approval by referendum, a State court or a Federal agency is required, the Attorney General may make a determination concerning the change prior to such approval if the change is not subject to alteration in the final approving action and if all other action necessary for approval has been taken.

§ 51.21 Party and jurisdiction responsible for making submissions.

(a) Changes affecting voting shall be submitted by the chief legal officer or other appropriate official of the submitting authority or by any other authorized person on behalf of the submitting authority. When one or more counties or other political subunits within a State will be affected, the State may make a submission on their behalf. Where a State is covered as a whole, State legislation (except legislation of local applicability) or other changes undertaken or required by the State shall be submitted by the State.

(b) A change effected by a political party (see § 51.7) may be submitted by an appropriate official of the political party.

§ 51.22 Address for submissions.

Changes affecting voting shall be mailed or delivered to the Assistant Attorney General, Civil Rights Division, Department of Justice, Washington, D.C. 20530. The envelope and first page of the submission shall be clearly marked: Submission under Section 5 of the Voting Rights Act.

§ 51.23 Withdrawal of submissions.

If while a submission is pending the submitted change is repealed, altered, or declared invalid or otherwise becomes unenforceable, the jurisdiction may withdraw the submission. In other circumstances, a jurisdiction may withdraw a submission only if it shows good cause for such withdrawal.

Subpart C—Contents of Submissions

§ 51.24 General.

(a) The source of any information contained in a submission should be identified.

(b) Where an estimate is provided in lieu of more reliable statistics, the submission should identify the name, position, and qualifications of the person responsible for the estimate and should briefly describe the basis for the estimate.

(c) Submissions should be no longer than is necessary for the presentation of the appropriate information and materials.

(d) A submitting authority that desires the Attorney General to consider any information supplied as part of an earlier submission may incorporate such information by reference by stating the date and subject matter of the earlier submission and identifying the relevant information.

(e) Where information requested by this subpart is relevant but not known or available, or is not applicable, the submission should so state.

§ 51.25 Required contents.

Each submission should contain the following information or documents to enable the Attorney General to make the required determination pursuant to Section 5 with respect to the submitted change affecting voting:

(a) A copy of any ordinance, enactment, order or regulation embodying a change affecting voting.

(b) If the change affecting voting is not readily apparent on the face of the document provided under paragraph (a) or is not embodied in a document, a clear statement of the change explaining the difference between the submitted change and the prior law or practice, or explanatory materials adequate to disclose to the Attorney General the difference between the prior and proposed situation with respect to voting.

(c) The name, title, address, and telephone number of the person making the submission.

(d) The name of the submitting authority and the name of the jurisdiction responsible for the change, if different.

(e) If the submission is not from a State or county, the name of the county and State in which the submitting authority is located.

(f) Identification of the person or body responsible for making the change and the mode of decision (e.g., act of State legislature, ordinance of city council, administrative decision by registrar).

(g) A statement identifying the statutory or other authority under which the jurisdiction undertakes the change and a description of the procedures the jurisdiction was required to follow in deciding to undertake the change.

(h) The date of adoption of the change affecting voting.

(i) The date on which the change is to take effect.

(j) A statement that the change has not yet been enforced or administered, or an explanation of wl such a statement cannot be m

(k) Where the change will affect less than the entire jurisdiction, an explanation of the scope of the change.

(l) A statement of the reasons for the change.

(m) A statement of the anticipated effect of the change on members of racial or language minority groups.

(n) A statement identifying any past or pending litigation concerning the change or related voting practices.

(o) A statement that the prior practice has been precleared (with the date) or is not subject to the preclearance requirement and a statement that the procedure for the adoption of the change has been precleared (with the date) or is not subject to the preclearance requirement, or an explanation of why such statements cannot be made.

(p) Other information that the Attorney General determines is required for an evaluation of the purpose or effect of the change. Such information may include items listed in § 51.26 and is most likely to be needed with respect to redistricting, annexations, and other complex changes. In the interest of time such information should be furnished with the initial submission relating to voting changes of this type. When such information is required, but not provided, the Attorney General shall notify the submitting authority in the manner provided in § 51.35.

§ 51.26 Supplemental contents.

Review by the Attorney General will be facilitated if the following

information, where pertinent, is provided in addition to that required by § 51.25.

(a) *Demographic information.* (1) Total and voting age population of the affected area before and after the change by race and language group. If such information is contained in publications of the U.S. Bureau of the Census, reference to the appropriate volume and table is sufficient.

(2) The number of registered voters for the affected area by voting precinct before and after the change, by race and language group.

(3) Any estimates of population, by race and language group, made in connection with the adoption of the change.

(b) *Maps.* Where any change is made that revises the constituency that elects any office or affects the boundaries of any geographic unit or units defined or employed for voting purposes (e.g., redistricting, annexation, change from district to at-large elections) or that changes voting precinct boundaries, polling place locations, or voter registration sites, maps in duplicate of the area to be affected, containing the following information:

(1) The prior and new boundaries of the voting unit or units.

(2) The prior and new boundaries of voting precincts.

(3) The location of racial and language minority groups.

(4) Any natural boundaries or geographical features that influenced the selection of boundaries of the prior or new units.

(5) The location of prior and new polling places.

(6) The location of prior and new voter registration sites.

(c) *Election returns.* Where a change may affect the electoral influence of a racial or language minority group, returns of primary and general elections conducted by or in the jurisdiction, containing the following information:

(1) The name of each candidate.

(2) The race or language group of each candidate, if known.

(3) The position sought by each candidate.

(4) The number of votes received by each candidate, by voting precinct.

(5) The outcome of each contest.

(6) The number of registered voters, by race and language group, for each voting precinct for which election returns a furnished. Information with respect to elections held during the last ten years will normally be sufficient.

(d) *Language usage.* Where a change is made affecting the use of the language of a language minority group in the electoral process, information that will

enable the Attorney General to determine whether the change is consistent with the minority language requirements of the Act. The Attorney General's interpretation of the minority language requirements of the Act is contained in Interpretative Guidelines: Implementation of the Provisions of the Voting Rights Act Regarding Language Minority Groups, 28 CFR Part 55.

(e) *Publicity and participation.* For submissions involving controversial or potentially controversial changes, evidence of public notice, of the opportunity for the public to be heard, and of the opportunity for interested parties to participate in the decision to adopt the proposed change and an account of the extent to which such participation, especially by minority group members, in fact took place. Examples of materials demonstrating public notice or participation include:

(1) Copies of newspaper articles discussing the proposed change.

(2) Copies of public notices that describe the proposed change and invite public comment or participation in hearings or that announce submission to and invite comments for the consideration of the Attorney General and statements regarding where such public notices appeared (e.g., newspaper, radio, or television, posted in public buildings, sent to identified individuals or groups).

(3) Minutes or accounts of public hearings concerning the proposed change.

(4) Statements, speeches, and other public communications concerning the proposed change.

(5) Copies of comments from the general public.

(6) Excerpts from legislative journals containing discussion of a submitted enactment, or other materials revealing its legislative purpose.

(f) *Minority group contacts.* For submissions from jurisdictions having a significant minority population, the names, addresses, telephone numbers, and organizational affiliation (if any) of racial or language minority group members who can be expected to be familiar with the proposed change or who have been active in the political process.

Subpart D—Communications From Individuals and Groups

§ 51.27 Communications concerning voting changes.

Any individual or group may send to the Attorney General information concerning a change affecting voting in a jurisdiction to which Section 5 applies.

(a) Communications may be in the form of a letter stating the name, address, and telephone number of the individual or group, describing the alleged change affecting voting and setting forth evidence regarding whether the change has or does not have a discriminatory purpose or effect, or simply bringing to the attention of the Attorney General the fact that a voting change has occurred.

(b) The communications should be mailed to the Assistant Attorney General, Civil Rights Division, Department of Justice, Washington, D.C. 20530. The envelope and first page should be marked: Comment under Section 5 of the Voting Rights Act.

(c) Comments by individuals or groups concerning any change affecting voting may be sent at any time; however, individuals and groups are encouraged to comment as soon as they learn of the change.

(d) Department of Justice officials and employees shall comply with the request of any individual that his or her identity not be disclosed to any person outside the Department, to the extent permitted by the Freedom of Information Act, 5 U.S.C. 552. In addition, whenever it appears to the Attorney General that disclosure of the identity of an individual who provided information regarding a change affecting voting "would constitute a clearly unwarranted invasion of personal privacy" under 5 U.S.C. 552(b)(6), the identity of the individual shall not be disclosed to any person outside the Department.

(e) When an individual or group desires the Attorney General to consider information that was supplied in connection with an earlier submission, it is not necessary to resubmit the information but merely to identify the earlier submission and the relevant information.

§ 51.28 Action on communications from individuals or groups.

(a) If there has already been a submission received of the change affecting voting brought to the attention of the Attorney General by an individual or group, any evidence from the individual or group shall be considered along with the materials submitted and materials resulting from any investigation.

(b) If such a submission has not been received, the Attorney General shall advise the appropriate jurisdiction of the requirement of Section 5 with respect to the change in question.

§ 51.29 Communications concerning voting suits.

Individuals and groups are urged to notify the Assistant Attorney General, Civil Rights Division, of litigation concerning voting in jurisdictions subject to the requirement of Section 5.

§ 51.30 Establishment and maintenance of registry of interested individuals and groups.

The Attorney General shall establish and maintain a Registry of Interested Individuals and Groups, which shall contain the name and address of any individual or group that wishes to receive notice of Section 5 submissions. Information relating to this registry and to the requirements of the Privacy Act of 1974, 5 U.S.C. 552a *et seq.*, is contained in Justice/CRT–004, 43 FR 44676 (Sept. 28, 1978).

Subpart E—Processing of Submissions

§ 51.31 Notice to registrants concerning submissions.

Weekly notice of submissions that have been received will be given to the individuals and groups who have registered for this purpose under § 51.30.

§ 51.32 Expedited consideration.

(a) When a submitting authority is required under State law or local ordinance or otherwise finds it necessary to implement a change within the 60-day period following submission, it may request that the submission be given expedited consideration. The submission should explain why such consideration is needed and provide the date by which a determination is required.

(b) Jurisdictions should endeavor to plan for changes in advance so that expedited consideration will not be required and should not routinely request such consideration. When a submitting authority demonstrates good cause for expedited consideration the Attorney General will attempt to make a decision by the date requested. However, the Attorney General cannot guarantee that such consideration can be given.

(c) Notice of the request for expedited consideration will be given to interested parties registered under § 51.30.

§ 51.33 Disposition of inappropriate submissions.

The Attorney General will make no response on the merits with respect to an inappropriate submission but will notify the submitting authority of the inappropriateness of the submission. Such notification will be made as promptly as possible and no later than

the 60th day following receipt and will include an explanation of the inappropriateness of the submission. Inappropriate submissions include the submission of changes that do not affect voting (see, e.g., § 51.12), the submission of standards, practices, or procedures that have not been changed (see, e.g., §§ 51.4, 51.13), the submission of changes that affect voting but are not subject to the requirement of Section 5 (see, e.g., § 51.16), premature submissions (see § 51.20), and submissions by jurisdictions not subject to the requirement of Section 5 (see §§ 51.4, 51.5).

§ 51.34 Release of information concerning submissions.

The Attorney General shall have the discretion to call to the attention of the submitting authority or any interested individual or group information or comments related to a submission

§ 51.35 Obtaining information from the submitting authority.

(a) If a submission does not satisfy the requirements of § 51.25, the Attorney General shall request such further information as is necessary from the submitting authority and advise the submitting authority that the 60-day period will not commence until such information is received by the Department of Justice. The request shall be made as promptly as possible after receipt of the original inadequate submission and no later than the 60th day following its receipt.

(b) A copy of the request shall be sent to any party who has commented on the submission or has requested notice of the Attorney General's action thereon.

(c) If, after a request for further information is made pursuant to this section, the information requested becomes available to the Attorney General from a source other than the submitting authority, the Attorney General shall promptly notify the submitting authority, and the 60-day period will commence upon the date of such notification.

(d) Notice of the request for and receipt of further information will be given to interested parties registered under § 51.30.

§ 51.36 Obtaining information from others.

(a) The Attorney General may at any time request relevant information from governmental jurisdictions and from interested groups and individuals and may conduct any investigation or other inquiry that is deemed appropriate in making a determination.

(b) If a submission does not contain evidence of adequate notice to the

878   Federal Register / Vol. 46. No. 2 / Monday. January 5. 1981 / Rules and Regulations

public. and the Attorney General believes that such notice is essential to a determination, steps will be taken by the Attorney General to provide public notice sufficient to invite interested or affected persons to provide evidence as to the presence or absence of a discriminatory purpose or effect. The submitting authority shall be advised when any such steps are taken.

§ 51.37 Supplementary submissions.

When a submitting authority provides documents and information materially supplementing a submission (or a request for reconsideration of an objection) or. before the expiration of the 60-day period. makes a second submission such that the two submissions cannot be independently considered, the 60-day period for the original submission will be calculated from the receipt of the supplementary information or the second submission.

§ 51.38 Failure to complete submissions.

If after 60 days the submitting authority has not provided further information in response to a request made pursuant to § 51.35(a), the Attorney General, absent extenuating circumstances and consistent with the burden of proof under Section 5 described in § 51.39(e). may object to the change, giving notice as specified in § 51.43.

§ 51.39 Standards for determination by the Attorney General.

(a) Section 5 provides for submission to the Attorney General as an alternative to the seeking of a declaratory judgment from the U.S. District Court for the District of Columbia. Therefore. the Attorney General shall make the same determination that would be made by the court in an action for a declaratory judgment under Section 5: whether the submitted change has the purpose or will have the effect of denying or abridging the right to vote on account of race. color. or membership in a language minority group.

(b) Guided by the relevant judicial decisions, the Attorney General shall base a determination on a review of material presented by the submitting authority, relevant information provided by individuals or groups. and the results of any investigation conducted by the Department of Justice.

(c) If the Attorney General determines that a submitted change does not have the prohibited purpose or effect. no objection shall be interposed to the change.

(d) If the Attorney General determines that a submitted change has the

prohibited purpose or effect. and objection shall be interposed to the change.

(e) The burden of proof on a submitting authority when it submits a change to the Attorney General is the same as it would be if the change was the subject of a declaratory judgment action in the U.S. District Court for the District of Columbia. Therefore. if the evidence as to the purpose or effect of a change is conflicting and the Attorney General is unable to determine that the submitted change does not have the prohibited purpose or effect. an objection shall be interposed to the change.

§ 51.40 Notification of decision not to object.

(a) The Attorney General shall within the 60-day period allowed notify the submitting authority of a decision to interpose no objection to a submitted change affecting voting.

(b) The notification shall state that the failure of the Attorney General to object does not bar subsequent litigation to enjoin the enforcement of the change.

(c) A copy of the notification shall be sent to any party who has commented on the submission or has requested notice of the Attorney General's action thereon.

§ 51.41 Failure of the Attorney General to respond.

It is the practice and intention of the Attorney General to respond to each submission within the 60-day period. However. the failure of the Attorney General to make a written response within the 60-day period constitutes preclearance of the submitted change. provided the submission is addressed as specified in § 51.22 and is appropriate for a response on the merits as described in § 51.33.

§ 51.42 Reexamination of decision not to object.

After notification to the submitting authority of a decision to interpose no objection to a submitted change affecting voting has been given. the Attorney General may reexamine the submission if. prior to the expiration of the 60-day period. information indicating the possibility of the prohibited discriminatory purpose or effect is received. In this event. the Attorney General may interpose an objection provisionally and advise the submitting authority that examination of the change in light of the newly raised issues will continue and that a final decision will be rendered as soon as possible.

§ 51.43 Notification of decision to object.

(a) The Attorney General shall within the 60-day period allowed notify the submitting authority of a decision to interpose an objection. The reasons for the decision shall be stated.

(b) The submitting authority shall be advised that the Attorney General will reconsider an objection upon a request by the submitting authority.

(c) The submitting authority shall be advised further that notwithstanding the objection it may institute an action in the U.S. District Court for the District of Columbia for a declaratory judgment that the change objected to by the Attorney General does not have the prohibited discriminatory purpose or effect.

(d) A copy of the notification shall be sent to any party who has commented on the submission or has requested notice of the Attorney General's action thereon.

(e) Notice of the decision to interpose an objection will be given to interested parties registered under § 51.30.

§ 51.44 Request for reconsideration.

(a) The submitting authority may at any time request the Attorney General to reconsider an objection.

(b) Requests may be in letter or any other written form and should contain relevant information or legal argument.

(c) Notice of the request will be given to any party who commented on the submission or requested notice of the Attorney General's action thereon and to interested parties registered under § 51.30. In appropriate cases the Attorney General may request the submitting authority to give local public notice of the request.

§ 51.45 Reconsideration of objection at the insistance of the Attorney General.

(a) Where there appears to have been a substantial change in operative fact or relevant law. an objection may be reconsidered. if it is deemed appropriate. at the insistence of the Attorney General.

(b) Notice of such a decision to reconsider shall be given to the submitting authority, to any party who commented on the submission or requested notice of the Attorney General's action thereon. and to interested parties registered under § 51.30. and the Attorney General shall decide whether to withdraw or to continue the objection only after such persons have had a reasonable opportunity to comment.

§ 51.46 Conference.

(a) A submitting authority that has requested reconsideration of an objection pursuant to § 51.44 may request a conference to produce information or legal argument in support of reconsideration.

(b) Such a conference shall be held at a location determined by the Attorney General and shall be conducted in an informal manner.

(c) When a submitting authority requests such a conference, individuals or groups that commented on the change prior to the Attorney General's objection or that seek to participate in response to any notice of a request for reconsideration shall be notified and given the opportunity to confer.

(d) The Attorney General shall have the discretion to hold separate meetings to confer with the submitting authority and other interested groups or individuals.

(e) Such conferences will be open to the public or to the press only at the discretion of the Attorney General and with the agreement of the participating parties.

§ 51.47   Decision after reconsideration.

(a) The Attorney General shall within the 60-day period following the receipt of a reconsideration request or following notice given under § 51.45(b) notify the submitting authority of the decision to continue or withdraw the objection, provided that the Attorney General shall have at least 15 days following any conference that is held in which to decide. The reasons for the decision shall be stated.

(b) The objection shall be withdrawn if the Attorney General is satisfied that the change does not have the purpose and will not have the effect of discriminating on account of race, color, or membership in a language minority group.

(c) If the objection is not withdrawn, the submitting authority shall be advised that notwithstanding the objection it may institute an action in the U.S. District Court for the District of Columbia for a declaratory judgment that the change objected to by the Attorney General does not have the prohibited purpose or effect.

(d) A copy of the notification shall be sent to any party who has commented on the submission or reconsideration or has requested notice of the Attorney General's action thereon.

(e) Notice of the decision after reconsideration will be given to interested parties registered under § 51.30.

§ 51.48   Absence of judicial review.

The decision of the Attorney General not to object to a submitted change or to withdraw an objection is not reviewable. However, Section 5 states: "Neither an affirmative indication by the Attorney General that no objection will be made, nor the Attorney General's failure to object, nor a declaratory judgment entered under this section shall bar a subsequent action to enjoin enforcement of such qualification, prerequisite, standard, practice, or procedure."

§ 51.49   Records concerning submissions.

(a) Section 5 files: The Attorney General shall maintain a Section 5 file for each submission, containing the submission, related written materials, correspondence, memoranda, investigative reports, notations concerning conferences with the submitting authority or any interested individual or group, and copies of any letters from the Attorney General concerning the submission.

(b) Objection files: Brief summaries regarding each submission and the general findings of the Department of Justice investigation and decision concerning it will be prepared when a decision to interpose, continue, or withdraw an objection is made. Files of these summaries, arranged by jurisdiction and by the date upon which such decision is made, will be maintained.

(c) Computer file: Records of all submissions and of their dispositions by the Attorney General shall be electronically stored and periodically retrieved in the form of computer printouts.

(d) The contents of the above-described files shall be available for inspection and copying by the public during normal business hours at the Civil Rights Division, Department of Justice, Washington, D.C. Materials that are exempt from inspection under the Freedom of Information Act, 5 U.S.C. 552(b), may be withheld at the discretion of the Attorney General. Communications from individuals who have requested confidentiality or with respect to whom the Attorney General has determined that confidentiality is appropriate under § 51.27(d) shall be available only as provided by § 51.27(d). Applicable fees, if any, for the copying of the contents of these files are contained in the Department of Justice regulations implementing the Freedom of Information Act, 28 CFR 16.9.

Subpart F—Sanctions

§ 51.50   Enforcement by the Attorney General.

(a) The Attorney General is authorized to bring civil actions for appropriate relief against violations of the Act's provisions, including Section 5. See Section 12(d).

(b) Certain violations may be subject to criminal sanctions. See Sections 12(a) and (c).

§ 51.51   Enforcement by private parties.

Private parties have standing to enforce Section 5.

Subpart G—Petition To Change Procedures

§ 51.52   Who may petition.

Any jurisdiction or interested individual or group may petition to have these procedural guidelines amended.

§ 51.53   Form of petition.

A petition under this subpart may be made by informal letter and shall state the name, address, and telephone number of the petitioner, the change requested, and the reasons for the change.

§ 51.54   Disposition of petition.

The Attorney General shall promptly consider and dispose of a petition under this subpart and give notice of the disposition, accompanied by a simple statement of the reasons, to the petitioner.

Appendix—Jurisdictions Covered Under Section 4(b) of the Voting Rights Act, as Amended

The preclearance requirement of Section 5 of the Voting Rights Act, as amended, applies in the following jurisdictions. The date in parentheses is the date that was used to determine coverage for the jurisdiction it follows.

Alabama (statewide) (Nov. 1, 1964)
Alaska (statewide) (Nov. 1, 1972)
Arizona (statewide) (Nov. 1, 1972)
(The following Arizona counties were covered individually through the use of earlier dates.)

Apache County (Nov. 1, 1968)
Cochise County (Nov. 1, 1968)
Coconino County (Nov. 1, 1968)
Mohave County (Nov. 1, 1968)
Navajo County (Nov. 1, 1968)
Pima County (Nov. 1, 1968)
Pinal County (Nov. 1, 1968)
Santa Cruz County (Nov. 1, 1968)
Yuma County (Nov. 1, 1964)
California (the following counties only)
Kings County (Nov. 1, 1972)
Merced County (Nov. 1, 1972)
Monterey County (Nov. 1, 1968)
Yuba County (Nov. 1, 1968)
Colorado (the following county only)
El Paso (Nov. 1, 1972)
Connecticut (the following towns only)
Groton Town (Nov. 1, 1968)
Mansfield Town (Nov. 1, 1968)
Southbury Town (Nov. 1, 1968)
Florida (the following counties only)
Collier County (Nov. 1, 1972)
Hardee County (Nov. 1, 1972)
Hendry County (Nov. 1, 1972)

Hillsborough County (Nov. 1, 1972)
Monroe County (Nov. 1, 1972)
Georgia (statewide) (Nov. 1, 1964)
Hawaii (the following county only)
Honolulu County (Nov. 1, 1964)
Idaho (the following county only)
Elmore County (Nov. 1, 1968)
Louisiana (statewide) (Nov. 1, 1964)
Massachusetts (the following towns only)
Amherst Town (Nov. 1, 1968)
Ayer Town (Nov. 1, 1968)
Belchertown (Nov. 1, 1968)
Bourne Town (Nov. 1, 1968)
Harvard Town (Nov. 1, 1968)
Sandwich Town (Nov. 1, 1968)
Shirley Town (Nov. 1, 1968)
Sunderland Town (Nov. 1, 1968)
Wrentham Town (Nov. 1, 1968)
Michigan (the following townships only)
Buena Vista Township (Saginaw County)
(Nov. 1, 1972)
Clyde Township (Allegan County) (Nov. 1,
1972)
Mississippi (statewide) (Nov. 1, 1964)
New Hampshire (the following political
subdivisions only)
Antrim Town (Nov. 1, 1968)
Benton Town (Nov. 1, 1968)
Boscawen Town (Nov. 1, 1968)
Millsfield Township (Nov, 1, 1968)
Newington Town (Nov. 1, 1968)
Pinkhams Grant (Nov. 1, 1968)
Rindge Town (Nov. 1, 1968)
Stewartstown (Nov. 1, 1968)
Stratford Town (Nov. 1, 1968)
Unity Town (Nov. 1, 1968)
New York (the following counties only)
Bronx County (Nov. 1, 1968)
Kings County (Nov. 1, 1968)
New York County (Nov. 1, 1968)
North Carolina (the following counties only)
Anson County (Nov. 1, 1964)
Beaufort County (Nov. 1, 1964)
Bertie County (Nov. 1, 1964)
Bladen County (Nov. 1, 1964)
Camden County (Nov. 1, 1964)
Caswell County (Nov. 1, 1964)
Chowan County (Nov. 1, 1964)
Cleveland County (Nov. 1, 1964)
Craven County (Nov. 1, 1964)
Cumberland County (Nov. 1, 1964)
Edgecombe County (Nov. 1, 1964)
Franklin County (Nov. 1, 1964)
Gaston County (Nov. 1, 1964)
Gates County (Nov. 1, 1964)
Granville County (Nov. 1, 1964)
Greene County (Nov. 1, 1964)
Guilford County (Nov. 1, 1964)
Halifax County (Nov. 1, 1964)
Harnett County (Nov. 1, 1964)
Hertford County (Nov. 1, 1964)
Hoke County (Nov. 1, 1964)
Jackson County (Nov. 1, 1972)
Lee County (Nov. 1, 1964)
Lenoir County (Nov. 1, 1964)
Martin County (Nov. 1, 1964)
Nash County (Nov. 1, 1964)
Northampton County (Nov. 1, 1964)
Onslow County (Nov. 1, 1964)
Pasquotank County (Nov. 1, 1964)
Perquimans County (Nov. 1, 1964)
Person County (Nov. 1, 1964)
Pitt County (Nov. 1, 1964)
Robeson County (Nov. 1, 1964)
Rockingham County (Nov. 1, 1964)
Scotland County (Nov. 1, 1964)

Union County (Nov. 1, 1964)
Vance County (Nov. 1, 1964)
Washington County (Nov. 1, 1964)
Wayne County (Nov. 1, 1964)
Wilson County (Nov. 1, 1964)
South Carolina (statewide) (Nov. 1, 1964)
South Dakota (the following counties only)
Shannon County (Nov. 1, 1972)
Todd County (Nov. 1, 1972)
Texas (statewide) (Nov. 1, 1972)
Virginia (statewide) (Nov. 1, 1964)
Wyoming (the following county only)
Campbell County (Nov. 1, 1968)

[FR Doc. 81-123 Filed 1-2-81; 8:45 am]
BILLING CODE 4410-01-M

9570   Federal Register / Vol. 46, No. 19 / Thursday, January 29, 1981 / Rules and Regulations

DEPARTMENT OF JUSTICE

28 CFR Part 51

Procedures for the Administration of Section 5 of the Voting Rights Act of 1965; Revision of Procedures; Correction

AGENCY: Department of Justice.

ACTION: Final rule; correction.

Federal Register / Vol. 46, No. 19 / Thursday, January 29, 1981 / Rules and Regulations   **9571**

SUMMARY: The Attorney General published as a final rule, effective January 5, 1981, a revision of 28 CFR Part 51. (Procedures for the Administration of Section 5 of the Voting Rights Act of 1965, as amended) (FR Doc. 81-125, appearing at 46 FR 870 January 5, 1981). That rule requires correction and is corrected as shown below.

EFFECTIVE DATE: January 5, 1981.

FOR FURTHER INFORMATION CONTACT:
David H. Hunter, Attorney, Voting Section, Civil Rights Division, Department of Justice, Washington, D.C. 20530, (202) 724-7189.

1. The rule is assigned Attorney General Order No. 921a-80.

2. In the Table of Contents, the headings for §§ 51.27 and 51.28 (both appearing at 46 FR 873, first column) should be changed to correspond to the headings as set forth in the text of the rule.

3. (a) The heading to § 51.45 (appearing at 46 FR 873, first column and 878, third column) should read: "§ 51.45 Reconsideration of objection at the instance of the Attorney General"

(b) In § 51.45(a) (appearing at 46 FR 878, third column), in the fifth line "insistance" should read "instance."

4. In § 51.14(a) (appearing at 46 FR 875, first column), in the third line "permists" should read "permits" and in the sixth line "institue" should read "institute."

5. In numbered clause (6) of paragraph (c) of § 51.26 (appearing at 46 FR 876, second column), the phrase "for which election returns a furnished" should read "for which election returns are furnished."

6. In § 51.39(d), the third line (appearing at 46 FR 878, second column) should read "prohibited purpose or effect, an" or rather than "prohibited purpose or effect, and."

7. In the Appendix, in the list of North Carolina counties in which the preclearance requirement of Section 5 of the Voting Rights Act applies (appearing at 46 FR 880, first column) "Graven County" should read "Craven County."

Stephen J. Wilkinson,

Department of Justice, Federal Register Liaison Officer (Alternate).

[FR Doc. 81-3057 Filed 1-28-81; 8:45 am]

BILLING CODE 4410-01-M

DOJ-1981-02

Table of Cases

Bibliography

BOOKS AND DOCUMENTS

Abraham, Henry J. *Freedom and the Court: Civil Rights and Liberties in the United States*. New York: Oxford University Press, 1972.

Appleby, Paul H. *Citizens as Sovereigns*. Syracuse, N.Y.: Syracuse University Press, 1962.

Anderson, James E. *Public Policy-Making*. New York: Holt, Rinehart and Winston, 1979.

Babbie, Earl R. *The Practice of Social Research*. Belmont, Calif.: Wadsworth, 1979.

Ball, Howard. *Courts and Politics: The Federal Judicial System*. Englewood Cliffs, N.J.: Prentice-Hall, 1980.

Bardach, Eugene. *The Implementation Game: What Happens After a Bill Becomes a Law*. Cambridge, Mass.: MIT Press, 1977.

Barker, Lucius and Barker, Twiley, Jr., eds. *Civil Liberties and the Constitution*. Englewood Cliffs, N.J.: Prentice-Hall, 1978.

Barker, Lucius and McCorry, Jesse J., Jr. *Black Americans and the Political System*. Cambridge, Mass.: Winthrop, 1976.

Barnard, Chester I. *The Functions of the Executive*. Cambridge, Mass.: Harvard University Press, 1938.

Bartley, Numan V. and Graham, Hugh D. *Southern Politics and the Second Reconstruction*. Baltimore: Johns Hopkins University Press, 1975.

Baum, Lawrence. "Judicial Impact as a Form of Policy Implementation." In *Public Law and Public Policy*, edited by John A. Gardiner. New York: Praeger Publishers, 1977.

Becker, Theodore L. and Feeley, Malcom M., eds. *The Impact of Supreme Court Decisions*. New York: Oxford University Press, 1973.

Benveniste, Guy. *Bureaucracy*. San Francisco: Boyd and Fraser Publishing Co., 1977.

Black, Earl. *Southern Governors and Civil Rights: Racial Segregation as a Campaign Issue in the Second Reconstruction.* Cambridge, Mass.: Harvard University Press, 1976.

Braybrooke, David and Lindblom, Charles E. *A Strategy of Decision: Policy Evaluation as a Social Process.* New York: The Free Press, 1963.

Casper, Jonathan. *The Politics of Civil Liberties.* New York: Harper & Row, 1972.

Dahl, Robert A. *A Preface to Democratic Theory.* Chicago: University of Chicago Press, 1956.

Davis, Kenneth Culp. *Discretionary Justice: A Preliminary Inquiry.* Baton Rouge: Louisiana State University Press, 1969.

Davis, Rufus S. *The Federal Principle: A Journey Through Time in Quest of Meaning.* Berkeley: University of California Press, 1978.

Derthick, Martha. *New Towns In-Town.* Washington, D.C.: The Urban Institute, 1972.

Dodd, Lawrence C. and Schott, Richard L. *Congress and the Administrative State.* New York: John Wiley and Sons, 1979.

Downs, Anthony. *Inside Bureaucracy.* Boston: Little, Brown and Co., 1967.

Dunsire, Andrew. *Control in a Bureaucracy.* New York: St. Martin's Press, 1978.

———. *Implementation, Evaluation and Change.* U.K.: The Open University, 1980.

Edner, Sheldon M. "Intergovernmental Policy Development: The Importance of Problem Definition." In *Public Policy Making in a Federal System,* edited by Charles O. Jones and Robert D. Thomas. Beverly Hills, Calif.: Sage Publications, 1976.

Edwards, George C., III. *Implementing Public Policy.* Washington, D.C.: Congressional Quarterly Press, 1980.

Elazar, Daniel J. *American Federalism: A View From the States.* New York: Thomas Y. Crowell, 1972.

Engstrom, Richard L. "Racial Discrimination in the Electoral Process: The Voting Rights Act and the Vote Dilution Issue." In *Party Politics in the South,* edited by Robert P. Steed, Lawrence W. Moreland, and Tod A. Baker. New York: Praeger Publishers, 1980.

Evans, Rowland and Novak, Robert. *LBJ: The Exercise of Power.* New York: New American Library, 1966.

Freeman, Howard. "Evaluation Research and Public Policies." In *Social Research and Public Policies,* edited by Gene M. Lyons. The Public Affairs Center, Dartmouth College. Hanover, N.H.: University Press of New England, 1975.

Fried, Robert C. *Performance in American Bureaucracy.* Boston: Little, Brown and Co., 1976.

Gardiner, John A., ed. *Public Law and Public Policy.* New York: Praeger Publishers, 1977.

Garrow, David J. *Protest at Selma: Martin Luther King, Jr. and the Voting Rights Act of 1965.* New Haven: Yale University Press, 1978.

Grodzins, Morton. "The Federal System." In *Goals for Americans.* New York: The American Assembly, Columbia University, 1960.

Grodzins, Morton and Elazar, Daniel. "Centralization and Decentralization in the American Federal System." In *A Nation of States: Essays on the American Federal System*, edited by Robert A. Goldwin. Chicago: Rand McNally, 1974.

Harris, Richard. *Justice: The Crisis of Law, Order and Freedom in America.* New York: E.P. Dutton, 1970.

Harvey, James. *Black Civil Rights During the Johnson Administration.* Jackson: University and College Press of Mississippi, 1973.

Holden, Matthew, Jr. *The Politics of the Black "Nation".* New York: Chandler, 1973.

Hood, Christopher C. *The Limits of Administration.* London: John Wiley, 1976.

Horowitz, Donald L. *The Courts and Social Policy.* Washington, D.C.: The Brookings Institution, 1977.

Hunter, David H. *Federal Review of Voting Changes; How to Use Section 5 of the Voting Rights Act.* Washington, D.C.: Joint Center for Political Studies, 1975.

————. *The Shameful Blight: The Survival of Racial Discrimination in Voting in the South.* Washington, D.C.: Washington Research Project, 1972.

Johnson, Lyndon Baines. *Vantage Point.* New York: Holt, Rinehart, and Winston, 1971.

Johnson, Richard. *The Dynamics of Compliance.* Evanston, Ill.: Northwestern University Press, 1967.

Joint Center for Political Studies. *Black Political Participation: A Look at The Numbers.* Washington, D.C., 1975.

Jones, Charles O. *An Introduction to the Study of Public Policy.* North Scituate, Mass.: Duxbury, 1977.

Jones, Charles O. and Thomas, Robert D., eds. *Public Policy Making in a Federal System.* Beverly Hills, Calif.: Sage Publications, 1976.

Krislov, Samuel. "The Perimeters of Power: The Concept of Compliance as an Approach to the Study of the Legal and Political Processes." In *Compliance and The Law: A Multi-Disciplinary Approach*, edited by Samuel Krislov. Beverly Hills, Calif.: Sage Publications, 1972.

————. *The Supreme Court in the Political Process*. New York: Macmillan Co., 1965.

Lawson, Steven F. *Black Ballots: Voting Rights in the South, 1944-1969*. New York: Columbia University Press, 1976.

Leach, Richard H. *American Federalism*. New York: W. W. Norton and Company, 1970.

Leege, David C. and Francis, Wayne L. *Political Research: Design, Measurement and Analysis*. New York: Basic Books, 1974.

Lipsky, Michael. *Street-Level Bureaucracy: Dilemmas of the Individual in Public Services*. New York: Russel Sage Foundation, 1980.

Lowi, Theodore J. *The End of Liberalism: Ideology, Policy, and the Crisis of Public Authority*. New York: W. W. Norton and Company, 1969.

Mayhew, Leon. *Law and Equal Opportunity*. Cambridge, Mass.: Harvard University Press, 1968.

Meier, Kenneth J. *Politics and the Bureaucracy*. North Scituate, Mass.: Duxbury Press, 1979.

Mosher, Frederick C. *Democracy and the Public Service*. New York: Oxford University Press, 1968.

Moreland, Lois B. *White Racism and the Law*. Columbus, Ohio: Charles E. Merrill Co., 1979.

Morris, Milton D. *The Politics of Black America*. New York: Harper and Row, 1975.

Myrdal, Gunnar. *An American Dilemma*, 2 vols. New York: McGraw-Hill, 1964.

Nachmias, David. *Public Policy Evaluation: Approaches and Methods*. New York: St. Martin's Press, 1979.

Nakamura, Robert T. and Smallwood, Frank. *The Politics of Policy Implementation*. New York: St. Martin's Press, 1980.

Navasky, Victor S. *Kennedy Justice*. New York: Atheneum, 1971.

Nixon, Richard M. *RN: The Memoirs of Richard Nixon*. New York: Grosset and Dunlop, 1978.

Palumbo, Dennis and Sharp, Elaine. "Process Versus Impact Evaluation of Community Corrections." In *The Practice of Policy Evaluation*, edited by David Nachmias. New York: St. Martin's Press, 1980.

Peltasen, Jack W. *58 Lonely Men*. Chicago: University of Chicago Press, 1970.

Pitkin, Hanna F. *The Concept of Representation*. Berkeley: University of California Press, 1967.

Pomper, Gerald M. and Lederman, Susan S. *Elections in America: Control and Influence in Democratic Politics*. New York: Longman, 1980.

Pressman, Jeffrey and Wildavsky, Aaron. *Implementation*. Berkeley: University of California Press, 1979.

Raines, Howell. *My Soul is Rested: Movement Days in the Deep South Remembered*. New York: Bantam Books, 1978.

Redford, Emmett S. *Democracy and the Administrative State*. New York: Oxford University Press, 1969.

Ripley, Randall B. and Franklin, Grace A. *Congress, The Bureaucracy and Public Policy*. Homewood, Ill.: The Dorsey Press, 1976.

Rodgers, Harrel R., Jr. and Bullock, Charles S., III. *Coercion to Compliance*. Lexington, Mass.: Lexington Books, 1976.

————.*Law and Social Change: Civil Rights Laws and Their Consequences*. New York: McGraw-Hill, 1972.

Rourke, Francies E. *Bureaucracy, Politics and Public Policy*. Boston: Little, Brown and Co., 1976.

Schattschneider, E. E. *The Semi-Sovereign People: A Realists's View of Democracy in America*. New York: Holt, Rinehart, and Winston, 1960.

Sigler, Jay A. *American Rights Policies*. Homewood, Ill.: Dorsey Press, 1975.

Simon, Herbert A. *Administrative Behavior*. New York: The Free Press, 1957.

Sundquist, James L. and Davis, David W. *Making Federalism Work: A Study of Program Coordination at the Community Level*. Washington, D.C.: The Brookings Institution, 1969.

Tannebaum, Arnold S. *Control in Organizations*. New York: McGraw-Hill, 1968.

Taylor, Frederick W. *The Principles of Scientific Management*. New York: W. W. Norton and Co., 1911.

Tribe, Lawrence. *American Constitutional Law*. New York: Foundation Press, 1978.

U.S. Commission on Civil Rights. *Political Participation: A Study of the Participation by Negroes in the Electoral and Political Processes in 10 Southern States Since Passage of the Voting Rights Act of 1965*. Washington, D.C., May 1968.

————. *The Voting Rights Act: Ten Years After*. Washington, D.C., 1975.

————. *The Voting Rights Act. . .The First Months*. November, 1965.

————. *Using the Voting Rights Act*. Washington, D.C.: U.S. Government Printing Office, 1976.

————. *The State of Civil Rights: 1979*. Washington, D.C., January, 1980.

U.S. Comptroller General, General Accounting Office. *Voting Rights Act—Enforcement Needs Strengthening*. February 6, 1978.

U.S. Congress. ("Extension of the Voting Rights Act,") Hearings Before the Subcommittee on Civil and Constitutional Issues, Committee on the Judiciary, House of Representatives. 94th Congress, 1st Session.

U.S. Department of Justice, Office of the Attorney General. "Procedures for the Administration of Section 5 of the Voting Rights Act of 1965. Revision of Procedures." *Federal Register*, vol. 46, no. 2, January 1981.

Van Horn, Carl E. and Van Meter, Donald S. "The Implementation of Intergovernmental Policy." In *Public Policy Making in a Federal System*, edited by Charles O. Jones and Robert D. Thomas. Beverly Hills, Calif.: Sage Publications, 1976.

Van Woodward, E. *The Strange Career of Jim Crow*. New York: Oxford University Press, 1957.

Walton, Hanes, Jr. *Black Politics: A Theoretical and Structural Analysis*. New York: J. B. Lippincott, 1972.

————. "Black Politics in the South: Projections for the Coming Decade." In *Public Policy for the Black Community*, edited by Marguerite Ross Barnett and James A. Hefner. New York: Alfred, 1976.

Wasby, Stephen J. "The Supreme Court's Impact: Some Problems of Conceptualization and Measurement." In *Compliance and the Law: A Multi-Disciplinary Approach*, edited by Samuel Krislov. Beverly Hills, Calif.: Sage Publications, 1972.

Webb, Eugene J. *Unobstrusive Measures*. Chicago: Rand McNally, 1966.

Williams, Walter. *The Implementation Perspective: A Guide for Managing Social Service Delivery Programs*. Berkeley: University of California Press, 1980.

Wirt, Frederick. *Politics of Southern Equality*. Chicago: Aldine Publishing, 1970.

Woll, Peter. *American Bureaucracy*. New York: W. W. Norton and Co., 1977.

ARTICLES AND PAPERS

Ball, H., Krane, D. and Lauth, T. "Judicial Impact on the Enforcement of Voting Rights Policy By Attorneys in the Department of Justice." Paper presented at the 1977 annual meeting of the Southern Political Science Association. New Orleans, La., November 3-5, 1977.

Black, Merle. "Racial Composition of Congressional Districts and Support for Federal Voting Rights in the American South." *Social Science Quarterly* 59, December 1978.

Button, James, Scher, Richard and Berkson, Larry. "The Quest for Equality: The Impact of the Civil Rights Movement on Black Public Services in the South." Paper presented at the annual meeting of the Midwest Political Science Association. Chicago, Ill., April 20-22, 1978.

Cavanaugh, Thomas E. "Changes in American Electoral Turnout, 1964-1976." Paper presented at the annual meeting of the Midwest Political Science Association. Chicago, Ill., April 1979.

Chayes, Abram. "The Role of the Judge in Public Law Litigation." *Harvard Law Review* 89, May 1976.

Cotrell, Charles and Stevens, R. Michael. "The 1975 Voting Rights Act and San Antonio, Texas: Toward a Federal Guarantee of a Republican Form of Local Government." *Publius: The Journal of Federalism* 8, Winter 1978.

Cox, Archibald. "Constitutionality of Proposed Voting Rights Act of 1965."*Houston Law Review* 3, November 1965.

———. "Foreward: Constitutional Adjudication and the Promotion of Human Rights." *Harvard Law Review* 80, November 1966.

Derfner, Armand. "Racial Discrimination and the Right to Vote." *Vanderbilt Law Review* 26, April 1973.

Edner, Sheldon M. "The Blind Men and the Elephant: How do Intergovernmental Actors Compensate for Their Handicap or is There a Cure for Hereditary Blindness." A paper presented at the annual meeting of the American Political Science Association. Washington, D. C., September 1-4, 1977.

Funston, Richard. "The Supreme Court and Critical Elections." *American Political Science Review* 69, September 1975.

Greshman, Eugene. "The Unhappy History of Civil Rights Legislation." *Michigan Law Review* 50, 1952.

Halpin, Stanley, Jr. and Engstrom, Richard L. "Racial Gerrymandering and Southern State Legislative Redistricting: Attorney General Determinations Under the Voting Rights Act." *Journal of Public Law* 22, 1973.

Hunter, David H. "The Administrators' Dilemmas for the Enforcement of Section 5 of the Voting Rights Act of 1965." Paper presented at the national conference of the American Society for Public Administration. Phoenix, AZ, April 9-12, 1978.

Ingram, Helen. "Policy Implementation Through Bargaining: The Case of Federal Grants-In-Aid." *Public Policy* 25, Fall 1977.

Jones, Mack H. "The 1965 Voting Rights Act and Political Symbolism." Paper presented at the 1979 Annual Meeting of the Southern Political Science Association. Gatlinburg, Tenn., November 1-3, 1979.

Leuchtenburg, William E. "The White House and Black America: From Eisenhower to Carter." In *Have We Overcome: Race Relations Since*

Brown, edited by Michael V. Namorato. Jackson: University Press of Mississippi, 1979.

Levine, James P. and Becker, Theodore L. "Toward and Beyond a Theory of Supreme Court Impact." *American Behavioral Scientist* 13, March /April, 1970.

Marshall, Burke. "The 1960's: The Civil Rights Movement and The Department of Justice." Paper presented at the 1978 National Archives Conference, Washington, D.C.

Note, "Federal Protection of Negro Rights." *Virginia Law Review* 51, October, 1965.

Note, "Voting Rights Act of 1965." *University of Texas Law Review* 4, July 1966

O'Connor, Robert and Ingersoll, Thomas. "The Impact of Judicial Decisions on the Implementation of the 1965 Voting Rights Act." Paper presented at the 1980 meeting of the Midwest Political Science Association, Chicago, Ill.

Parker, Frank R. "County Redistricting in Mississippi: Case Studies in Racial Gerrymandering." *Mississippi Law Journal* 44, June 1973.

Pottinger, J. Stanley. *Statement on Extension of the Voting Rights Act*, Subcommittee on Civil Rights and Constitutional Rights, House Judiciary Committee, March 5, 1975.

Roman, John J. "Section 5 of the VRA: The Formation of an Extraordinary Federal Remedy." *American University Law Review* 22, 1972.

Rosenthal, Donald B. "Bargaining Language in Intergovernmental Relations: What to do Until a Theory Arrives." Paper presented at the annual meeting of the American Policital Science Association, August 31-September 3, 1978, New York, N.Y.

Sabatier, Paul and Mazmanian, Daniel; "The Implementation of Public Policy: A Framework of Analysis." *Policy Studies Journal* 8, 1980.

Sherwood, Frank P. "Dealing with Dominance: The Center's Role in an Increasingly Unbalanced System." *Public Administration Review* 35, December 1975.

Snow, Deborah P. "Justice Department Implementation of Section 203 of the Voting Rights Act." Paper presented at the National Conference of the American Society for Public Administration, Phoenix, Ariz., April 1978.

Stern, Mark. "Southern Congressional Civil Rights Voting and the New Southern Democracy." Paper presented at the annual meeting of the American Political Science Association, Washington, D.C., August 31-September 3, 1979.

Stillman, Richard H., II. "The Bureaucracy Problem at DOJ," *Public Administration Review* 36, July/August 1976.

Stover, Robert and Brown, Don. "Understanding Compliance and Non-compliance with Law: The Contributions of Utility Theory." *Social Science Quarterly* 56, December 1975.

Stuart, Reginald. "Where the Right to Vote Was like Reaching the Moon." *New York Times*, April 14, 1981.

———. "Local Governments Hurt Rural Black Belt Schools Despite Integration, Report Claims." Jackson, Mississippi *Clarion-Ledger*, April 8, 1981.

Thompson, Joel A. "The Voting Rights Act in North Carolina: A Quasi-Experimental Analysis of Policy Effectiveness." Paper presented at the Citadel Symposium on Southern Politics, Charleston, S.C., March 27-29, 1980.

Ulmer, S. Sidney, "Earl Warrren and The Brown Decision" *Journal of Politics* 33, 1971.

Van Meter, Donald S. and Van Horn, Carl E. "The Policy Implementation Process: A Conceptual Framework." *Administration and Society* 6, February 1975.

Weiss, Carol. "The Politicization of Evaluation Research," *Journal of Social Issues* 26, Autumn 1970.

Wernz, William. " 'Discriminatory Purpose,' 'Changes', and 'Dilution': Recent Judicial Interpretations of Section Five of the Voting Rights Act." *Notre Dame Lawyer* 51, December 1975.

Williams, Walter. "Implementation Analysis and Assessment." *Policy Analysis* 1, Summer 1975.

———. "Special Issue on Implementation: Editor's Comments." *Policy Analysis* 1, Summer 1975.

Wilson, James Q. "The Bureaucracy Problem." *The Public Interest*, Winter, 1967.

———. "On Pettigrew and Armor." *The Public Interest* 31, Spring 1973.

Wilson, Woodrow. "The Study of Administration." *Political Science Quarterly* 2, 1887.

Zimmerman, Joseph F. "The Federal Voting Rights Act: Its Impact on Annexation." *National Civic Review*, June 1977.

Index

About the Authors

HOWARD BALL is Professor and Head of the Department of Political Science at Mississippi State University. His earlier works include *The Vision of Hugo Black, Courts and Politics*, and *Judicial Craftsmanship or Fiat?* (Greenwood Press, 1978).

DALE KRANE is Associate Professor, Department of Political Science at Mississippi State University. He has contributed to *Public Administration Review, Southern Studies*, and other scholarly journals.

THOMAS P. LAUTH is Associate Professor, Department of Political Science at the University of Georgia in Athens, Georgia. His earlier works include *Changing Perspectives in Contemporary Political Analysis*, as well as articles for numerous scholarly journals.